ASA Monographs 23

Social Anthropology and Development Policy

Edited by
Ralph Grillo and Alan Rew

Social Anthropology and Development Policy

Tavistock Publications
London and New York

First published in 1985 by
Tavistock Publications Ltd
11 New Fetter Lane, London EC4P 4EE

Published in the USA by
Tavistock Publications
in association with Methuen, Inc.
733 Third Avenue, New York, NY 10017

© 1985 Association of Social Anthropologists

Printed in Great Britain at the
University Press, Cambridge

*British Library Cataloguing in
Publication Data*

Social anthropology and development
policy.—
 (ASA monograph; 23)
 1. Developing countries—Economic
policy
 2. Ethnology
 I. Grillo, R. D.   II. Rew, Alan
 III. Series 330.9172'4   HC59.7

ISBN 0-422-79790-1
ISBN 0-422-79620-4 Pbk

*Library of Congress Cataloging in
Publication Data*
Main entry under title:
Social anthropology and development
policy.

 (ASA monographs; no. 23)
 Bibliography: p.
 Includes index.
 1. Applied anthropology—
Congresses.
 2. Economic development—Social
aspects—Congresses. 3. Developing
countries— Economic policy—
Congresses. I. Grillo, R. D. II. Rew,
Alan, 1942–   . III. Series: A.S.A.
monographs; no. 23.
 GN397.5.S65 1985   306   84-26821
 ISBN 0-422-79790-1
 ISBN 0-422-79620-4 (pbk.)

Contents

vi

List of Contributors

Raymond Apthorpe is Professor of Social Anthropology and Sociology of Development, Institute of Social Studies, The Hague/International Centre for Economics and Related Disciplines, LSE.

A. P. Cheater is a Lecturer in Sociology at the University of Zimbabwe.

S. Conlin is a Social Development Adviser at the Overseas Development Administration.

Donald Curtis is a Lecturer in the Sociology of Development at the Development Administration Group, Institute of Local Government Studies, University of Birmingham.

Ralph Grillo is Reader in Social Anthropology at the University of Sussex.

P. H. Gulliver is Professor of Social Anthropology at York University, Toronto.

Polly Hill is a Fellow of Clare Hall, Cambridge.

Robert Layton is Reader in Social Anthropology at the University of Durham.

M. R. Redclift is Lecturer in Latin American Rural Sociology at the Institute of Latin American Studies and Wye College, University of London.

Alan Rew is Chief Social Science Consultant, W. S. Atkins and Partners.

Andrew Strathern is Director, Institute of Papua New Guinea Studies, Port Moresby.

M. G. Whisson is Professor of Social Anthropology at Rhodes University, Grahamstown.

Acknowledgements

The papers in this volume came from the Third Decennial Conference of the Association of Social Anthropologists of the Commonwealth (ASA), held at Robinson College, Cambridge, 4–8 July 1983. The editors would like to thank Professors Jean La Fontaine, Emanuel Marx, and Paul Stirling, who chaired the various sessions at which the papers were presented, and Professors Lorraine Baric, Jeremy Boissevain, Scarlett Epstein, and Dr Michael Redclift, who formed a panel of speakers for a discussion of Alan Rew's paper.

The Association would like to thank its local organizer, Dr Malcolm Ruel of Clare College, for his major contribution to the Meeting's success, Professor Jack Goody and the Faculty of Archaeology and Anthropology, University of Cambridge, for providing us with a reception in the course of the Conference, and the Warden and Fellows of Robinson College for their hospitality throughout.

Generous grants from the British Council and the Esperanza Trust enabled several overseas speakers to attend the proceedings.

Ralph Grillo*

1 Applied Anthropology in the 1980s:
retrospect and prospect

This volume contains papers presented to the second part of the third Decennial Conference of the Association of Social Anthropologists of the Commonwealth (ASA) at Cambridge in July 1983. The theme of the Conference as a whole was 'Anthropology in the Eighties', that of Part Two, 'Anthropology and Policy'. It is not usually necessary to set an ASA conference in its local, British, social context, but on this occasion it is, for that context in large part determined the shape of the third Decennial, and, hence, the nature of this monograph.

When, at its Annual Business Meeting, in April 1980, the ASA first considered the programme for the proposed 1983 Decennial, one member suggested that 'future . . . conferences might take into account the particular problems and needs of those members working outside the academic sphere' (ASA *Annals*, 1 (1980): 8). By this was meant mainly those members employed in what is conventionally, though often inaccurately, called 'applied anthropology', e.g. engaged in advising on or monitoring the social and cultural implications of policies concerned with economic and technical change. Subsequently it was agreed that in the light of 'the growing interest in the profession in the theoretical and other problems associated with the practical application of the subject' (ASA *Annals* 2 (1981): 15), a substantial part of the proceedings of the Decennial would be devoted to policy issues.

That such a proposal was made and accepted reflects important changes in the profession and its working environment in recent years. For although the desire to make anthropology useful is almost as old as the discipline (Firth 1981), and some British anthropologists, especially during the colonial era, were always concerned with its practical relevance, for many years after

* I would like to thank Dr A. V. Akeroyd and Professor A. L. Epstein for their considerable help with the preparation of this chapter.

World War II, application was considered a marginal activity, and applied professionals were few and far between.

From the early 1960s, however, and increasingly during the 1970s, anthropologists began to enter the important policy field of development, and/or engage in research in Third World countries which, as those countries often demanded, was directly related to their needs and problems. At the same time, anthropologists became increasingly involved with 'relevant' research, as it was sometimes called, in Britain and Europe, notably in the field of ethnic relations.

Much of this research was undertaken by professional anthropologists working outside the academy, but it should not be thought that their interest in applied anthropology was inspired by want of an orthodox academic job or by shortage of funds for more traditional types of research. Most of those who entered these fields in the 1960s and 1970s did so because they believed that anthropology could and should illuminate the urgent and pressing issues of the day, and could do so in ways which at least complemented the perspectives of other disciplines. They also believed that it was possible to find ways of resolving some, if not all, of the difficult intellectual, moral, and political problems which, as an earlier generation had recognized, application undoubtedly poses.

During the 1970s, those engaged in such work began to come together formally and informally, for the most part outside the ASA. In 1976, a British Medical Anthropology Society was founded in Manchester. In 1977, the Royal Anthropological Institute (RAI) set up a Development Anthropology Committee 'to promote the involvement of anthropology in development in the Third World' (*RAIN* (December 1978): 16). In 1978, the Social Science Research Council (SSRC) financed a series of workshops convened by Professor T. S. Epstein, which brought together many anthropologists working in the development field, and in 1981, during the Edinburgh meeting of the American Society for Applied Anthropology (SfAA), a British applied anthropology group was founded. Later that year, AAG (as it was first called) became GAPP, the Group for Anthropology in Policy and Practice, which by 1983 had over 150 members (*Annals*; *RAIN*; *GAPP* newsletter).

In comparison with the USA, where the SfAA was founded in 1941, the formal organization of applied practitioners was a late development in Britain, though in other respects the history of anthropology's experience of application in the two countries is surprisingly similar (cf. Barnett 1956; Eddy and Partridge 1978, Foster 1969; Goldschmidt 1979; Spicer 1976; Stewart 1983). Nonetheless, by the early 1980s applied anthropology was firmly established on the professional agenda in Britain. By that time, however, and this certainly parallels the experience of our American colleagues, another factor had become predominant, the problem of professional (un)employment.

By the end of the 1970s it was clear that the period of resource growth which had, since World War II, sustained traditional research in anthropology, and an academic career structure, in particular since the Robbins Report and the expansion of higher education in the 1960s, was over. Partly in response to this change, which had already evoked concern among some of the proponents of the RAI's Development Committee, the ASA, in conjunction with the SSRC, convened in September 1980 a meeting attended, *inter alia*, by representatives of all UK anthropology departments. A section of this meeting examined prospects for the employment of anthropologists in development, in industry, in commerce, and in the public services (Akeroyd, Grillo, and Tapper 1980). A number of problems faced by those working outside the academy were identified, including those connected with their professional status and training. But above all the task was creating new opportunities for trained post-graduates who wished to exercise their profession, allowing them to obtain employment in a contracting job market. Events since 1980 – government cuts in university and polytechnic funds, the restructuring of the SSRC, and the continuing high levels of general unemployment – only served to underline the importance and difficulty of that enterprise.

These changing circumstances gave the 1983 Decennial a particular significance. They also made it, frankly, a particularly difficult conference in that discussion, not surprisingly, was dominated by the seemingly intractable problems of training and employment. However, the papers, and in many respects the discussion too, ranged far beyond these immediate issues, and since they have been taken up elsewhere (see Baric, Conlin, Grillo, and Wallman 1983) it was not felt necessary to address them here. This book should not, therefore, be seen as a guide to anthropological employment outside the academy or in any simple way as a practitioner's handbook. Our concern is with some of the wider issues raised by such employment.

Reflecting on the proceedings of Part Two of the Decennial in the light of sixty years' experience as a working anthropologist, Sir Raymond Firth, the ASA's Life President, commented that he had a sense of *déjà vu, déjà connu* and *déjà conçu*. Those familiar with the detailed history of anthropology might well agree. What we debate here has been discussed many times in the past by anthropologists in Britain and elsewhere. This is hardly surprising, for the issues are quite fundamental, raising problems which lie at the heart of the discipline. They are concerned with what the limits of anthropology are, or might be, and with what its practitioners can or should do, intellectually, morally and politically, and each generation needs to review such matters afresh, reaching its own conclusions in the context of its own time.

In this volume we tackle such questions by focusing on the role of the professional anthropologist in research which is concerned with devising, implementing or reviewing policies for development in Third World countries, a field which in the past (such as during the colonial era), and probably until recently, has been the most significant one for British applied anthropologists. We do not deny the importance of application in other contexts, for example, in industrial society (Gowler and Clarke 1983), but in planning the conference and this volume, we felt that concentration on one broadly defined field, in which there is a wealth of anthropological expertise, would enable us to evaluate that expertise as systematically as possible.

This contribution surveys a number of interrelated topics which are covered in various ways in each of the chapters. There is, first, an unavoidable review of what applied anthropology has meant to British anthropologists and what such activity has signified to the profession in this country. This is accompanied by a survey of the experience of application during the colonial period which, it is suggested, shaped the prevailing attitude towards application after World War II. Gulliver's chapter, which is an important contribution to the ethnography of applied anthropology during the late colonial era in East Africa, reflects on that experience from the viewpoint of the 1980s.

The insights drawn from it, and those by Cheater, Conlin, Layton, Rew, Strathern, and Whisson, inform the examination of the way in which the context of application has and has not changed in the transition from a colonial to a post-colonial world. That discussion enables us to examine what, specifically, is the contribution that anthropologists have expected to make, and what they might actually make, to the development process. This theme runs through many of the papers, but it is central to those by Apthorpe, Curtis, Hill, Rew, and Strathern. The anthropologist's contribution, however, cannot be understood apart from the nexus of relationships into which the anthropologist is drawn by applied research. Any account of the anthropologist in development must itself be anthropological, and that perspective is emphasized throughout this volume. Last, but certainly not least, are the important ethical and political questions which any assessment of the anthropologist's contribution to development policy must necessarily tackle, something of special concern to Redclift.

The Meaning of Applied Anthropology

'Malinowski sent me to study social change because, he said, I didn't know enough anthropology for fieldwork of the standard type. Nobody today regards the study of social change as an occupation for the half-baked. But that is rather the status of applied anthropology.'

(Mair 1969: 8)

It is tempting to state simply that this volume is concerned with the anthropologist who is involved in devising, implementing and/or reviewing policies affecting human groups, provide that as a definition of 'applied anthropology', and leave the matter there. That is not possible, for it is soon obvious that any such definition is prescriptive rather than descriptive, representing a view of what applied anthropology *really* is, or what applied anthropology and its subject matter *should* constitute. It is also likely to encode a view of the nature of anthropology as a branch of knowledge, and its relationship to the society in which it is embedded.

When, for example, the American anthropologist, Foster, says that applied anthropology refers to the professional activities of anthropologists 'in programs which have as primary goals changes in human behavior believed to ameliorate contemporary social, economic and technological problems, rather than the development of social and cultural theory' (Foster 1969: 54), he is offering a conception of the field with which many who might otherwise accept the label, 'applied anthropologist', would profoundly disagree. Indeed, because the term has been used in so many different ways, as we shall see, and has referred to so many different sorts of activity, or because, alternatively, it is thought to be associated with one kind of activity or school or style or period of research rather than another, the very label itself has been questioned (e.g. by Cochrane 1971 and Goldschmidt 1979). We are manifestly dealing with a value-laden notion, and it is worth reviewing in some detail its meaning and significance to anthropologists of different times and places.

It has frequently been suggested (e.g. Firth 1981; Hogbin 1957) that the phrase 'applied anthropology' was first used in print by Radcliffe-Brown (1931), though it is well known that the linking of similar terms with anthropology occurred much earlier (e.g. Temple 1914), and it was in 1929 that Malinowski published his famous paper on what he called, 'practical anthropology'. During the 1930s, a period discussed in greater detail below, four sorts of activity were generally referred to as practical or applied: research on contemporary society, especially on 'culture contact', later to be called social change, in the colonies; research into a number of specific problems of concern to colonial administrations (not always or even usually at their request); provision of information and/or advice to those administrations; and the involvement of anthropologists in the training of administrators.

Subsequent debate about applied anthropology during the colonial period has often included argument as to whether one or other of these activities should be allowed the term. Regarding the first, for example, Lucy Mair, the only person in Britain to have held a chair in applied anthropology, comments in the Introduction to her *Anthropology and Social Change* – which interestingly republished a number of essays previously issued under the title, *Studies in Applied Anthropology* – that it was the Fellows of the International African Institute (IAI, see below) who pioneered the study of social change, and 'if applied anthropology is indeed the study of social change, they can be said to have introduced it' (Mair 1969: 2–3). Brokensha, however, in a survey of applied research in Anglophone Africa, uses the criterion not of subject matter but of value: 'all anthropological research which has been helpful to governments' (1966: 4). With this criterion he casts what is in theory, though not perhaps in practice, a very wide net. It is far too wide for Gulliver who in a personal communication cited by Brokensha (see Gulliver in this volume) argued for a much narrower definition: 'Research specifically oriented to administrative and development problems, together with some degree of responsible participation in utilizing the results of such research' (Gulliver in Brokensha 1966: 4; cf. Forde 1953: 841).

Not surprisingly, in view of this definition, Gulliver also questions the association of applied anthropology with a particular kind of subject matter, such as social change. Although Gulliver was right in that the study of social change was not of itself 'applied' in the sense used by him (or by Foster), no matter how useful or interesting to government it might have been, it was certainly more likely to be policy-relevant than research concerned with the 'reconstruction of a hypothetical untouched society' (Mair 1969: 3), as Malinowski was prone to point out. But, to claim that it is 'not really applied anthropology' is to miss the point that there has always been a variety of research which might legitimately be termed applied. As Redclift remarks in his comment on Rew's paper in this volume, to stress one kind of activity – in Rew's case that of the anthropologist as policy professional – is to overlook other ways in which anthropologists have believed it possible for their discipline to make a practical contribution to human affairs.

In both Brokensha's and Gulliver's definition, and indeed in at least three of the four types of activity usually considered applied anthropology in the 1930s, the crucial criterion is clearly something to do with government, though Brokensha wanted a much broader definition than Gulliver's, so that he could include a 'wide spectrum of possible collaboration' (1966: 12) between anthropologist and administrator. For Firth, and for many others, collaboration with government is, however, only one possible kind of applied activity. There are, he suggests, 'different degrees of absorption in a problem' (1981: 197). He lists five tasks which any anthropologist might undertake, each of which he or she might reasonably claim to be applied: crisis aid to the society studied; mediating with outside authorities; interpreting the culture to outsiders; helping form public opinion on a problem; and conducting 'client-oriented' research. His list could be further extended to include a wide range of activities under the general heading, 'practical'. For example:

(a) Pursuing fundamental research (see below), but interested, even pleased, should someone make use of it (e.g. Lewis 1977).
(b) Researching issues of contemporary social or political concern, to contribute to knowledge about them and perhaps inform public debate (e.g. Firth).
(c) Researching issues known to be of interest to policy makers or other potential users while not oneself engaging in policy making (e.g. Mair).
(d) Researching the anthropology of development (see below and in various ways, Charsley 1980, 1982; Colson 1971; Condominas 1979; Epstein 1962).

(e) Problem-oriented research undertaken on a customer–contractor basis (see below).

(f) Researching and participating in policy formation as a policy professional (e.g. Cochrane 1971, 1980; Rew in this volume).

(g) Acting as mediator, broker, spokesperson, advocate or expert witness for a society or group in their relationship with another body (e.g. in various ways Beattie 1965; Dobyns 1978; Weber and McCall 1978; Layton in this volume).

(h) 'Action anthropology' (as defined by Huizer 1979b; Schensul and Schensul 1978; Tax 1975).

(i) 'Revolutionary anthropology' (Gough 1968; Stavenhagen 1971); 'Partisan anthropology' (Lewis 1973: 589); 'Committed anthropology' (Polgar 1979); 'Liberation anthropology' (Huizer 1979a; Polgar 1979).

This is not a comprehensive typology, nor is it intended to be. Nor are the categories necessarily homogeneous. It is merely a list of activities which could be – and have been – described as anthropology applied or put to practical use, even if those precise labels have not been employed. Some will be more familiar to British anthropologists than others: much recent discussion in Britain has focused on (e) or (f), for example, whereas few in this country have had any experience of 'action anthropology' as that is usually defined. Finally, these categories should not be seen as necessarily exclusive, though they may well represent different kinds and degrees of absorption or engagement, and as such some may be thought by their advocates to preclude other possibilities.

If the first point to emerge from this is that there is a range of activities which the terms 'applied' or 'practical' might embrace, the second is that we are dealing essentially with *activities* which involve a variety of goals (some perhaps mutually exclusive), and a variety of somewhat different relationships, or relationships, perhaps with the same people, of a somewhat different kind. This suggests that 'applied anthropology' might be discarded as a term of art and replaced with a much broader notion of contextually defined professional activity.

Such an approach has several virtues, as we will show, but we should not allow it to blind us to the fact that applied anthropology – in its now discarded emic capacity – was never just a label for a type of professional activity. To treat it as such is to ignore its evaluative connotation. Foster, writing mainly from an American perspective, remarks that 'only in time of war has it been fully respectable for anthropologists to devote themselves wholeheartedly to non-theoretical goal-oriented research' (1969:132, cf. Goldschmidt 1979; Partridge and Eddy 1978; Spicer 1976; Stewart 1983). On both sides of the Atlantic after World War II the status of any applied anthropology was low, and for many years the orthodox view in British anthropology was to abjure all application of research outside the academy, even perhaps 'helping form public opinion'. A mid-1970s study (Landman 1978) of some sixty British applied anthropologists found overwhelming evidence of their sense of inferiority *vis-à-vis* the rest of the profession, and Lucy Mair's comment cited at the head of this section shows that this is no recent phenomenon.

'For many anthropologists there are few things more alarming than applied anthropology' (Cochrane 1971: 8). Objections to application have been made on a number of practical, intellectual, ethical, and political grounds – see Evans-Pritchard 1946 for a classic, much-cited example, and Fuller 1982 for a more recent one – and later we consider in more detail what these are. One we mention here because it is important to put it in its place early on. It pertains to the frequently made opposition between 'applied' research and that which is termed 'pure', and the idea that applied work is for the 'half-baked', 'the refuge of the less intelligent' (Landman 1978: 323).

Such sentiments are difficult to document because they rarely appear in print in such a direct way. Nonetheless, they have been widespread in British anthropology and are still influential, as anyone who was closely involved with the recent enquiry into the work of the SSRC, and the place within it of social anthropology, will be able to testify.

In 1982, the Secretary of State for Education and Science asked Lord Rothschild to investigate the work of the SSRC. The terms of reference of the inquiry were couched in the language of an earlier Report by Rothschild (1971) into scientific research and development. There Rothschild had identified a type of research which he termed 'customer–oriented': addressed to specific problems and undertaken on a 'customer–contractor' basis, i.e. where there was an identifiable, paying, end-user for a product. (In illustrating his argument Rothschild used the homely examples of a tank or gun.) The SSRC inquiry was to ask whether research in the social sciences might be undertaken on such a basis.

As his report showed (Rothschild 1982), if the funding of the social sciences were left to the end-user, then much of the research now carried out would simply not be supported, a point made many times over during the inquiry when social scientists, anthropologists among them, had expressed the fear that they would be driven to undertake theoretically less demanding and academically less important work because that would be the only research to attract funds. In one respect this objection has considerable force: what academic discipline would wish its research priorities determined solely by the market place? Yet such fears also reflect a persistent distinction between research which is applied, practical or engaged and that which is pure, abstract and theoretical.

Rothschild's earlier report had in effect attempted to do away with such a distinction by drawing what is essentially a sociological contrast between research involving a customer–contractor relationship, and all other research which, he argued, was *basic*. There are, as we shall see, problems in using such a model for anthropology, but it is in line with our own view that varieties of research should be treated as varieties of activity, and is a useful one if it helps dissolve the crude distinction between 'applied' and 'pure' which has bedevilled so much of the thinking in Britain about anthropology outside the academy. For there is no logical reason for supposing that research in one context is necessarily intellectually less demanding than research in another, and the empirical evidence to support such a contention appears to be lacking. And where is the evidence to suggest that applied research, in the contextual sense, does not raise theoretical questions of major importance to the subject as a whole, though in some cases they may be different questions from those that are pursued in another, more traditional, context? Nor, finally, should it be supposed that research from within the academy, or indeed anthropology at large, can be characterized as ethically or politically neutral or conducted in a moral or political void (cf. Nadel 1951, 1953).

Yet we must face the fact that an applied/theoretical opposition persists in anthropology and affects both 'sides': one abjuring practice, the other theory. Why does anthropology, more than any other social science, appear to make such heavy weather of this distinction? What, one wonders, would Keynes have made of it? If, then, the meaning of applied anthropology is to be found in its rejection by those in the mainstream of the subject, we have to ask why this rejection has occurred. This means tracing the historical experience of applied anthropology in Britain, and that entails a consideration of the experience of applied anthropology during the colonial period.

Applied Anthropology and the Colonial Experience

'A new branch of anthropology must sooner or later be started: the anthropology of the changing Native . . . This anthropology would obviously be of the highest importance to the practical man in the colonies.'
(Malinowski 1929: 36)

This is not the place to rehearse in its entirety the debate of the 1960s and 1970s on the role of British, French and Dutch anthropologists in colonialism, or of American anthropologists in Latin America and South-east Asia. The issues are well known, if not always well argued by the various protagonists. Although the contributors to that debate were not usually concerned specifically with applied anthropology (obvious exceptions are Bastide 1973; Faris 1973; Frank 1979; Onoge 1979), it did, however, raise important questions concerning the nature of applied research during the colonial period, especially in Anglophone Africa. Here we comment on some of these questions from the point of view, mainly, of the anthropologists who participated in such research.

For reasons of space, this chapter ignores what might be termed the 'pre-history' of application, i.e. before Malinowski and Radcliffe-Brown stood at the centre of the subject. It is sufficient for our purposes simply to note that already by the 1920s a number of anthropologists had been for some time working directly with colonial administrations, for example, in West Africa, and in other parts of the world, too, such as New Guinea and the Pacific (for the earlier period, see references in Barnett 1956; Feuchtwang 1973; Firth 1938, 1981; Forde 1945, 1953; Kuper 1973; Mair 1957a; Richards 1977; and in greater detail Foster 1969; Lackner 1973; Reining 1962; Robertson 1975). A crucial development in the history of applied anthropology, and in the subject at large, was the foundation in 1926 of what became the International African Institute, the IAI (Barnett 1956; Feuchtwang 1973; Firth 1981; Forde 1953; Foster 1969; Hogbin 1957; Kuper 1973; Mair 1957a, 1957b, 1960, 1969; Onoge 1979; Owusu 1979; Richards 1944).

In the first issue of the IAI's journal, *Africa*, Lord Lugard had observed that 'Its aims will not be restricted exclusively to the field of scientific study but will be directed also towards a closer association of scientific knowledge and research with practical affairs.' Although the Institute's constitution precluded direct concern with policy matters, he continued by pointing out that this left 'a wide field in which . . . the results of scientific study may be brought into closer relations with the practical tasks which are being carried out in Africa' (Lugard 1928: 2), and suggested as suitable matters for research questions of land tenure, native customary law, the economic effects of contact, and the introduction of new technology. The then Minister for the Colonies (Leo Amery) expressed an interest in the Institute's activities.

Lugard's theme provided the basis for the IAI's subsequent research policy. It was taken up, for example, in the Institute's Five Year Plan (1932) which in promoting the types of inquiry suggested by Lugard, as well as other kinds of research, sought 'the collaboration of those engaged in the practical tasks of administration . . . and . . . to bring the [IAI's] inquiries into living and fruitful relation with the problems with which they are concerned' (*Africa* 5(1): 9). And it was, of course, in *Africa* that Malinowski presented his case for practical anthropology.

There he argued that the IAI could fulfil the important function of 'bridging the gap between theoretical anthropology and its practical application' (Malinowski 1929: 37). By anthropology he meant his 'new branch' of the discipline, and in explaining the difference between it and the anthropology of the past he is at pains to emphasize its administrative value. It would, he claimed, be 'of the highest importance to the practical man in the colonies' (Malinowski 1929: 36).

In this paper which, with its favourable comments on Indirect Rule (pp. 23–4) and its reference to the *Dual Mandate* (p. 30), clearly has Lugard as one of its addressees, Malinowski was proselytizing on behalf of the 'new' discipline of functionalism. Much has been made of his remarks: the hostile comments on colonial anthropology in, for example, Bastide (1973) and Onoge (1979) are largely based on extracts from them. There is a danger of selective quotation from Malinowski, as Huizer (1979a) points out. For although on several other occasions (e.g. Malinowski 1939: 35–6, 1961: 7, 138 ff.) he did indeed write favourably on the policy of Indirect Rule, as did his student, Mair (1936: 12, 264; 1957a: 73), the context makes it clear that such a policy was seen as the only, and better, alternative to *direct* rule. As James (1973) has cogently demonstrated, Malinowski was far from uncritical of colonial policy in general and in particular, and on several points his views changed considerably over a period of some fifteen years. It is nevertheless true that in the early 1930s he sought through the IAI to establish a practical relationship between anthropology and colonial administration. The new anthropology was promoted, in part at least, as applied anthropology.

What, under certain circumstances, application might mean was demonstrated in a book published in 1935 which is now little known or read, though Kuper (1973) provides a good account of it. This was the report on a self-styled 'experiment' in Tanganyika in 1932 involving close collaboration between an IAI financed anthropologist (Brown) and a local District Officer (Hutt). The introduction to the report, written by the then Chief Secretary of Tanganyika Territory, P. E. Mitchell, sets out what were, in effect, the terms of reference of the experiment. The anthropologist, who had already undertaken intensive research in the area, was to be responsible, with the administrator, for considering two principal questions: 'Is the local government based on tribal loyalties and traditional authority, deriving from the past, acceptable in the present? And are the people well governed and content?' (Mitchell 1935: xiv–xv). These and other remarks (e.g. pp. xi–xii) firmly place the collaboration in the context of the then prevailing system of Indirect Rule.

Working alongside one another, the two parties were to keep to their own sphere of competence: the anthropologist was not to question policy, and the administrator was not to question the scientific findings of the anthropologist. The report enables us to see how this worked. Its Appendix C contains a long list of questions put to the anthropologist: (Q 58): 'What is the Native interpretation of the plural wives' tax? Is it unpopular? Does it affect polygyny?' (Brown and Hutt 1935: 254). The anthropologist showed that this measure was seen as a tax on women, not husbands, who obliged their wives to find the money themselves (pp. 202–4). (Q 63): 'What are the effects of whipping as a punishment?' (p. 254). (Answer): '[The people] are, on the whole, inclined to think that it is less effective than fining [which is] more akin to native concepts' (p. 207).

If all applied anthropology of the 1930s were like this, then there might be some justification for describing it as 'applied colonialism' (Onoge 1979: 63), but this experiment is interesting precisely because such close collaboration was highly unusual, not to say unique. For a start, many anthropologists were extremely reluctant to become involved with such a relationship, even when they were sought by officialdom. Leach, for example, reports that his Hpalang research was originally intended as a study monitoring the anthropologist-administrator Stevenson's 'Kachin regeneration scheme' (Leach 1977). As we know, it became nothing of the kind. Reluctance to collaborate was by no means all on one side, however, and the relationship between anthropology and the colonial service was always a difficult one.

Richards has observed that before World War II 'the colonial office . . . gave no financial support to anthropological research . . . and might be said to be famous for *not* doing so' (1977: 169). Strictly speaking, this is true only of the Colonial Office in London, for various administrations in Africa (such as the Sudan (Ahmed 1973) and Northern Rhodesia (Brown 1973)) did fund some anthropological research. Funding is not the issue here, however.

Malinowski, as we have seen, argued that anthropology could be of value to the practical person. That argument undoubtedly convinced – if it did not echo the views of – a number of influential senior people such as Lugard (see his preface to Nadel's *Black Byzantium*), and perhaps above all Lord Hailey, who in 1938 wrote enthusiastically of the potential contribution of anthropologists to colonial administration (1938: 45 ff.), but many administrators were, and remained, sceptical. Among the sceptics was Mitchell who, before the Tanganyika experiment, had published in Africa (1930) a critical reply to Malinowski's 'Practical Anthropology' paper (see Malinowski's rejoinder of 1930). The Brown–Hutt experiment, which one presumes was sired by this controversy, apparently did little to change Mitchell's mind, for he returned to the attack twenty years later (Mitchell 1951, and Schapera's reply (1951)).

One major reason for scepticism was that anthropologists, including those supported by private bodies such as the IAI, seemed to produce very little of direct value to administrators. For some anthropologists this was not for want of trying. *Africa*, for example, continued through the 1930s to provide a forum for problem-oriented anthropology (e.g. Mair 1938), to which both anthropologists and administrators contributed. Volume VIII (4) (1935) of the journal provides one illustration, with important papers on witchcraft by Evans-Pritchard, Nadel, and Richards alongside articles on 'Witchcraft and British Colonial Law' (Orde Browne) and 'Witchcraft and Colonial Administration' (Clifton Roberts). The work of Richards, who was closely associated with, but not supported by, the IAI (Smith 1934), and who took up the themes of the IAI's Five Year Plan in her preliminary account of her Bemba study (1932), was certainly considered administratively useful (Hailey 1938: 48; Brown 1973: 179), but, as Kuper (1973: 138) notes, when Wilson, who held influential views on the nature of applied anthropology, tried to set out the practical value of anthropological knowledge and expertise (in *Africa* 1940), the evidence he was able to adduce in support of his contention seems slight. Indeed, for the period through to the mid-1940s, there is only a handful of studies (notably Read 1942; Schapera 1947) which are constantly cited as outstanding examples of applied anthropology, much in the way that the episode of the Golden Stool and the Vicos Project are 'repeated in many introductory texts' (Cochrane 1971: 37–8).

In her 1944 survey of the IAI's achievements, Richards in fact admits to 'only a very moderate success' in fulfilling the original aims, adding: 'It looks as though the anthropologist has been advertising his goods, often rather clamorously, in a market in which there is little demand for them' (1944: 292). Yet despite this, and despite the critics, anthropology still had at that time its influential supporters, the most important of whom was Hailey, described by Richards as a good friend of the subject (1954: 173).

Hailey's support appears to have been crucial for the development of anthropology in the years following World War II. Shortly before the War Hailey had produced the authoritative *African Survey* (1938), in which the work of the IAI figured prominently. The *Survey* led to the Colonial Development and Welfare Act (1940) and the establishment of a fund to support a Colonial Research Committee. A branch of this committee was the Colonial Social Science Research Council (CSSRC), set up in 1944 with a strong anthropological contingent: Richards was a member, Firth was its Secretary (see, among others, Brown 1973; Chilver 1951, 1977; Forde 1953; Hailey 1944, 1957; Kuper 1973; Lee 1967; Mair 1957a, 1960; Richards 1977).

There was a direct line of descent from the IAI (and Lugard) to the CSSRC (and Hailey), and thus to the expansion of anthropological research that occurred after the War. Through the CSSRC were funded a large number of individual scholars as well as three major research institutes in East, West, and Central Africa. The success of anthropology in securing CSSRC and other funding during this period may be gauged from any list of the personnel of the institutes, and may be seen in figures for 1956 which show that of 214 British and Commonwealth social scientists then working in Africa, 90 were anthropologists or sociologists (Lee 1967: 24).

Like the IAI, the CSSRC was supposedly an 'experiment in applied research' (Richards 1977: 174, cf. 1944: 289). What type of research was it to support? Soon after the War the CSSRC funded a number of short 'look-see' tours, e.g. by Firth in West Africa, Schapera and Stanner in East Africa, and Leach in Sarawak. Many of the projects recommended by their reports were in policy-relevant areas. Firth, for example, argued that in West Africa 'there are social and economic problems of great urgency . . . sociological research in its widest meaning is needed to provide data for action and guidance in action' (1947: 180). He cited urban surveys, studies of trade and marketing, labour migration, land tenure and African commerce as priorities for investigation. A similar range of projects emerged from other reports, and in Gluckman's Seven Year Plan for the CSSRC-supported Rhodes Livingstone Institute, where labour migration was identified as of central importance for the Institute's work, as it was 'one of the most important social problems confronting the government' (Gluckman 1945: 7).

From this it might seem that despite the scepticism in official quarters, and the misgivings of many anthropologists (see below), post-War social anthropology was set on being an applied discipline, and, indeed, several applied studies, based mainly on the institutes, were undertaken with CSSRC funds. One example was the East African Institute of Social Research's survey of migrant labour in Uganda which Stanner and Schapera had recommended should be initiated by the Protectorate government. The survey thus became 'an experiment' (note how frequently that word occurs) 'in using the resources of a local research Institute on the study of a practical problem at the request of government' (Richards 1954: xiii). Preliminary work was done by two Colonial Social Research Fellows (the Sofers) and a lecturer at Makerere University College (Powesland), but later research was organized by the Institute through a steering committee comprising representatives of government departments. Several Institute Fellows (Fallers, Middleton, Southall), carrying out their own independent fieldwork in Uganda, were also drawn into the survey.

In all, this was a substantial project, but although it undoubtedly stimulated subsequent urban and industrial research in Uganda, it is not at all clear what the government was able to make of its principal conclusions (set out in Richards 1954: 223). In any case, by the time they were published the Protectorate almost certainly had other more important issues – the growing demand for independence – to consider. Elsewhere, similar 'experiments' were all too often a grave disappointment to the keener advocates of applied anthropology. Frequently the local administration was not interested in recommendations that might be made, or sometimes viewed them as an embarrassment. By the end of the 1950s, Richards was led to conclude that probably 'the most important contribution of the anthropologist to government policy has been his influence on the climate of opinion than his answers to specific questions' (1961: 7). On the other side, Hailey who had earlier been one of anthropology's strongest administrative supporters, commented in the revised edition of *An African Survey* that 'the claims of anthropologists to provide a solution to specific administrative problems' had not been substantiated (1957: 60; cf. Lee 1967: 98 ff.). Despite the flow of studies concerned with contemporary problems in the colonies there was a diminishing confidence in applied anthropology (cf. Mair 1957a: 13, 1957b: 243; Kaberry 1961: xi).

This, however, is only part of the story. For some of the leading figures in the discipline had long held fundamental reservations about this type of research. In 1938, for example, Firth had sounded 'a note of caution'. 'If the anthropologist is asked to help in making a policy of Indirect Rule more efficient, is this with the ultimate object of fitting natives for self-government . . . or . . . is it with the aim of simply getting a more cohesive community within the framework of an imperial system?' (Firth 1938: 156; cf. Firth 1977). Later he asked: 'How far can [the anthropologist] join in a policy of development which may tend to perpetuate the conditions to which he does not subscribe?' (Firth 1944: 21). Similar reservations concerning the ethical and political implications of applied anthropology, which here clearly means research in collaboration with government, are implicit in Wilson's discussion (1940) and are apparent in the cautious way in which Gluckman (1945) formulates the future relationship between the Rhodes Livingstone Institute and the administration in Central Africa.

There were also academic reservations. Evans-Pritchard began his 1946 *Africa* paper apparently endorsing applied research, but went on to warn against what would happen to research on fundamental issues such as kinship and ritual 'if we allow considerations of utility to guide and limit our research' (1946: 94). Firth, too, recorded the fear 'lest the colonial tail wag the anthropological dog . . . colonial affairs as such can have only a limited interest for anthropologists' (Evans-Pritchard and Firth 1949: 138). Anthropologists had created, and now wished to defend, their own agenda (cf. Schapera 1951: 128). Moreover, by the mid-1940s when it was clear to some (e.g. Firth 1944, 1946: 306) that the colonial era had a limited future, the security for anthropology and of the career anthropologist was thought to lie within the academy.

Evans-Pritchard returned to the theme of the academic agenda in a broadcast talk on 'Applied Anthropology' (1951) and in the Marett Lecture of 1950 (Evans-Pritchard 1950/1962). Here he developed a further objection to applied anthropology. Malinowski and others had argued that what the anthropologist provided the administration was *scientifically discovered* cultural and sociological knowledge (hence the language of 'experiments'), and a scientific framework for its explanation. Anthropologists knew, as scientists, how social and cultural systems worked. It was frequently suggested that the anthropologist should be accorded the same status in the colonial system as other scientific officers: they might be experts in, say, horticulture, while the anthropologist was the expert in culture or social structure (Schapera 1951: 135). Evans-Pritchard, however, urged the view that anthropology was a kind of history rather than a kind of natural science, and the non-scientific status of the discipline precluded application.

In sum, there was in the post-War years a movement against applied anthropology, which neither the continuing involvement in experiments with applied research by the institutes, nor the employment of the occasional anthropologist in a government advisory capacity (e.g. Gulliver) did anything to discourage. There were several reasons for this movement: a wish to distance the subject from colonialism because of disagreement with policy, or sometimes because it was foreseen that the future lay in self-government; a desire to pursue research of the discipline's own choosing, and the need for career purposes to establish academic credentials (here the snobbishness about pure research becomes relevant); and finally a growing disbelief in the possibility of application for either practical reasons – the minimal impact made on government, for instance, or intellectual ones of the kind advanced by Evans-Pritchard.

In a judicious summary of the 'colonial encounter' debate, Kuper remarks that anthropologists 'slipped into accepting that their speciality was the colonial subject . . . the consequence has been to identify anthropology with the mass humiliation of colonialism' (1973: 149). Ironically, anthropologists had often sought to distance themselves from colonial administrations, and the movement from applied anthropology may now be seen as an aspect of that distancing. Whether that was in the long run wise or not is difficult to decide. Certainly, the rejection of the applied role may have saved anthropology from being dragged down with the colonial system – if not from an identification with colonialism – but there was a cost. In the immediate post-War period anthropology had a good standing in the field of colonial development which it was able to exploit to the extent of a large amount of CSSRC funding. There is a sense, however, in which that funding was obtained under false pretences, for anthropologists were often unwilling or unable to deliver the goods. Their standing diminished in official eyes, and in other ways, too, anthropology appears to have lost ground in the changes taking place in the Colonial Office during the 1950s (Lee 1967). In consequence, when, in the 1960s, colonial regimes became post-colonial, and development became the order of the day, anthropology was in no position to offer its services or to take advantage of the opportunities that now arose. There was, it appears, no anthropologist involved in the establishment of the Overseas Development Ministry in 1964. Those anthropologists interested in development issues, entering a world dominated intellectually by economists, in which the credentials of the anthropologist were suspect, both at home and abroad, had to rebuild their profession almost from scratch.

Changing and Unchanging Contexts of Applied Research

'I consider "development anthropology" a kind of neo-colonialism.'
(Leach 1982: 50)

Aside from the intellectual objections proposed by Evans-Pritchard, the most telling arguments against application have probably been the practical and, in a broad sense, political ones: no-one really listened to what the anthropologist had to say, and in any case application was likely to mean intervening in a society or culture – itself something to which exception might be taken – for and on behalf of a system whose values the anthropologist did not share, nor wished to be seen sustaining. What, if anything, changed during the 1960s and after in such a way as to allow anthropologists to overturn the conclusions of a previous generation? One way of approaching this question is by locating applied anthropology, as an activity, in the context in which it occurs. In this section we will consider the broad, macro-political context.

To draw a stark contrast between an old-style applied anthropology of the colonial period and a new-style development anthropology of the post-colonial world (where every government came to power to implement a five-year plan for change in a climate in which formally at least very different values were at stake, ones as often as not more congenial, politically, to many anthropologists) has a certain validity, though it disguises important differences within, and similarities between, each era. Undoubtedly, as many have said, colonialism was far from homogeneous, and differences between regimes (for example, in Burma or the Pacific or in Central Africa) had implications for the work of anthropologists and for their relations with the colonizing power. Nonetheless, accepting the value of a degree of generalization, we would agree that in the colonial world 'the basic reality which made pre-War social anthropology a feasible and effective enterprise was the power relationship between dominating (European) and dominated (non-European) cultures' (Asad 1973: 17). There was a fundamental structural precondition for anthropology, a structural context formed by a global system of social, economic, and political relations in which anthropology – pure or applied – could be constituted as a subject-discipline, and of which it was inevitably a part.

Anthropologists were by no means as insensitive to this global system as is sometimes implied. Gluckman, for example, influenced by Wilson, saw the task of the Rhodes-Livingstone Institute as precisely that of studying how societies in Central Africa were 'absorbed in the modern world-system' (1949: 90). Nor was he alone in this, as Firth's writings amply demonstrate. However, within that system, and here Asad and Kuper are right, anthropology was allowed to become in effect the *specialized* study of groups caught up in the process of absorption. Nowhere was this more so than in applied research or research concerned with social change, as is illustrated by the topics (migration, the cash economy, local government, land tenure) with which that research was concerned.

To digress for a moment, it is interesting to compare what happened in colonial anthropology with what occurred in a seemingly very different field, the anthropology of Europe. Between roughly 1955 and 1977, British and American anthropologists researching in Europe, including Britain in Europe, concentrated on a limited number of themes, concerned, for example, with the culture of small rural communities, or with ethnic minorities. To some extent these themes emerged from relatively autonomous professional paradigms, but the social and political context in which anthropology was located clearly had a major influence. The vast majority of researchers came from the 'core' cultures and societies to study 'marginal' populations: inhabitants of peripheral regions such as the Celtic fringe, South Italy, Northern Norway; minorities such as immigrants or Gypsies; and, latterly, the inner cities and the 'hidden' economy. These are readily identifiable communities at the margin of society as that is defined by the centre. They are marginal to the central institutions and their relationship to those institutions is often problematic, in the way that the relationship of the 'natives' to a colonial regime was often problematic. It is not a matter of chance that there is a literature in which such groups in Europe and America are described as 'internal colonies'. That such people are seen as exotic, because different, appears to call for the expertise of the anthropologist, *par excellence* the student of the Other, and their study is frequently assigned to the anthropologist in the division of labour in the social sciences.

At this level of generalization there is a striking similarity between the anthropology of Europe, and that of the colonial era, especially in its applied form. At this level, too, contemporary anthropological research in the Third World is not so very different. The bulk of applied fieldwork over the past twenty years has been in former colonial territories, and in areas such as Latin America and the Middle East, which are all in profound ways incorporated in the modern world system. Students of the sociology or anthropology of development, Long, for example (1977: 4), in fact define their subject matter as precisely the processes of transformation which accompany that incorporation. In each case (in the colonial world, in the contemporary Third World, and in that Europe which anthropologists study) we find what may be termed 'disjunctive' social, political, and economic systems. Often over a long period, previously disparate formations have been conjoined, with varying degrees of tightness and looseness, as a roughly connected system. The process of connection itself generates various kinds of differentiation and difference between and within the constituent elements. Relations of centrality and peripherality are created, with those at the margin having problems – or indeed being themselves seen as problems – for which plans and policies are required. What seem to be gaps appear, and it is in those gaps that we find the anthropologist.

To stress in broad terms the similarities between the context of colonial applied research and that of the contemporary work in development from a perspective which is close to that of many theorists of underdevelopment (see Cheater in this volume), is not to deny the differences. These might include the way in which Third World societies are enmeshed in the world system: for example, the way that throughout the post-War period they have been used in a Cold War conflict between superpowers in which aid channelled through a complex system of national, international, and supranational agencies is itself one of the weapons. That complex system of agencies appears to Firth to be a major difference between past and present:

> 'Even with bodies such as the League of Nations, FAO and WHO, there was nothing like the pervasive modern system of highly financed, articulate, bureaucratic organizations directly concerned with development and welfare of so-called Third World and more wealthy countries, and providing channels for anthropological opinion and inquiry, of applied as well as of theoretical kind.'   (Firth 1981: 196)

A further difference stems from the political changes in the countries themselves. There are, now, few colonies left and almost everywhere indigenous governments, formally independent, rightly seek to define for themselves what kind of social research is undertaken, and to what end. Strathern's chapter in this volume discusses at length the implications of this for the work of anthropologists in one country, New Guinea. He calls for a 'long term and multiplex' reciprocity between the researcher and the country in which the research is located. A reciprocal relationship is not, however, an easy one to establish and maintain especially in the applied field in which 'projects' (the centrepieces of the development process) may well be part of the local as well as international political currency.

Here it is difficult to generalize, but many of the countries with which we are concerned share a number of features characteristic of what have been termed 'post-colonial states'. On the basis of Kenyan experience, and allowing for variation between systems, Sandbrooke offers this description:

'All underdeveloped countries pursuing a capitalist economic strategy will share certain common features of social structure . . . a small native bourgeoisie, a small capitalist-farmer stratum or perhaps a landed olig-archy, a small salariat, employed by the state, an external estate of rep-resentatives of international corporations (temporarily *in* society though not *of* it), a working class, a sub-proletariat of the unemployed and unpro-ductively employed, and a large peasantry.'

(Sandbrooke 1975: 10)

He and others have written extensively of the clientelistic politics of such societies and the way in which resource distribution, which includes aid distribution, is entangled with them.

Not all countries are like this – Kenya is not Tanzania or Mozambique – and indeed one of the striking features of the modern world is precisely the variety of regimes and roads to development, and sometimes the rapidity with which change occurs (Grenada 1979, 1982, 1983). Nevertheless, because of the way in which the international aid system operates, many of the projects on which the development anthropologist is likely to work are located in post-colonial systems of this classic kind, and 'development' has to be understood in terms of this national and international context of which it forms a part.

Many anthropologists recognize this now, as some of them recognized the significance of the imperial system for their research (pure and applied) in the colonial era. This is one of the commonest reasons for rejecting application as a viable enterprise, and must underly Leach's description of development anthropology as a 'kind of neo-colonialism'. Leach does not, unfortunately, fully explain what he means. If he means that development anthropology, and the role of the development anthropologist, has to be set in the context of a contemporary system of neo-colonialism, then he is surely right, though equally surely that must be true of any social research in Third World countries, no matter how abstruse.

To argue that development anthropology, or any anthropology, is *ipso facto* neo-colonialist in intention or effect, and should therefore be rejected, is quite a different matter. Some development anthropology might be, but then so might any kind of anthropology. Nonetheless, despite important differences, more apparent in some respects than in others, the structural context of contemporary development anthropology and that of old-style applied anthropology is broadly similar – *déjà vu, déjà connu* – and both raise similar ethical and political dilemmas.

What precisely these dilemmas are, what the possible criteria for evaluating them are, what the argument of the 'rejectionists' is, and what might be said to them, are matters to be considered more fully later in this chapter. There is, first, another dimension by reference to which applied research, and the relationships in which the applied anthropologist engages, may be contextualized: what Foster (1969) calls the 'interaction setting', the socio-political environment at a micro-level.

The Anthropologist in the Middle

'Application normally involves the pursuit of interests rather than of truth.'
(Charsley 1982: 195)

The Rothschild Report of 1971 drew attention to research, which may be identified as one kind of applied activity, in which there is a customer-contractor relationship. Though this model has the virtue of being essentially sociological, specifying a type of relationship rather than a type of subject matter, it is not an entirely adequate one through which to examine the situation of the anthropologist, even at the micro-level. The nature of the inadequacy is revealed if we glance at the ethical code of the Society for Applied Anthropology which lists not two, but four parties, to each of whom, the code suggests, the anthropologist owes a responsibility: 'our employers or other sponsors', 'our colleagues', 'society as a whole', and 'the community being served'. It is difficult to write anything about a relationship as diffuse as that between the anthropologist and 'society as a whole', but clearly Rothschild's dyad must be expanded at least to a triad to incorporate not only the contractor-anthropologist and the customer-sponsor, but also that party which for many anthropologists is probably the most important: the community being served, the subjects of enquiry.

It is useful to think in terms of such a triad (cf. Butcher n.d.) though it must be recognized for the oversimplification that it is. There may be a multiplicity of customer institutions layered in complex ways which often makes it difficult to know who is the ultimate customer. There may be a variety of bodies, formal and informal, local, national, and international, directly or indirectly concerned with the administration, planning, distribution, extraction, etc., or at least with an interest in it which they may seek to have represented

(Belshaw 1976: 214 ff.). Nor should the subjects be considered a homogeneous group, nor the anthropologist thought always to be an autonomous third or fourth or *n*th party. The micro-political environment of applied research is always a complex one. This is true of any research in the modern world, but the difference in applied research is that the anthropologist is always structurally involved in the complexity, and in many ways contributes to it. Nonetheless, simplification is justified if it allows us to concentrate on certain key features of that environment.

In some cases, and these are considered later, customer/subject are one and the same, but often in applied anthropology they are not. Development research, for example, is often sponsored by and designed for large scale bureaucratic enterprises, sometimes 'in' the society, but not 'of' it, which form part of the 'pervasive modern system' to which Firth refers. The subjects of research, who may or may not be a community, and who may or may not be being served, are those to whom the bureaucratic enterprises and institutions are oriented in various ways: administering, planning for, distributing resources to, extracting resources from, solving the problems of, instituting changes affecting, or simply considering the implications of, any of these. Frequently the object of attention is an aspect of the system of production or collective consumption in which the subjects are engaged, sometimes both, and as was suggested in the previous section, it becomes the object of attention because of large scale, long term processes of incorporation of which the particular matter to hand is an instance.

Of the three relationships in the triad, most has been said of that between customer and subject: the literature of development is largely about it. Least well documented has been that between anthropologist and customer, though recently there has emerged a distinctive ethnography of it, to which Gulliver's chapter in this volume is an important historical contribution. The emergence of that ethnography, the existence of which represents a major difference between the development anthropology of today and the applied anthropology of the colonial era, is partly a function of the self-reflexive mood that pervades the subject. It also stems from the elementary practical problems encountered by those engaged in applied research within the kind of system described above, for example, how to write a report. These seemingly trivial issues are not new – Hailey once advised anthropologists to think about 'the manner of presentment of the results of inquiry' (1944: 15) – but it is notable how important they have seemed in recent debate. Their significance is greater than if they were a simple practical difficulty which might be overcome by suitable training. To understand why this is so a digression is necessary; what do anthropologists believe they bring to applied research?

There is surprising agreement among anthropologists past and present on the nature of their contribution. Essentially it consists in a perspective, usually described as holistic, in which units of study are conceived as complex wholes consisting of a multiplicity of related elements. The totality of relationships, in the Maussian sense that each has a multiplicity of aspects, is emphasized, as is the emic or actor's perspective (see Mair 1984 for a recent restatement of these themes). In addition the indispensability of even the most trivial piece of information is emphasized. Everything is considered potentially as part of the datum of inquiry. There is also a preference for work in depth, and over a long period of time. Quality is preferred to quantity, and there is suspicion of the general as against the particular. There is an unwillingness to be pressed on cause and effect.

This, the anthropological perspective, is reinforced by our constant habit of addressing a defined literature through a language which is ours, and by a history through which we are inculcated into an unshakable commitment to certain values: a method of work (fieldwork, remember, was once described as 'our blood of the martyrs'), and a peculiar conception of time (fifteen months for fieldwork, ten years to write a monograph). We have too, or had from World War II until now, our own career structure with its own system of personal and professional evaluation. In short, we have a culture, and it is that culture which often seems to be at stake in the interaction setting of applied anthropology.

For a profession which is fully aware of the culture of its subjects, we are surprisingly slow to recognize that the 'customers' also have their culture or cultures, which in complex ways differ from our own, and we are frequently bewildered by systems which are the staple of political science and the sociology of bureaucracy. If there is one gap, between customer and subject, which the anthropologist is prepared to fill (see below), then there is another between social scientist and customer. This gap is apparent, often, in differences of life style and career expectations, but it is also apparent in differences of professional discourse: how a problem and information concerning it is encoded, what constitutes social reality and how it works. Off the record, anthropologists seem aghast at what seems to them the 'narrowness' of officialdom. In turn, the anthropologist often seems arrogant, and it is no wonder that to the colonial administrator, for example, it appeared that 'the anthropologist often offers his help but seldom actually condescends to give it' (Richards 1944: 296).

Conlin's chapter in this volume, originally written in the form of a report, illustrates the problems posed by the ways in which anthropologists and their customers, where these are bureaucracies, encode knowledge. He touches on what are seen as some of the most difficult practical problems facing the anthropologist in development. That our virtues are to others vices is nowhere better demonstrated than in the oft-cited difficulty of persuading others of the evidential value of qualitative data collected by our traditional methods of fieldwork, as against that collected by extensive surveys. Difficulties also arise through unwillingness to be pressed on cause and effect, with the result that conclusions seem inconclusive. Many social scientists will have encountered statements like the following from a senior British policy administrator:

'You people never know where you stand. Every year you have a different theory. I want you to tell me now, in this meeting, does such and such a practice have positive or negative consequences.'

Can anthropologists, asks Firth, 'give a straight answer to blunt questions of the order, what do I do now?' (Firth 1981: 198). There is, in fact, a long history of what is reported as the anthropologist's unwillingness 'to make a recommendation'. It will be recalled that the IAI's constitution precluded a concern specifically with policy, though Lugard interpreted this injunction somewhat loosely. During the 1930s, the orthodox view in anthropology was that the anthropologist *qua* scientist, objectively reported the facts (Wilson 1940: 45–6). For Firth, the 'ideal role' of the anthropologist was 'diagnosis and prediction'. By that he meant: 'to state what a situation is, and that if certain results are desired, then certain methods should be followed; and alternatively, if certain methods are followed, then certain results will probably occur' (1938: 197). Nadel, described by Foster (1969: 162) as 'more realistic', was one of the few to urge anthropologists to go beyond this position (Nadel 1951: 54–5, 1953) but this was firmly rejected by Mair: 'I do not agree that to confine oneself to indicating the implications of policy as a cowardly shirking of issues, still less a refusal to put one's knowledge at the service of humanity' (1957a: 19; cf. 1957b: 243).

If disciplinary orthodoxy compels seemingly dispassionate formulae, not of immediate use to the customer, the conclusions offered, or more generally the way in which an issue is attacked, frequently seem unpalatable to the recipient. In a memorable phrase, Firth describes anthropology as the 'uncomfortable science' (1981: 198). Sponsors often get more than they bargained for. This is not just a matter of more information than they need, though Richards recalls a colonial governor telling her to provide 'just half a sheet – just the salient facts' (1977: 178). It is rather that the findings of the anthropologist, starting from different premises, may challenge the recipient's assumptions.

Barnett provides an interesting illustration of this in his description of an episode in the Trust Territory of the Pacific Islands where an anthropologist was brought in as a 'trouble-shooter' to advise on an emergency that had arisen in connection with a strike. In his report, the anthropologist argued, presumably against the prevailing view, that the strike was only a symptom of existing economic, social and political conditions, and that 'no permanent or lasting gain can come from treating [it] as the problem to be solved' (Barnett 1956: 161). The report proposed a number of far-reaching measures to deal with what the anthropologist diagnosed as the fundamental issues.

In this way anthropological knowledge often seems, and often is, dangerous, or embarrassing. This is not because we are good at digging dirt (though we do, professionally, pay a lot of attention to gossip), or because we try to unravel 'what actually happens', but because we are likely to treat the customers themselves as part of the datum of enquiry, and thus as part of the problem under consideration. Superficial acquaintance with anthropology may make it seem a safe discipline, especially appropriate when 'other cultures' are the object of attention, but our interpretation of 'other' may be very wide indeed.

This subversive potential of anthropology, which stems from our methodology, could be seen as one of our greatest strengths, but it has to be recognized that in reality the customer–contractor relationship is one in which the power to define what is and is not possible resides usually with the customer. This means that the anthropologist is inevitably caught in a web of compromise. Traditional methods may have to be abandoned in favour of rapid surveys which satisfy the demand for 'a table on every page' (cf. Richards 1944: 296). Restraints on access to persons and evidence, on the dissemination of findings, and – most important – the ability to define the nature of the problem under investigation, may have to be accepted. The anthropologist may have to be reconciled to the selective reading of a detailed research report and its incorporation as, say, one line in a ministerial brief, or even perhaps to the fact that a study has been undertaken to enable an institution to declare that a study has been undertaken (Epstein 1980: 453). The question that all this raises is how far are we prepared to go, and on what terms, and yet retain our professional and personal self-respect?

Applied research, in which the customer is a large, bureaucratic enterprise always involves, too, the danger that the anthropologist is led into compromising his or her relationship with those who constitute for many of us the most important party, the subjects themselves. This has led some to conclude that the only kind of acceptable application is that which is for and on behalf of the subjects themselves. Judith Okely, for example, in a comment on the ASA's third Decennial, remarked: 'A prevailing assumption seemed to be that policy research would be done only for the power élites; obviously they pay the piper. A few voices reminded us that policy research could and should be put at the disposal of subordinate groups with whom anthropologists have claimed to empathize' (1983: 12; cf. Sarsby 1984). Yet this type of application poses its own problems, too.

It was suggested that Rothschild's dyad was inadequate because it ignored the subject. Interestingly, anthropology used to present its enterprise in dyadic terms also. Many, chief among them Evans-Pritchard ('During fifteen years during which I worked on sociological problems [in the Sudan] I was never once asked my advice on any question at all' (1946: 97, cf. Morris 1977: 210), effectively wrote out that other third party, who in this case might be loosely identified with Firth's 'outside authority'. The idea that the anthropologist might be at one apex of a triangular relationship was hardly perceived, other than in exceptional circumstances of the kind encountered by Evans-Pritchard in Cyrenaica where he was 'able to acquaint myself at first hand with Arab needs and difficulties and bring them to the notice of the head of the administration' (Evans-Pritchard 1946).

In fact, much traditional research, not of a consciously applied kind, has involved anthropologists in a triadic relationship in which they take on the role of mediator, broker or spokesperson between their subjects and the 'outside authority' (see Barnett 1956; Cochrane 1971; Firth 1977, 1981; Lewis 1977; Lloyd 1977; Mair 1957a; Schapera 1947; Schensul and Schensul 1978; Strathern 1979). This may happen so casually as to pass without notice, disguised as the multiplicity of services rendered to informant-friends. Driving them to hospital is a common enough example. But rendering service by liaising with government, missionaries, schools, employers or police may pass in easy stages to a form of 'gatekeeping' of the kind with which we are familiar from the literature on mediators, brokers, patrons and clients, though that literature rarely mentions the anthropologist.

Sometimes, through such mediation, the subjects become in effect customers. Layton's paper provides an account of one situation where this has occurred extensively: Australian courts adjudicating Aboriginal land claims. There, the anthropologist testifies as an expert witness, reporting anthropological data on behalf of a group of clients on which he or she may be cross-examined in open court. This role has been less common among British anthropologists than it has been among their counterparts in the United States (see Dobyns 1978; Schensul and Schensul 1978), though examples did occur during the colonial period. Layton comments that in these cases there is 'a danger that anthropologists will cease objective reporting and analysis, and become advocates for particular groups'. His implied contrast between the objectivity of the expert witness and the commitment of the advocate, and his concern at the spectacle of 'anthropologists opposing each other in court', troubles others besides anthropologists. That concern was shared by American linguists involved in the recent Ann Arbor court case which raised highly controversial linguistic, and political, issues (Labov 1982). There, as in the Aboriginal land cases, the professional social scientists agreed to testify on behalf of a group of claimants to certain rights whose cause they espoused. Need this always be the case? Or should the expert witness be prepared, lawyer-like, to offer professional services to anyone, whatever is privately felt to be the merits of the client's case. If the anthropologist can testify for the Aborigines, why not for the mining companies too?

In fact, where subjects are in effect customers, the engagement of the anthropologist usually derives from a commitment to their cause. A number of writers, especially in the United States, would, however, argue that commitment alone is insufficient. What is sometimes termed 'advocacy anthropology' seeks to go far beyond the provision of expert evidence marshalled on behalf of a group. 'The aim of the "expert"', say Schensul and Schensul, 'must be to increase the capability of client group members to speak for themselves in political, planning and service areas' (1978: 122). This is the approach taken by those who favour 'action anthropology' of the kind developed through participation in the Fox Project (Lurie 1973; Peterson 1978; Tax 1975; Van

Willigen 1976). The emphasis is on working with and through a local community 'to facilitate indigenous social action programs by supplying data and results which can make significant contributions to the effectiveness of their efforts' (Schensul 1973: 111–12). Gerrit Huizer puts it more romantically: 'To learn from people about their lives, to help them look, with an emancipatory perspective, at their society and themselves, to experience with them the tremendous potential for united effort, to help them find ways to channel this potential, and to experience together the actual emancipatory activities' (1979b: 417).

There are few, if any, adherents of this kind of applied anthropology in Britain, though the kind of commitment it espouses is surely apparent in Strathern's paper in this volume (and see also Sarsby 1984). It has emerged in a political culture very different from that experienced by most British anthropologists, though its relevance to certain kinds of community politics which are present in Britain should be obvious. More usually British experience is of a much more indirect kind of representation.

Gulliver, in this volume, says he assumed two responsibilities while working as government anthropologist in Tanganyika: 'to act as spokesman for African interests, attitudes and expectations . . . (and) as protester where inefficacies and injustices existed'. He shows that such responsibilities emerged from the structural relationship between Africans and administrators in the colonial system, and from the social, economic, cultural and linguistic gap between the two parties. As anthropologist, he bridged the gap.

This phenomenon is a feature of all disjunctive systems, and is not confined to the colonial context. It is the phenomenon which action or advocacy anthropology attacks. How successful can that attack be? Cheater's paper, in this volume, concludes that in recently independent Zimbabwe 'the anthropologist's colonial role as mediator between government and people has already given way to the ability of wealthier people to negotiate directly with their popularly elected, but not always popularly supported governments'. Yet the reality is that because of their structural position in disjunctive systems many of those who are anthropologists' subjects are forced into inarticulateness *vis-à-vis* those in power and at the centre. The anthropologist is often in a position to make their case with greater effect. At that point the anthropologist becomes a 'translator'.

That the anthropological enterprise as a whole constitutes a kind of translation, in several senses, has long been influential, and has recently been restated by Ardener (1983). Whisson, in this volume, draws attention to Monica Wilson's discussion of this point in which she identifies two interpretative functions: a primary one of communication, and a secondary one of negotiation (Wilson 1972: 20). Whisson comments: 'The "pure" anthropologist will limit himself to Wilson's primary function, the "applied" anthropologist will be no less concerned with the second.' It should go without saying, however, that no act of interpretation, neither in Wilson's nor

Ardener's senses, occurs in a social, cultural or political void. We need to be clear about the context in which they occur, and indeed in which they are possible.

Gulliver's discussion of the administrative culture of colonial Tanganyika enables us to see what interpretation meant and why it occurred. Gulliver felt obliged to undertake this role, but many anthropologists resent the position of apparent power into which they feel they are manoeuvred by systems which create a structural need for articulators and negotiators. It is then that the dangers of neo-colonialism or at least neo-paternalism seem greatest. But if we accept that inarticulacy in the face of external authority is often part of the reality of the situation, how can the anthropologist hope to avoid this role? The choice is often between accepting the status of articulator, thereby sustaining, if only temporarily, the system which created the need for it, and allowing matters to take their course, perhaps to the detriment of the subjects' well-being.

This discussion of the micro-politics of the customer–anthropologist–subject triad has not encompassed every aspect of the relationships involved, nor could it in a chapter of this kind. But enough has been said in this, and in the previous section on the wider political context of the development process, to suggest that the dilemmas and difficulties which face those who engage in development anthropology, or indeed any kind of applied research, are such as to justify those who would wish to have nothing to do with it. Paradoxically, perhaps, this is not the conclusion to be reached here, though it may be wished that anyone who engages in applied work, or who contemplates so doing, is fully aware of the problems that such work poses.

Anthropologists in Development: Choice and Responsibility

'He had no illusions about his work: he had put his knowledge in the service of whatever power happened to be in the land, and never took an attitude. Thus he had served the colonial regime with the same relentless unsparing energy that he did an independent African government . . . His secret ambition was one day to set up a private practice . . . so that, like a lawyer or priest, his services could be hired by anybody.'

(Ngũgĩ wa Thiong'o 1977: 43)

For those who reject the theoretical possibility of application, because of their view of anthropology's subject matter, or because they conceive anthropology to be no more, or no less, than a form of self-reflexive philosophy, or a kind of history – and the idea of an 'applied history' is absurd – there is no problem. They need read no further. It is to those, perhaps the majority now, who accept at the very least a theoretical potential for application that the following remarks are addressed.

It was suggested earlier that there is widespread agreement about the sort of contribution that an anthropologist, as opposed to another kind of social scientist, might make to a field such as development; the bringing to bear of a certain frame of mind or manner of thinking which illuminates the social and cultural dimensions of a problem. This is our main, and long-standing claim to attention, made years ago by Malinowski and Radcliffe-Brown, though few now would justify that claim by any reference to the *scientific* status of anthropological knowledge, at least in the way that Malinowski and Radcliffe-Brown did (but see Partridge and Eddy 1978: 42).

In recent years, in the development field, the case for the social and cultural dimension has been argued in opposition to the views of economists and other technical experts (see Hill in this volume; Colson 1971; Epstein 1976). Disillusionment with programmes and projects conceived mainly in economic and technological terms, in development as well as in other fields too, such as industry, has led to a growing acceptance of the anthropologists' view of the importance of social and cultural factors, and the dire consequences which follow their neglect. Foster (1969) provides a huge number of examples which demonstrate this lesson, and the work of Cochrane (1971, 1979, 1980) is a systematic account of the relevance of what he terms 'cultural appraisal'.

For those who accept these arguments, or at the very least are struck by what Sandra Wallman has called 'a chronic desire to be useful', the problem is whether there *should* be application, and under what conditions. At that point the debate is unavoidably ethical and political (Barnes 1983).

The various perspectives that are taken may be grouped roughly into three. First there are the principled rejectionists, of whom there are several kinds. Some would argue that the anthropologist has no special right *qua* anthropologist, to intervene in social affairs, and that to do so entails a form of élitism or paternalism: 'the gentleman in Whitehall really does know better' (Jay 1947: 258). Another view is that faced with the complexity of the setting within which application takes place, and the distastefulness of almost all regimes, the anthropologist must turn away and hope for better times. This has been the response of many anthropologists in the United States to revelations about social scientists' involvement in Project Camelot and in south-east Asia (Belshaw 1976; Partridge and Eddy 1978, among others). It is worth noting that British anthropologists have never been tested in quite that way. Others would argue on more obviously political grounds that the theorists of development, for example, are correct, and what is at issue is the system as a whole, and that anthropologists must resist incorporation within it. We will see shortly what might be said to this group.

A second position may be described as 'monitorist'. The anthropologist must monitor what happens, 'diagnose and predict', understand what occurs and bring that understanding to the public's attention. This is an honourable tradition in the subject, established by concerned anthropologists of the colonial era such as Firth, Mair, Read, Richards and Schapera, and later by writers such as Colson (1971) and Epstein (1962). More recently Charsley has urged the importance of 'an anthropological study of development which is entirely separate from application and logically prior to it' (1982: 194). This is what he and others call the 'anthropology *of* development'. The aim of this research is to investigate specific plans, policies or projects and their implementation. The importance throughout the development world of 'the project' as the principal unit of organization suggests that 'project ethnographics' (Rew in this volume) should be a central feature of such an anthropology. Charsley, following Foster (1969: 96, 113) has indicated that the study of development bureaucracies is another urgent task. Apthorpe, also in this volume, considers that the rhetoric of development policy, treated as political discourse, is a rich field of study, with important implications for our understanding of how that policy works.

The monitorists' aim need not, of course, be confined to policy specialists. It could be argued that where, as frequently happens, a project is implemented in an area which has been intensively studied by any anthropologist, there is an opportunity – some would say duty – to monitor what occurs, and if necessary comment publicly on its impact. This might be one way of repaying the debt that anthropologists owe their subjects and actualizing the exchange which Strathern rightly believes so crucial.

What distinguishes an anthropology *of* development from what Cochrane and others term 'development anthropology' is precisely a separation of study and application to which Charsley refers. The anthropologist of development is usually at some distance from the action, so to speak. Slightly closer to it are those who seek collaboration with development anthropologists, or what Rew calls 'policy professionals', without themselves being directly involved.

Conlin, in the ASA's 1983 *Newsletter*, drew attention to the fact that in his work as an anthropologist in overseas development he had difficulty in finding research which would be useful to a social adviser. He warned: 'Unless British social anthropology responds to the demand for basic research in areas of policy concern it will be increasingly marginalized.' Hill's paper might be read as a response to that plea. It explores the way in which detailed cross-cultural evidence can be collated and compared in such a way as to provide a number of models of different kinds of agrarian system in a form which would be of direct use to policy planners. Her chapter, and that of Curtis, point to gaps in contemporary anthropological theory of the middle range which ought, in their view, to provide the foundations on which those directly concerned with the devising and implementing of policies might base their judgements.

This research, which is basic in Rothschild's sense, is an important area of possible collaboration between anthropologists inside and outside the academy, but it is research which is in the strict sense irresponsible: the producer is not accountable for the end use of the product. That brings us to the third group, represented by Conlin and Rew, and in some aspects of their work by others in this volume who are actively engaged in customer–

contractor relationships in which they are called upon to devise and review development policies. Let us call them 'activists'; they stand at the opposite end of the spectrum to the rejectionists.

It is in contrasting the two perspectives that we come to the heart of the ethical and political issues that are at stake in this field. Let us return to the dilemma of the anthropologist who refuses as a matter of principle the role of articulator or spokesperson. The justification of that refusal, other than on grounds of humility, must inevitably be of an anti-reformist kind, similar to that which leads the rejectionist to refuse incorporation within the process of (under) development: no amelioration, however small, is justifiable if it perpetuates a system which is wrong. The activists, on the other hand, unless they would want to claim they accept the system in its entirety, or that they are 'only doing a job', must justify their position through some version of reformism. Development is happening, it might be said, much of it bad, but some perhaps useful and wanted by those who are affected, with or without the participation of anthropologists. But there is a reasonable chance that the application of anthropological knowledge will moderate the bad and enhance the good (Belshaw 1976: 257).

Cochrane makes this point particularly strongly: 'At a time when anthropological knowledge is badly needed in the emerging nations there is little justification for moralizing to the extent that nothing gets done' (1971: 9). This, generally, is Rew's position, too, but it leads Redclift to ask: 'Is it better that anthropologists get involved in development on the wrong side, for the wrong people, for the wrong reasons, than they stay motionless on the touchline?' Clearly a reformist perspective – the belief that in the long run development, say, is better with anthropology than without it, cannot absolve the anthropologist from all political and ethical choice. Many would argue to the contrary that there must always be limits, that the anthropologist must exercise choice and retain the freedom to accept or reject participation in a particular project or programme (Foster 1969: 178; cf. Firth 1944: 21). Gulliver (in this volume) sets one limit when he urges that applied research must have a 'benevolent environment', one in which there is 'reasonable opportunity for the anthropologist to work and genuinely to be heeded' (see also Mair 1984: 135).

There may obviously be some environments which are more benevolent than others, but the criterion of room for anthropological manoeuvre is a useful one to bear in mind if we consider another question which often seems the most important: what dealings can there be with regimes of which the anthropologist actively disapproves? This was a dilemma constantly faced by colonial anthropologists, many of whom, as Gulliver reminds us, could be categorized in Memmi's phrase as 'colonizers who refuse': those who benefited from the colonial system while ultimately rejecting it and doing what they could to ease its impact, or in some cases hasten its end.

In the contemporary world nowhere is this dilemma more acute than in

South Africa (cf. Gluckman 1975). Whisson's use of 'collaboration' in his assessment of the choices open to those who elect to stay in such a country is presumably deliberate. It inevitably calls to mind the experience of those in occupied Europe. His discussion reminds us of three things. First, that the ethical and political dilemma of the anthropologist in South Africa is not the dilemma solely of the *applied* anthropologist. Second, that few contemporary anthropologists, pure or applied, have ever been confronted with problems as difficult as those faced day by day by colleagues in South Africa. Third, even in such conditions there is room for manoeuvre; participation does not inevitably mean collaboration.

The profession in Britain has so far refrained from establishing an ethical code to guide the conduct of its members, and it is difficult to envisage one which steered a satisfactory course between pious generality and what many would believe to be oppressive restriction on their freedom as researchers. All that can be urged is a high degree of awareness of the issues, a consciousness of the framework within which the applied anthropologist works and within which decisions on principle must be made. This may seem limp, but it is probably all that can be said at this time, though what might happen if (when?) British anthropology encounters its Project Camelot remains to be seen.

The argument sketched here leads, then, to a perspective which might be termed conditional reformism. Anthropology has much to offer the world of development – though that world has yet to be completely convinced of its value. But we must be fully aware of what involvement in that world means, ethically, politically and practically. Applied anthropologists need an especially high degree of consciousness of what is and is not possible, of what has historically been possible and what has not; optimism – yes – but also realism, and a stronger sense of scepticism, too. They will also need an exceptionally thick skin.

References

AHMED, A. G. M. (1973) Some Remarks from the Third World on Anthropology and Colonialism: the Sudan. In T. Asad (ed.) *Anthropology and the Colonial Encounter*. London: Ithaca Press.
— (1979) The Relevance of Contemporary Economic Anthropology. In G. Huizer and B. Mannheim (eds) *The Politics of Anthropology*. The Hague: Mouton.
AKEROYD, A., GRILLO, R. D., and TAPPER, N. (1980) Training and Employment of Social Anthropologists. *Royal Anthropological Institute Newsletter* December 1980: 5–7.
ARDENER, E. (1983) Social Anthropology, Language and Reality. In D. J. Parkin (ed.) *Semantic Anthropology*. London: Academic Press, ASA Monographs 22.
ASAD, T. (ed.) (1973) *Anthropology and the Colonial Encounter*. London: Ithaca Press.
BARIC, L., CONLIN, S., GRILLO, R. D., and WALLMAN, S. (1983) Report of the ASA Action Committee for Employment and Training in Applied Anthropology. Cyclostyled.

BARNES, J. A. (1983) Why Bother about Ethics? *Australian Anthropological Society Newsletter* September.

BARNETT, H. G. (1956) *Anthropology and Administration*. Evanston, Illinois: Row, Peterson.

BASTIDE, R. (1973) *Applied Anthropology*. London: Croom Helm.

BEATTIE, J. (1965) *Understanding an African Kingdom: Bunyoro*. New York: Holt, Rinehart, & Winston.

BELSHAW, C. (1976) *The Sorcerer's Apprentice: An Anthropology of Public Policy*. New York: Pergamon Press.

BROKENSHA, D. (1966) *Applied Anthropology in English-speaking Africa*. Ithaca, NY: Society for Applied Anthropology Monograph 8.

BROWN, G. and HUTT, A. MCD. B. (1935) *Anthropology in Action: An Experiment in the Iringa District of the Iringa Province, Tanganyika Territory*. London: Oxford University Press for the International Institute of African Languages and Cultures.

BROWN, R. (1973) Anthropology and Colonial Rule: Godfrey Wilson and the Rhodes–Livingstone Institute, Northern Rhodesia. In T. Asad *Anthropology and the Colonial Encounter*. London: Ithaca Press.

— (1979) Passages in the life of a White Anthropologist: Max Gluckman in Northern Rhodesia. *Journal of African History* 20: 525–41.

BUTCHER, D. (n.d.) The Applied Anthropologist in Development Projects. Cyclostyled.

CHARSLEY, S. (1980) Comment on Cochrane. *Current Anthropology* 21 (4): 452.

— (1982) *Culture and Sericulture: Social Anthropology and Development in a South Indian Livestock Industry*. London: Academic Press.

CHILVER, E. (1951) The Institutes of Social and Economic Research in the African Colonies. *Journal of African Administration* III: 178–86.

— (1977) The Secretaryship of the Colonial Social Science Research Council: a Reminiscence. In P. Loizos (ed.) Anthropological Research in British Colonies: Some Personal Accounts. *Anthropological Forum* IV (2).

COCHRANE, G. (1971) *Development Anthropology*. New York: Oxford University Press.

— (ed.) (1976) *What Can We Do For Each Other? An Interdisciplinary Approach to Development Anthropology*. Amsterdam: B. R. Gruner.

— (1979) *The Cultural Appraisal of Development Projects*. New York: Praeger Special Studies.

— (1980) Policy Studies and Anthropology. *Current Anthropology* 21 (4): 445–58.

COLSON, E. (1971) *The Social Consequences of Resettlement: The Impact of the Kariba Resettlement upon the Tonga*. Manchester: Manchester University Press.

CONDOMINAS, G. (1979) Notes on the Present-day State of Anthropology in the Third World. In G. Huizer and B. Mannheim *The Politics of Anthropology*. The Hague: Mouton.

DOBYNS, H. F. (1978) Taking the Witness Stand. In E. M. Eddy and W. L. Partridge (eds) *Applied Anthropology in America*. New York: Columbia University Press.

EDDY, E. M. and PARTRIDGE, W. L. (eds) (1978) *Applied Anthropology in America*. New York: Columbia University Press.

EPSTEIN, T. S. (1962) *Economic Development and Social Change in South India*. Manchester: Manchester University Press.

— (1976) The Ideal Marriage between the Economist's Macro Approach and the Anthropologist's Micro Approach. In G. Cochrane (ed.) *What Can We Do For Each Other?* Amsterdam: B. R. Gruner.

— (1980) Comment on Cochrane. *Current Anthropology* 21 (4): 453.

EVANS-PRITCHARD, E. E. (1946) Applied Anthropology. *Africa* 16 (1): 92–8.

— (1950) Social Anthropology Past and Present. (The Marett Lecture 1950.) In E. E. Evans-Pritchard (1962) *Essays in Social Anthropology*. London: Faber & Faber.

— (1951) *Social Anthropology*. London: Cohen & West.

— and FIRTH, R. (1949) Anthropology and Colonial Affairs. *Man* XLIX: 137–38.

FARIS, J. C. (1973) Pax Britannica and the Sudan: S. F. Nadel. In T. Asad (ed.) *Anthropology and the Colonial Encounter*. London: Ithaca Press.

FEUCHTWANG, S. (1973) The Colonial Formation of British Social Anthropology. In T. Asad *Anthropology and the Colonial Encounter*. London: Ithaca Press.

FIRTH, R. (1938) *Human Types* (first edition) London: T. Nelson and Sons.

— (1944) The Future of Social Anthropology. *Man* XLIV: 19–22.

— (1946) *Malay Fishermen*. London: Routledge & Kegan Paul.

— (1947) Social Problems and Research in British West Africa. *Africa* 17: 77–92; 170–80.

— (1958) *Human types* (second edition). New York: Mentor Books.

— (1977) Whose Frame of Reference? In P. Loizos (ed.) *Anthropological Research in British Colonies*. Some Personal Accounts. *Anthropological Forum* IV (2).

— (1981) Engagement and Detachment: Reflections on Applying Social Anthropology to Social Affairs. *Human Organization* 40 (3): 193–201.

FORDE, D. (1945) Social Development in Africa and the Work of the International African Institute. *Journal of the Royal Society of Arts* XCIII (4682): 71–83.

— (1953) Applied Anthropology in Government: British Africa. In A. L. Kroeber *et al. Anthropology Today*. Chicago: University of Chicago Press.

FORSTER, P. (1973) Empiricism and Imperialism: A Review of the New Left Critique of Social Anthropology. In T. Asad (ed.) *Anthropology and the Colonial Encounter*. London: Ithaca Press.

FOSTER, GEORGE M. (1969) *Applied Anthropology*. Boston: Little, Brown and Co.

FRANK, A. G. (1979) Anthropology = Ideology, Applied Anthropology = Politics. In G. Huizer and B. Mannheim (eds) *The Politics of Anthropology*. The Hague: Mouton.

FULLER, C. J. (1982) Is Anthropology Special? *Royal Anthropological Institute Newsletter* 48: 16–17.

GLUCKMAN, M. (1945) The Seven Year Research Plan of the Rhodes–Livingstone Institute. *Human Problems in British Central Africa* IV: 1–32.

— (1949) The Village Headman in British Central Africa. *Africa* XIX (2): 89–94.

— (1975) Anthropology and Apartheid: The Work of South African Anthropologists. In M. Fortes and S. Patterson (eds) *Studies in African Social Anthropology*. London: Academic Press.

GOLDSCHMIDT, W. (ed.) (1979) *The Uses of Anthropology*. Washington: American Anthropological Association, Special Publication 11.

— and SANDAY, P. R., The Present Uses of Anthropology, An Overview. In Goldschmidt (ed.) *The Uses of Anthropology*. Washington: American Anthropological Association, Special Publication 11.

GOUGH, KATHLEEN (1968) New Proposals for Anthropologists. *Current Anthropology* 9(5): 403–07.

GOWLER, D. and CLARKE, G. (1983) The Employment and Training of British Social Anthropologists. Report to the Social Science Research Council. Cyclostyled.

HAILEY, LORD WILLIAM (1938) *An African Survey*. London: Oxford University Press.

— (1944) The Role of Anthropology in Colonial Development. *Man* XLIV: 10–15.

— (1957) *An African Survey Revised* (1956). London: Oxford University Press.

HOGBIN, H. I. (1957) Anthropology as Public Service and Malinowski's Contribution to it. In R. Firth (ed.) *Man and Culture*. London: Routledge & Kegan Paul.

HUIZER, G. (1979a) Anthropology and Politics: From Naïveté toward Liberation? In G. Huizer and B. Mannheim *The Politics of Anthropology*. The Hague: Mouton.

— (1979b) Research-through-action: Some Practical Experiences With Peasant Organization. In G. Huizer and B. Mannheim (eds) *The Politics of Anthropology*. The Hague: Mouton.

34   Ralph Grillo

— and MANNHEIM, B. (eds) (1979) *The Politics of Anthropology*. The Hague: Mouton.
International Institute of African Languages and Cultures (1932) A Five Year Plan of Research. *Africa* 5 (1): 1–13.
JAMES, W. (1973) The Anthropologist as Reluctant Imperialist. In T. Asad (ed.) *Anthropology and the Colonial Encounter*. London: Ithaca Press.
JAY, D. (1947) *The Socialist Case*. London: Faber & Faber.
KABERRY, P. (1961) Introduction. In B. Malinowski *The Dynamics of Culture Change*. New Haven: Yale University Press.
KUPER, A. (1973) *Anthropology and Anthropologists: The British School 1922–72*. London: Penguin.
LABOV, W. (1982) Objectivity and Commitment in Linguistic Science: The Case of the Black English Trial in Ann Arbor. *Language in Society* 11 (2): 165–201.
LACKNER, H. (1973) Social Anthropology and Indirect Rule. In T. Asad (ed.) *Anthropology and the Colonial Encounter*. London: Ithaca Press.
LANDMAN, R. H. (1978) Applied Anthropology in Post-colonial Britain: The Present and the Prospect. *Human Organization* 37 (3): 323–27.
LEACH, E. R. (1977) In Formative Travail with Leviathan. In P. Loizos (ed.) *Anthropological Forum* IV (2).
— (1982) *Social Anthropology*. London: Fontana.
LEE, J. M. (1967) *Colonial Development and Good Government*. Oxford: Clarendon Press.
LEWIS, DIANA (1973) Anthropology and Colonialism. *Current Anthropology* 14 (5): 581–91.
LEWIS, I. M. (1977) Confessions of a 'Government' Anthropologist. In P. Loizos (ed.) *Anthropological Forum* IV (2).
LLOYD, P. C. (1977) The Taming of a Young Turk. In P. Loizos (ed.) *Anthropological Forum* IV (2).
LOIZOS, P. (ed.) (1977) Anthropological Research in British Colonies: Some Personal Accounts. *Anthropological Forum* IV (2): 137–248.
LONG, N. (1977) *An Introduction to the Sociology of Rural Development*. London: Tavistock Publications.
LUGARD, F. D. (1922) *The Dual Mandate in British Tropical Africa*. Edinburgh: Blackwood.
— (1928) The International Institute of African Languages and Cultures. *Africa* 1: 1–12.
— (1942) Foreword to S. F. Nadel, *A Black Byzantium*. London: Oxford University Press for the International African Institute.
LURIE, N. (1973) *Anthropology and the American Indian*. San Francisco: Indian Historical Press.
MAIR, L. P. (1936) *Native Policies in Africa*. London: George Routledge and Sons.
— (ed.) (1938) *Methods of Study of Culture Contact in Africa*. International African Institute Memorandum XV.
— (1957a) *Studies in Applied Anthropology*. London: LSE Monographs on Social Anthropology 16, Athlone Press.
— (1957b) Malinowski and the Study of Social Change. In Firth, *Man and Culture*. London: Routledge & Kegan Paul.
— (1960) The Social Sciences in Africa South of the Sahara: The British Contribution. *Human Organization* 19: 98–107.
— (1969) *Anthropology and Social Change*. London: LSE Monographs on Social Anthropology 38, Athlone Press.
— (1984) *Anthropology and Development*. London: Macmillan.
MALINOWSKI, B. (1929) Practical Anthropology. *Africa* 2 (1): 22–38.
— (1930) The Rationalization of Anthropology and Administration. *Africa* 3 (4): 405–30.

— (1939) The Present State of Studies in Culture Contact. *Africa* 12 (1): 27–48.
— (1961) *The Dynamics of Culture Change*. New Haven: Yale University Press.
MITCHELL, P. E. (1930) The Anthropologist and the Practical Man: A Reply and a Question. *Africa* 3 (2): 217–23.
— (1935) Introduction to G. Brown and A. Hutt *Anthropology in Action*.
— (1951) Review of Lord Hailey's 'Native Administration in the British Territories in Africa'. *Journal of African Administration* III: 55–65.
MORRIS, H. S. (1977) Constraints on Research in Colonial and Post-colonial Sarawak. In P. Loizos (ed.) *Anthropological Forum* IV (2).
NADEL, S. F. (1951) *The Foundations of Social Anthropology*. London: Cohen.
— (1953) *Anthropology and Modern Life: An Inaugural Lecture, 10 July, 1953*. Canberra: Australian National University.
NGŪGĪ WA THIONG'O (1977) *Petals of Blood*. London: Heinemann.
OKELY, J. (1983) A View from the Terraces. *Royal Anthropological Institute Newsletter* 58: 12.
ONOGE, O. F. (1979) The Counter-revolutionary Tradition in African Studies: The Case of Applied Anthropology. In G. Huizer and B. Mannheim (eds) *The Politics of Anthropology*. The Hague: Mouton.
OWUSU, M. (1979) Colonial and Post-Colonial Anthropology of Africa: Scholarship or Sentiment? In G. Huizer and B. Mannheim, *The Politics of Anthropology*. The Hague: Mouton.
PARTRIDGE, W. L. and EDDY, E. M. (1978) The Development of Applied Anthropology in America. In E. M. Eddy and W. L. Partridge (eds) *Applied Anthropology in America*. New York: Columbia University Press.
PETERSON, J. H., jnr (1978) The Changing Role of an Applied Anthropologist. In E. M. Eddy and W. L. Partridge (eds) *Applied Anthropology in America*. New York: Columbia University Press.
POLGAR, S. (1979) From Applied to Committed Anthropology: Disengaging from Our Colonialist Heritage. In G. Huizer and B. Mannheim (eds) *The Politics of Anthropology*. The Hague: Mouton.
RADCLIFFE-BROWN, A. R. (1931) Applied Anthropology. *Proceedings of the Australian and New Zealand Association for the Advancement of Science*. 20th Meeting, Brisbane 1930: 267–80.
READ, M. (1942) Migrant labour in Africa and its Effects on Tribal Life. *International Labour Review* 45: 605–31.
REINING, C. C. (1962) A Lost Period of Applied Anthropology. *American Anthropologist* 64: 593–600.
RICHARDS, A. I. (1932) African Problems in North-eastern Rhodesia. *Africa* 5 (2): 121–44.
— (1944) Practical Anthropology in the Lifetime of the International African Institute. *Africa* 14 (6): 289–301.
— (ed.) (1954) *Economic Development and Tribal Change*. Cambridge: Heffers.
— (1961) Anthropology on the Scrap-Heap? *Journal of African Administration* XIII (1): 3–10.
— (1977) The Colonial Office and the Organization of Research. In P. Loizos (ed.) *Anthropological Forum* IV (2).
ROBERTSON, A. F. (1975) Anthropology and Government in Ghana. *African Affairs* 74: 51–64.
ROTHSCHILD, LORD (1971) *A Framework for Government Research and Development*. Cmnd. 4814. London: HMSO.
— (1982) *An Enquiry into the Social Science Research Council 1981–82*. Cmnd. 8554. London: HMSO.
SANDBROOKE, R. (1975) *Proletarians and African Capitalism: The Kenya Case, 1960–72*. Cambridge: Cambridge University Press.

SARSBY, J. (1984) Advocacy and Anthropology. *Royal Anthropological Institute News-letter* 60: 4–5.

SCHAPERA, I. (1947) *Migrant Labour and Tribal Life*. London: Oxford University Press.

— (1951) Anthropology and the Administrator. *Journal of African Administration* III: 128–35.

SCHENSUL, S. L. (1973) Action Research: The Applied Anthropologist in a Community Mental Health Program. In A. Redfield (ed.) *Anthropology Beyond the University*. Athens, Georgia: University of Georgia Press.

— and SCHENSUL, J. J. (1978) Advocacy and Applied Anthropology. G. H. Weber and G. J. McCall (eds) *Social Scientists as Advocates*. London: Sage Publications.

SMITH, E. W. (1934) The Story of the Institute: A Survey of Seven Years. *Africa* 7 (1): 1–27.

SPICER, EDWARD H. (1976) Beyond Analysis and Explanation? Notes on the Life and Times of the Society for Applied Anthropology. *Human Organization* 35 (4): 335–43.

STAVENHAGEN, R. (1971) Decolonizing Applied Social Sciences. *Human Organization* 30: 333–44.

STEWART, OMER C. (1983) Historical Notes about Applied Anthropology in the United States. *Human Organization* 42 (3): 189–94.

STRATHERN, A. (1979) Anthropology, 'Snooping', and Commitment: A View from Papua New Guinea. In G. Huizer and B. Mannheim (eds) *The Politics of Anthropology*. The Hague: Mouton.

TAX, S. (1975) Action Anthropology. *Current Anthropology* 16: 514–17.

TEMPLE, SIR R. (1914) *Anthropology as a Practical Science*. London: G. Bell.

VAN WILLIGEN, J. (1976) Applied Anthropology and Community Development Administration: A Critical Assessment. In M. V. Angrosino (ed.) *Do Applied Anthropologists Apply Anthropology?* Athens: University of Georgia Press.

WEBER, G. H. and MCCALL, G. J. (eds) (1978) *Social Scientists as Advocates*. London: Sage Publications.

WILSON, G. (1940) Anthropology as a Public Service. *Africa* 13 (1): 43–61.

WILSON, M. (1972) *The Interpreters*. (The Third Dugmore Memorial Lecture.) Grahamstown: The 1820 Settlers National Monument Foundation.

P. H. Gulliver

2 An Applied Anthropologist in East Africa during the Colonial Era

This is a retrospective account and assessment of a small piece of history in a corner of social anthropology. I make no apology for what is mainly a subjective account, for it may be that understanding can be gained and lessons learned from one person's experience as an applied anthropologist. This chapter is, then, a kind of case study which I shall also use in order to consider some general issues and policy options.

At the outset, it is useful to define and circumscribe the meaning of 'applied anthropology'. In my view, derived from practical experience, 'applied anthropology' involves *both* a particular orientation of research and a mode of presentation and use of its results. Research and its findings are specifically directed to the concerns of governments and their officers and are intended to be applied to policy making and administration. Thus, 'applied anthropology' may include ethnographic and historical survey directed to problems and issues of importance to a government, impact assessment of current or projected policies, and research into particular areas where the anthropologist serves as an identifier and/or clarifier of issues and policy options. In all cases, the anthropologist reports in a form relevant to and usable by officers concerned, so as to present both factual information and advice and recommendations.

What I do *not* include under the rubric of 'applied anthropology' are anthropological research and its results which are devised and oriented for non-governmental purposes (e.g. academic and scholarly) and which are not sought by a government, even though official permission is sought and granted. Thus I dissent from Brokensha's wider, and vaguer, definition: 'All anthropological research which has been helpful to governments' (1966: 4). On that basis, it is impossible to distinguish applied from any other kind of anthropology. In particular I wish to exclude anthropological work, whether or not with formal governmental permission, which has not direct and deliberate reference to application and which is not presented in a form that facilitates application.

Second, it also seems unwise either to limit 'applied anthropology' to the study of social change (Mair 1969: 3) or to assume that all such studies are 'applied anthropology'. Such definition not only disregards some equally valid kinds of applied research (say, the current rules of succession and inheritance) but it ignores the crucial point that 'applied anthropology' involves actual applicability.

Third, after World War II, several colonial governments in Africa and elsewhere subsidized research by particular social anthropologists who were attached to research institutes or were based in a metropolitan university. It was expected that such research would yield information useful to colonial administrations. However, with a few exceptions, I would not include this kind of research as 'applied anthropology'. One reason is that the actual research itself was not primarily dictated by needs for governmental information and advice but rather by academic and scholarly requirements. A second reason is that subsequent reports of research findings were not directed specifically to the needs of governments and their officers. Indeed, most reports were delayed (sometimes lengthily) by the need to fulfil academic requirements and were in due course published in forms not readily available to, or understandable by, colonial officers.

From this brief introduction, I turn first to the kind of anthropological research which I undertook as one of the government sociologists in Tanganyika and, second, to the kinds of reporting and their consequences.

Applied Anthropological Research in Tanganyika

Applied anthropologists were employed by some British colonial governments before 1945.[1] Thus, when the government of Tanganyika Territory created an establishment for three permanent 'government sociologists' soon after World War II, this was not itself novel. It was, however, the only case of its kind in Africa in the post-War era.

Bureaucratically, as an establishment officer, each government sociologist was directly responsible to the Provincial Commissioner (PC) of the province in which he was working at a particular time, although there was privileged access to the Member for Local Government on the Governor's Executive Council. The allocation of a sociologist to a province was made by the Member for Local Government, with general research requirements in mind. Directives for specific research or approval of a sociologist's suggestions for research were made by the PC, although local requests for information could be made by other officers. Like other specialist officers, a government sociologist obtained facilities (e.g. office space, house, access to information) from the District Commissioner of the district in which he was working, but without being subject to his authority.

At the risk of inducing confusion with ethnographic details beyond the interests of all but East Africanists, a brief chronological account of my research activities will best demonstrate why and how I conducted successive projects.

On arrival in Tanganyika in August 1952, I was directed by the Member for Local Government to go to the Songea District, Southern Province. Characteristically, requirements were couched in rather general terms: to investigate economic conditions in the Ngoni chiefdoms of the district, with particular reference to labour migration and to the prevailing poor results of tobacco cultivation as a cash crop.[2] I was informed by the PC that there was governmental concern because the Ngoni had remained a conservative people who showed little inclination to accept or promote economic change. How I was to investigate these general problems was left entirely to me and my suggestion was accepted that, in an area for which there was almost no existing anthropological information, I should need about a year to do the field research.

I embarked on the field research in the same way as I had previously done elsewhere. My plan was, first, to make an ethnographic and historical survey and, thereafter, to concentrate on the study of labour migration and the economy. As the research continued, enquiries and suggestions were made by local officers about particular topics for enquiry.[3]

After about six months of field research, a political crisis developed in one of the chiefdoms as dispute over succession to the chiefship was complicated by a secessionist demand by one ethnically discrete section. The PC requested me to enquire into the rules and history of Ngoni succession and into the history of the dissident section. Although I had some information already, this required a modification of my field plans. I requested a month in which to make enquiries and then presented confidential reports to the PC. After a briefing session, I attended a large meeting between colonial officials and Africans, at which I deliberately sat aside from the two parties. After the issues were resolved, the successful parties assumed (largely correctly) that my intervention had helped to win their cases. As a result, my role as spokesman for African interests was emphasized and further fieldwork facilitated.

After a little less than a year in the field, I suspended research and spent some three months compiling a report dealing with history, political tradition, local government, and economics. This report, presented formally to the Member for Local Government, was cyclostyled and distributed to concerned officers in the district, province and capital. The timing of the report was largely determined by my own need to take a break from the field and to review the data collected. It contained only a few recommendations, being primarily a presentation of information for the immediate use of government officers.

After this report, the PC agreed to my suggestion that I should continue field research and give priority to further detailed enquiries relating to labour migration and economic conditions. In addition, however, my anthropological imagination had been caught by the opportunity to study the dynamics of kinship and dispute management in Ndendeuli local groups and I continued that study simultaneously.

After another eight months in the field, interrupted by a visit to the capital to consult archives, brief visits to employment areas and participation in the District Development Committee, I finished my research and wrote two reports: one on the causes, conditions and consequences of labour migration and the other on economic change. Both contained recommendations for relevant government policies.

Following these reports, I recommended further and comparative studies of labour migration and local economic conditions. It was agreed that I should study these matters among the people of the eastern shorelands of Lake Nyasa. After a couple of months, my new research was cut short. This was the only instance of such curtailment during my career as an applied anthropologist. Partly this was a result of my recommendations for further research; but, more importantly, issues concerning labour migration had become crucial in several regions of Tanganyika, especially migration to the Rhodesias and South Africa. The Governor-in-Council called for a full-scale examination of the magnitude, causes and effects of labour migration with the aim of formulating policy at the Territorial level. As the official view understood it, widespread labour migration from most of the Territory's rural areas to estates, farms, mines and towns was disrupting local economies, frustrating economic development and raising international issues where countries to the south encouraged and actively recruited migrants from Tanganyika. I was directed to move to south-western Tanganyika, there to study and report on labour migration with particular reference to migration southwards. Exactly where and how I should conduct this research was left to me. After some reconnaissance, I decided on intensive investigation among the Nyakyusa among whom migration was highest, together with extensive enquiries at a more general level among other peoples of the region.[4] Because of expressed urgency to provide results, the project was completed in about four months, followed immediately by the wide circulation of my report.

Following this work, I recommended continuation of research among the Nyakyusa in order to study further the effects of large-scale labour migration and the problems arising out of economic development, rapid population growth, and an apparent shortage of agricultural land. This proposal was accepted: I spent a further six months among the Nyakyusa and completed a report. During that time, in addition to the agreed research aims, and in response to requests from the District Commissioner, I provided information on the working of the local government system and on the high rate of divorce suits in the local courts.

About this time, the government sociologist in northern Tanganyika resigned and I was invited to move to that region. This I accepted largely because of a desire to work in a region entirely new to me. There, after consultation with central and provincial officers, it was agreed that, as a first priority, I should investigate the voluntary settlement of labour migrants in a major region in which they found work: the sisal-growing region of north-eastern Tanganyika. With the completion of that project and my report after about six months, I suggested a full-scale investigation of contemporary conditions among the Arusha people. This was accepted by the Member for Local Government and the PC because of the apparent seriousness of a number of related issues among the Arusha: rapid population growth, an increasing shortage of agricultural land and an alleged landless class which had been involved in near-riots; the ineffectiveness of local government; deteriorating relations between the Arusha and both government officers and local non-African farmers; the apparent refusal of the Arusha to accept socio-economic innovation, and the low level of economic development despite a most favourable environment.

At the end of a year's field research, I prepared a report for general distribution. This dealt with demography, the land question, agriculture, and economic conditions and included a brief ethnographic survey, a presentation of Arusha views and attitudes towards the Administration and the contemporary world, and recommendations for government policies. I then proposed that my research work among the Arusha should continue and this was agreed. In the second period of field research I was able to follow my anthropological inclinations and study the age-set system, dispute management processes, and the conservative commitment of the people despite increasingly acute land shortage (with population densities well over 1,000 people per square mile). During this continued fieldwork, I was also requested to provide information on the indigenous political system and on the operation of local government and to collaborate with the District Commissioner in formulating reforms that would encourage greater participation by the people and increased effectiveness of local government services.

During this period, I also acted as consultant to the Administration on various matters where, it was thought, my specialist knowledge would be useful: for example, the planning of a sociological survey of the capital city, policy in regard to resettlement projects and to the use of the lands left vacant by the failure of the post-war groundnuts scheme, and the question of so-called detribalization. It was also expected that I should comment on various government reports and on applications from overseas by anthropologists wishing to undertake research in the Territory. In addition, I dealt with ethnographic enquiries from individual officers in various parts of the country.

From the preceding description, it may be clear that sometimes my research resulted from directives by senior officers of the government and sometimes from proposals that I myself made to, and discussed with, those officers. In either case, officers were often rather unclear about what they wanted and were fairly open to my suggestions to clarify the dimensions of issues and problems. I had a great deal of freedom – and responsibility – during the course of field research to work out what seemed to be the most important matters. It was left to me to decide the emphases to be given to various kinds of information and analysis.

It should also be clear that fieldwork was carried out in essentially the same way as any academic anthropologist would – as I had done previously and would again in later years. I always acknowledged my employment by the government to the people among whom I worked and lived; to have done otherwise would have been foolish, for my appointment was no secret matter. However, I took care to distance myself from government officers. I consistently refused to divulge information on individuals or on what I knew were sensitive matters to the African peoples; and I refused to act as disseminator of governmental information. Despite some exasperation and failure by government officers to understand, my policy was accepted. In the field, I took care that informants were aware that I had information (e.g. crimes, tax evasion, witchcraft) which I did not pass on to officers and courts; and I deliberately cultivated my own ignorance of governmental actions. During the longer research projects, I learned and used the local language as best I could, otherwise using Swahili (the Territory's lingua franca), and I worked with participant observation, open-ended interviewing, questionnaire surveys, and the like.[5] My field research files and notebooks remained entirely confidential: no-one ever asked to see them. Research locations and methods were always my own choice. I was not dependent on officers of the government. On the other hand, I did seek to learn what I could from the knowledge and experience of officers and their records. They too were informants of variable trustworthiness.

My relations with African officials were, as far as I could make them, not those of a colonial officer to subordinates. No more than any independent anthropologist in that era, could I avoid being a white man, with therefore potentially superior status in the class hierarchy. However, by normal anthropological field methods I was able, by my life style and non-authoritarian behaviour, to distinguish myself from the ascribed roles of other Europeans, to gain the trust and confidence of many of the people among whom I worked and to be accepted as friendly, sympathetic and eccentric. Invariably, I sought to explain what my interests were and why, and the advantages of my research to the people themselves.

Reports and Recommendations

In the foregoing account of field research, I have indicated briefly the reports of my work, and a detailed list of these is given in the Appendix to this chapter. Bureaucratically, the form was that reports were made to the PC of the province in which I worked, although in practice some were directed to the Member for Local Government whilst others were directed to meet purely local concerns. Reports were of three general kinds. There were fairly lengthy ethnographic and analytical ones which were cyclostyled and roughly bound: with governmental encouragement and minimal financing, and these were distributed quite widely to provincial and local officers and to those in the capital and elsewhere who were concerned and interested. These were invariably produced rather hastily, there being no time for intellectual deliberations. They were written in non-technical language as far as possible so that busy officers would not be deterred from reading them. A summary version of findings and recommendations was always given in a few pages at the beginning of a report. Other reports were briefer and related to particular topics of concern and interest to local officers. These had limited distribution in so far as they were directed to specifically local matters not of general interest, although copies were made available on request from other officers.[6] Third, there were a few confidential reports made to senior administrators concerning politically delicate matters on which I was specifically requested to provide information and advice.

It was made clear to me from the start that I was expected not only to provide information but also to identify and clarify issues of importance, to proffer advice and to make appropriate recommendations for governmental policy and action. Increasingly, as I was accepted as a knowledgeable specialist and as my experience grew, my confidence also grew in making recommendations and arguing their merits, both in written and oral form. That is to say, my responsibility as an applied anthropologist went beyond supplying information which officers might use to assess or formulate policy: there were opportunities and obligations to present informed opinion and to participate in processes leading to decision making.

Some of my recommendations were rejected or tacitly ignored. An example was my proposal to reorganize the structure of the Ngoni chiefdoms so that each sub-chief and headman would be responsible for all the residents of a clearly prescribed geographical-administrative area. Another example was my proposal that an agency be established to facilitate communication and the transfer of money between labour migrants and their families and to provide facilities to labour migrants in difficulties, both within and beyond Tanganyika. This proposal was rejected on the grounds of cost.

Some recommendations were accepted and, sometimes with modifications, put into practice: for example, that the Ndendeuli gain autonomy from the Ngoni chiefdom and establish their own local government authority; that labour migrants choosing to settle permanently in the employment areas were experiencing little difficulty in their new life and therefore, contrary to some official views, special provisions and treatment were unnecessary; that additional land, with at least minimal services, be made available for Arusha settlement in order to relieve the critical pressures of a very dense agricultural population on existing lands; that Arusha local government be reformed to include an elected tribal council with legislative responsibilities.

Some recommendations were referred to African local authorities for consideration and possible action. For example, I proposed that immigration into the more congested areas of Nyakyusa country be restricted, that non-residents there should not acquire arable land and that sales of individually held land should be freely permitted. These, in modified form, were put into force by the Nyakyusa Tribal Council. Some of my proposals were of a less specific kind, referring to more general administrative or technical arrangements and these, sometimes successfully and sometimes not, were considered in conjunction with the development of ongoing programmes.

In addition to such particular proposals, in my reports I attempted to indicate matters relevant to local conditions and to current governmental policies where it seemed that information and advice might be helpful in assessing those policies and the operation of institutions. For example, I noted the inadequacy of local courts which were located long distances from potential plaintiffs in Ngoni country, and I emphasized the severe restrictions on agricultural development in the lowland areas of Arusha as a result of the iniquitous distribution of limited water supplies.

Briefer memoranda were written in response to particular points raised by officers. Examples are the rules regarding trespass and damage by straying animals and those concerning individual rights in newly pioneered lands among the Arusha – both instances arising out of current court cases – and information and explanation concerning the high rate of divorce suits by Nyakyusa women.

In these various, written reports, as also in formal and informal discussions with colonial officials, I assumed two other responsibilities which arose out of my special knowledge of, and relations with, the African peoples with whom, for most of the time, I lived. Neither of these responsibilities was requested or expected of me by the Administration but both were accepted. The first was to act as spokesman for African interests, attitudes and expectations. Exceedingly few colonial officers had close and intimate knowledge of, and personal relations with, the African people and their institutions: all were limited by their roles in a bureaucracy. Thus, like bureaucrats everywhere, there was a common tendency among officers to work in some ignorance of the ideas and needs of the people with whom they dealt, to lose empathy during the application of rules and procedures, and to exercise authority complacently and thoughtlessly. These conditions were, of course, much exacerbated by severe cultural and status differences between officers and Africans. Therefore, in addition to providing socio-cultural information, I took care to represent African opinion and ideas, both on particular matters and on more general issues within the colonial regime.

Second, and closely related, I took upon myself to act as protester where inefficacies and injustices existed. For example, I drew officers' attention to situations where chiefs extorted payments from applicants for agricultural land, magistrates discriminated against women seeking divorce, and witnesses were subpoenaed to attend distant courts without recompense.

In taking up these responsibilities, I was frequently asked by Africans to speak on their behalf because they assumed that, as well as re-emphasizing grievances and needs, I would be heard more attentively by officers. There were difficulties in exercising these parts of my role. I was not always listened to. Sometimes my intervention was considered to be misplaced or naïve, especially from an officer lacking seniority. Moreover, there was a danger that I could be used for partisan purposes by some local faction. Nevertheless, I persisted as equitably as possible, since there was such an obvious need for a mediator who, as I saw it, was both knowledgeable of, and favourable towards, African interests in a political situation where the distribution of power was so distorted.

Assessment and Overview

Within its quite limited scope – one colonial territory at a particular time in history and in the development of social anthropology – I think in retrospect, as I believe I did at the time, that my role as applied anthropologist was moderately successful. It was not, and could not have been, of course, successful in the views of those, anthropologists and others, who have considered that anthropology was hopelessly enmeshed in, ideologically distorted and theoretically castrated by, the colonial–imperial system of that period. However, at least it has been generally acknowledged that many of us in social anthropology then were critical of colonial regimes, both for what they represented – an arm of Western metropolitan exploitation and paternalism, tinged with racialism – and for their inequities and inefficiencies and the downright oppression by particular regimes in particular contexts. With such a critical attitude, it nevertheless seemed to me in 1952, when I applied for the appointment in Tanganyika, that colonialism was the going regime and it seemed reasonable and attractive to try to work within it, to contribute towards amelioration and improvement and even, just a little, to hasten its end.

On the other hand, although my imagination was caught by an apparent opportunity to ameliorate, and my vanity was touched that professionally I might achieve something, I took the job principally for two other reasons. Having completed my doctorate and enjoyed enormously the fieldwork it entailed, I wished to continue anthropological research rather than to teach with what seemed to me an inadequate basis of experience and knowledge. Second, I wished to continue to have the personal freedom, excitement, and stimulation of living and working in the African plains and bushlands, rather than accept the offer of a university lectureship and live in London. The appointment as applied anthropologist appeared to offer opportunities for plenty of varied field research, for investigating some of the anthropological interests that had caught my curiosity, and for building the foundation of a personally experienced, comparative orientation. My expectations were well fulfilled in the event: in six years I accomplished three major research projects, one lesser one, and several minor ones.

However, I reiterate that my applied anthropology was moderately successful, indeed perhaps as successful as it could be in the context. By that I mean that a good deal of my research results were seriously considered by responsible officers in the formulation and/or administration of policies and programmes. Particular recommendations for policy and action were accepted and taken up, sometimes with modifications arising out of other specialists' advice and African opinion. More commonly, I think, the knowledge, understanding, assumptions, and attitudes of colonial officers were affected and, as I saw it, improved as a result of my reports and subsequent discussions. Administrative and technical officers better comprehended the people with whom they were dealing and the socio-economic and cultural conditions in which they operated. This it is scarcely possible to prove in any definitive way, nor do I wish to make inflated claims that I left behind me a trail of enlightened and empathetic officers. To be sure, some were adamant in their ignorance and assumed superiority; but many were not, as they admitted and as I observed. It is altogether too facile, in the righteous indignation of anti-colonialism, to picture colonial officers as ignorant, unteachable, authoritarian figures, wholly disregardful of the rights and interests of the colonized and much concerned for their own status and comfort. Moreover, too often the proponents of that kind of picture have chosen to go to the earlier days of colonialism in Africa when the worst excesses occurred and when comprehension, experience and benignity were at their lowest level. My own experience, and therefore my frame of reference, applies to the last decade of the colonial regime in East Africa. At that time, a colonial officer was enmeshed in the intricacies and manoeuvres of a bureaucracy and of technical operations. He had neither the opportunity nor the inclination to make detailed enquiries into the complexities of a land tenure system, or the diverse consequences of social change, among a people whose language he typically did not speak and for whom he was responsible for only two or three years. Yet administrative officers who had read history or philosophy for a bachelor's degree, or technical officers with their specialist university training, were not usually unintelligent, and their minds were not normally closed. They were very often susceptible to new information and fresh ideas, despite their professional socialization into the going system. They were especially likely to be flexible if they were not put on the defensive by direct attack; thus it was important that they perceived me as another specialist with something genuine to offer. Consequently, and despite some disappointments and some direct antagonism, I was pleasantly surprised enough times to come to believe that I was able to get messages across.

It is worth pointing out to a scholarly audience that, as an academically trained anthropologist now become an applied research officer, I too had a great deal to learn. I came to appreciate that 'a commanding characteristic of the academic outlook – namely its orientation to goals and standards set on very wide horizons . . . .[was in contrast with the fact that] administrators' problems are essentially local, specific and immediate' (Apthorpe 1961: ii). And I had to understand that, as he goes on to say, 'often . . . the scientist forgets or fails to transfer his scientific method from his research field to others, particularly to the delicate issues of public relations which must be so carefully handled if sociological and social anthropological investigations are to proceed', and if their results are to be sympathetically received and considered. It was necessary, too, to recognize that there were other points of view, that other specialists had information and ideas that could be as pertinent as my own, and that sometimes there were ineluctable technical, logistical, and financial impediments to even the best proposals for change. I had to take realistic account of what seemed to be other people's prejudices and what seemed to them to be my own prejudices. Retrospectively, I think that my earlier recommendations were possibly too tentative because of my responsibility to officers of many years' seniority. Be that as it may, I had to learn my way through the system and how to manipulate it towards the ends I sought; and I had to learn how best to defend and propagate my proposals and ideas before practical men of experience. Working as an applied anthropologist, as I understood and practised the role, involved a great deal more than carrying out field research and presenting its results. I am convinced that the most effective applied anthropology must involve more than that.

The research freedom that I was given and the degree of success achieved might have been greater had I remained longer than six years in the appointment, with an increase in seniority, acceptance, and cumulative experience.[7] Yet that success, and indeed the whole *modus operandi*, might not have occurred in another colonial territory at another time. At that time, Tanganyika had a special status in the British colonial world in that it was a United Nations Trust Territory. Its government was responsible and had to report to the UN as well as to the Colonial Office. The affairs of Tanganyika were reviewed and debated at the UN and delegations came to make inspection and enquiry. It was explicit UN policy that Britain should promote progress towards the political independence of the Territory. There was, therefore, an awareness among officers that their work was in international view and policies seem to have been adjusted as a result. The establishment of a sociological research service was probably one consequence of this. In addition, it is probably not unimportant that there was no politically significant European minority, nor demographically and politically dominant 'tribes', to beset the government with acute political issues. To many officers at all levels, the way seemed clear to what might be called progressive development, economically and politically. Tanganyika was poor in natural resources, mostly rather sparsely populated and ethnically much sub-divided. Since German times, before World War I, there had been little political unrest and, with some local exceptions, rather little economic change. As a result, although complacent paternalism was rife, at least it was largely in benevolent form. By the 1950s, issues of local economic development were prominent: general policy was to encourage and foster cash-cropping agriculture in order to increase local incomes and standards of living. The Territory-wide problems of persisting, large-scale labour migration were matters of major concern: the development of improved local agriculture was intended in part to eliminate the necessity for labour migration and the presumed disruption it had caused for half a century. It was general policy, too, to continue to limit and control the power of chiefs by progressive democratization of local government through elective councils and meritocratic appointments. The door was, then, open for information, analysis and recommendations concerning such matters from a government sociologist.

An important feature of my role as applied anthropologist, and one I wish to emphasize strongly, is that I was, from the bureaucratic point of view, an insider – neither an outsider like most anthropologists from universities in Britain and North America, nor yet a visitor coming, perhaps by invitation, to undertake a single job of research and report. I was an officer of the government, subject to the same regulations and privileges as other officers and with full right to be there and carry out my own line of work. I was expected to be there for a long time and not to disappear to some distant ivory tower. I was held responsible for my work, my reports, my views and proposals, both to the government in general and to individual colleagues. I could be legitimately expected to answer questions, supply facts, give opinion and advice and contribute to ongoing or new policy. It was not necessary to importune me or tactfully invite me to produce, with the anticipation that I might, at a time of my own choosing, from London or California, offer something which could (but might not) be useful – even though written for another purpose, such as obtaining a degree or academic rewards. As Government Sociologist, I was trusted at least as much as any other officer, whilst under as much responsibility to accomplish my work; yet at the same time I was always allowed freedom to carry out research and to prepare reports without interference of any kind other than, occasionally, a limitation of time and the tacit expectation that compilation of reports should be speedy and done in a straightforward manner. These conditions held despite the fact that, for anthropological purposes, I deliberately cultivated a role rather different from that of other officers, and that my life style was thought to be eccentric by many of my colleagues.

To those anthropologists who have complained that colonial officials never asked their advice about features of the social life of the people they studied (e.g. Evans-Pritchard 1946: 98), I am much inclined to reply, 'Why should you have been asked? You were an outsider, a visitor soon to be gone, often talking about concepts, ideas and assumptions that were foreign and not understood by officers.' Many field anthropologists were young, naïve, perhaps brash, and inexperienced, moving hopefully towards a university career. There was some not unnatural umbrage among officials, and also some dog-in-the-manger resentment. This is not an adequately satisfactory answer, of course, but it helps to explain the official reticence. I myself was able to make good use of the fact that I had research experience, a doctorate, and publications and that I was not committed to another career elsewhere. To the best of my knowledge, my presence, work, and opinion were not resented; rather, I was accepted as a specialist – one of several kinds of specialist employed by the government – who, though a little odd in his ways, could be asked for specialist opinion and participation and was there precisely for that purpose. It is pertinent that Evans-Pritchard (1946) remarked on his similar insider status whilst he served as Tribal Affairs Officer in the British Military Administration in Cyrenaica during World War II. He contrasted this with his outsider status previously in the Sudan.

My general, retrospective conclusion, then, is that my work as an applied anthropologist was moderately successful in terms of amelioration, information, advice and the widening of perspectives, and as spokesman and protestor.

This conclusion does not take account of latter-day criticism of the relations between colonialism and the nature and development of social anthropology.[8] Such criticism can, for present purposes, be briefly summarized as follows:

1. Social anthropology was made possible and developed in the era of metropolitan colonialism and it was, therefore, in large part dependent on colonial power and patronage and was intimately affected by it in methodology, theoretical assumptions and analytical interests;
2. Social anthropologists failed to give the careful analytical study, which they developed in their local-level research, to investigation of the colonial system itself; and they failed to take account of the dependency of local societies and cultures upon the wider, embracing political economy;
3. Social anthropology was ahistorical at both micro- and macro-levels.

This is not the place to renew the whole debate and here I am only concerned with the critique in so far as it affects the assessment of applied anthropology in the colonial world and the chances for its success in the contemporary world. As an anthropologist and one-time applied anthropologist, I agree in general with those kinds of critical accusation and therefore do not seek to argue against them. It is, of course, easy to be wise retrospectively – perhaps a little too easy – and especially if one believes in a paradigm that purports to supply all the answers. I am no true believer. No doubt the provenance of functionalism and its concern for order and continuity lay in some degree in anthropologists' work and semi-clientage in the colonial system and its genitor, the expanding Western capitalist system. But it may be remembered that functionalism also had some older and deeper roots in Western thought, nor is it entirely absent in some latter-day Marxist theorizing. Instead of renewing the debate, let me make some observations relevant to the anthropological experience, and in particular to applied anthropology, within the colonial regime.

My own inclination in the 1950s was to be an ameliorist, a gradualist, unconvinced that the revolution was at hand and, indeed, rather hoping that it was not since I had no great faith, no doubt affectual as much as intellectual, in the efficacy of revolution. Colonialism was the going system in Africa at the time, as it seemed to me, and it appeared preferable to try to work within it and do what one could. Colonialism was also going in the sense of perceptibly moving to an end. Political nationalism was gaining strength, whilst the costs of the system were evidently becoming too great for the metropolitan powers. In that context, it seemed useful, practicably possible, and ethically defensible to attempt to do something that could help the colonized, make their voices heard more clearly and articulately and even, perhaps, assist in hastening the process towards decolonization.

My assumption, when becoming an applied anthropologist, was that my research interests and theoretical ideas would not be dictated either overtly or tacitly by my employers, although I accepted that I would be required to investigate some matters which otherwise I might well have ignored. As far as I can now tell, my assumption was justified. Under other circumstances, I should probably not have given so much research time and effort to, for example, the investigation of labour migration; yet that did allow me to study local economies, social change, and local group dynamics, all of which were of overt interest to me anthropologically, and it also gave me some improved understanding of the colonial economy of Tanganyika. In investigating local government operation in order to meet government requirements for information and assessment, it is true that I was studying aspects of order and control; but at the same time I was stimulated to study the historical processes of local-level political development and my attention was caught more than before by the need and opportunity to study conflict, discontinuity, and contradiction, both structurally and at the inter-personal level. In practice, prescribed research opened up new intellectual interests. Neither by overt injunction nor by tacit demand was I limited in what I chose to investigate nor in how it was done. In so far as I was a 'child of imperialism', this would have been no less so had I not worked in the applied field. In short, it was always possible to study those matters of direct interest and concern to the government whilst looking more deeply at their implications within the local social systems and simultaneously investigating what other matters interested me. Moreover, I was in a good strategic position to act as 'radical critic' (James 1973: 43).

In Memmi's terms, I was a 'colonizer who refuses': one who rejects the nature of colonialism and supports the demands of the colonized, but who nevertheless benefits from belonging to the colonizers' group. Because of the inherent dilemma which that role entails, Memmi argued that the colonizer who refuses 'applies to one and to the other [the colonizer and the colonized] those ulterior motives which he deems convenient and portrays a colonized according to his reconstruction. In short, he begins to construct myths' (1965: 32). Whilst accepting the dilemma, I would query Memmi's conclusion that the colonizer who refuses constructs myths, if by that he implies that there is some genuine, mythless reality in a colonial situation which is well perceived by either the colonizers or the colonized. Moreover, the two main parties in the colonial situation had their own dilemmas to take care of, although dilemmas of a different order from that of the colonizer who refuses. Each of the three parties constructed its own 'myths' to take care of its own dilemma and to rationalize the position in which it found itself. All were *ex parte* constructs and representations. It may be arrogant to suggest that the anthropologist as a colonizer who refuses was, in some sense, more able to comprehend both sides. Yet, with caution, I do suggest that; it was certainly what I believed in that earlier era. It is not that the anthropologist's constructs were 'correct', whatever that might mean, but that at least they had the potential to take account of both sides and of the built-in dilemmas of each. Maybe in saying that, I am constructing a Memmi-like myth. I did not believe it to be so then nor do I altogether accept it today. I do not see, now, that the inherent dilemma of the applied anthropologist (or of any anthropologist, at any time) is an inevitable barrier to useful research and reporting.

And yet . . . There is considerable truth in Asad's assertion that the anthropologists of that era 'chose to live *professionally* at peace' (1973: 18, his italics), not only because they chose not to attack the system head on but also because they wanted to get on with doing anthropology. This was close to my own view as an applied anthropologist. I was trained as a social anthropologist: I greatly enjoyed the work and wished to do more. In this, I had to an extent to suppress other feelings and beliefs concerning the inequity of the system, indefensible though that may now seem, especially under the emotional impact of such contemporary words as oppression, power, exploitation, racialism, and the like. Most of us still live more or less 'professionally at peace' within a going political economy in which we perceive injustices and exploitation. Some, it is true, man the barricades intellectually or even sometimes in practice. Most do not, preferring to get on with their own lives and their private and scholarly pursuits. Maybe that is morally wrong. Nevertheless, at that time, and recognizing my inadequacy as a political animal, it seemed likely that I could combine professional aims and amelioratory intervention. The possibility that my efforts 'probably acted to inhibit oppressed peoples from overtly attacking the colonial regime' (Faris 1973: 154) scarcely occurred to me, and in retrospect I would still give it little weight. I believe that I was able to help people in need and suffering some injustice. I did not believe that I could destroy the system which, in large part, had created those needs and injustices.

Then there is the valid criticism that anthropologists, in their professional concentration on the study of small-scale, local systems – often in a near vacuum and ahistorically – signally neglected the wider system in which those local systems were enmeshed. Anthropologists did fail to study the colonial system itself with the care they devoted to micro-studies, nor did they give it adequate weight in their analyses. Nowadays, the two-way interlinkages of local, regional, national, and international levels are taken for granted as essential features of most anthropological enquiry. Nevertheless, no-one can achieve everything, however estimable: there must be specialization. It seemed to me in that earlier era, as it still does today, that the persisting *raison d'être* of social anthropology has been, and remains, its concern with, and expertise in, investigating the local level. Today, I believe that we should draw freely and extensively, and also critically, on the macro-specialists in order to have the best available information and understanding about the wider systems. At that earlier time I scarcely recognized the need and, in so far as I did, it appeared that there were rather few macro-materials available. Nevertheless, I will defend the anthropological specialization in local-level investigation and analysis. Earlier, we almost had this field to ourselves and, despite some incursions by a few historians, sociologists, and others, we still predominate there. It is the field in which the methods and theory of social anthropology have been concentrated and with results of considerable value. Social anthropologists are micro-sociologists; it was in that role that I worked as an applied anthropologist, although with the then-unrecognized handicap of largely failing to consider forms and consequences of dependency. It remains my opinion that an applied anthropologist can and should work at the local level and not seek some spurious standing as a macro-specialist. He can and should take every advantage of increasingly available macro-data, and with a genuine historical perspective, so that he may attempt to see both how things are today and how they came to be that way and also to assess the likely consequences in the future of current and alternative policies. However, it is also incumbent on the anthropologist to seek to explain the palpable fact that local-level systems are not all the same and that they change in somewhat different ways, despite their common dependency.

In conclusion, two questions and two brief answers. First, can applied anthropology be effectively undertaken? In my view, it can, but it requires a benevolent environment in which the anthropologist is relatively free to work in his own way, and in which he has the opportunity to put his findings and opinion to willing listeners and to participate in the evaluation of those findings, in conjunction with those of other specialists, in developing and modifying policy and action. Among other things, this means that the applied anthropologist has to tailor his research and his reports so that they are both genuinely relevant to matters in hand and are given in a form understandable to others. For example, should he consider it essential to enquire into the complexities of kinship or of cultural meanings, he should demonstrate in relatively non-complex ways the pertinence of his results.

My experience in colonial Tanganyika illustrates one mode of relatively effective applied anthropology. Not all applied anthropology requires that the anthropologist be in long-term employment by the government. Single research projects are, of course, possible, although the anthropologist will then miss the undoubted advantage of being an accepted insider. There is, however, another serious problem here. In practice, in recent times, as no doubt in earlier periods too, the very real danger of single applied anthropology projects is that the employment of an anthropologist is too often a form of window-dressing. Governments are seeking to give the appearance that account is being taken of the interests of the people at the local level who are to be affected by some governmental policy. The work of the anthropologist is neither taken seriously nor given weight in decision-making or policy planning by administrators. In such cases, anthropologists are being used, not for the expertise, information, and advice they can give, but to present a public image, whilst politicians and administrators proceed unchanged in their intentions and their self-advantageous policies. Unfortunately, as it seems to me, anthropologists tend to collude in this deception because they are able to obtain fees, foreign travel, research opportunities, and data for themselves and their students; and, I am afraid, some anthropologists are seduced by the seeming importance offered to them in their applied roles. I have the most serious doubts that a hasty two or three months in an academic summer vacation, or even a longer period on sabbatical, can produce much of genuine applied value if it results merely in the filing of a report. Thus, I re-emphasize that what I have called a benevolent environment for applied anthropology should include the authentic opportunity for the anthropologist to follow up his report by participation in planning deliberations.

Second, should anthropologists work in the applied field if and where that involves work in a regime that is colonialist, neo-colonialist, oppressive or otherwise abhorrent? This is less easy to answer, if only because moral and ideological views differ as much among anthropologists as among any other people. The probable fact that in many regimes there is not an environment benevolent to the anthropological enterprise should debar applied anthropology there. The work would be a failure, a cover-up, and quite possibly to the disadvantage of the people studied. On the other hand, where some policy is in prospect – say, the building of a large dam or the definition and registration of land titles – and where there is reasonable opportunity for the anthropologist to work and genuinely to be heeded, his involvement in the applied field can be advantageous. I think it is easy to exaggerate the probable contribution of anthropology under almost any regime; nevertheless, it is no

54   P. H. Gulliver

less easy to exaggerate its uselessness and to abandon anthropological skills and perceptions in the face of the real difficulties of making them in any way effective.

Appendix

Researches and Reports as Government Sociologist, Tanganyika, 1952–58

FIELD RESEARCH

After each research area, the main research interests are indicated in two general categories: (a) topics of direct interest to government officials: (b) other topics not necessarily of direct interest to government officials:

1. August 1952–June 1954 (23 months): *Ngoni, Ndendeuli* (Songea)
   (a) ethnography, labour migration, cash-cropping, local government, chiefly succession, demography, history;
   (b) kinship, shifting cultivation, local group dynamics, dispute management.
2. July–September 1954 (2 months): *Nyasa Lakeshore* (Songea)
   (a) labour migration, local economy;
   (b) history, kinship.
3. September 1954–February 1955 (5 months): *Nyakyusa* (Rungwe) and south-western Tanganyika
   (a) labour migration;
   (b) ethnography.
4. July 1955–January 1956 (6 months): *Nyakyusa* (Rungwe)
   (a) land tenure, demography, agriculture, local government, divorce, social change;
   (b) age-villages, kinship, history.
5. January–July 1956 (6 months): *Tanga region* (Tanga Province)
   (a) labour migrants on estates, local settlement of migrants, detribalization;
   (b) kinship, ethnic relations, Swahili culture.
6. July 1956–June 1958 (22 months): *Arusha* (Northern Province)
   (a) ethnography, demography, land tenure, landless people, economic conditions, local government, law, history, social change;
   (b) age institutions, kinship, dispute management.

REPORTS (other than short memoranda)

1. *Administrative Survey of the Ngoni and Ndendeuli* (Cyclostyled, General Distribution.

An Applied Anthropologist in East Africa during the Colonial Era 55

Ngoni Chiefship: History and Rules of Succession (Confidential Report)
Ndendeuli: History of Relations with the Ngoni (Confidential Report)
Tobacco Cultivation in Songea District (Limited Circulation)
Labour Migration from Songea District: Causes, Conditions and Consequences (Cyclostyled, General Distribution).

2. *The Nyasa* Lakeshore Region (Limited Circulation)
3. *The Migration of Workers from Tanganyika to the South* (Cyclostyled, General Distribution)
4. *Land Tenure and Social Change among the Nyakyusa* (Cyclostyled, General Distribution)
  Rice and Coffee Cultivation in Nyakyusa (Limited Circulation)
  Traditional and Administrative Chiefship in Nyakyusa (Confidential Report)
  Local Government in Nyakyusa (Limited Circulation)
5. *Migrant Workers in the Tanga Region* (Cyclostyled, General Distribution)
  Detribalization (Limited Circulation)
6. *Report on Land and Population in the Arusha Chiefdom* (Cyclostyled, General Distribution)
  Administrative Reform in the Arusha Chiefdom (Limited Circulation)
  Indigenous Local Government among the Arusha (Limited Circulation)
  Arusha Land Law (Limited Circulation)
  Arusha History (Limited Circulation)

PUBLICATIONS arising directly and principally out of field research

1. (1955) *Labour Migration in a Rural Economy*. East African Institute of Social Research (East African Studies, 6).
  (1956) A History of the Songea Ngoni. *Tanganyika Notes and Records* 49.
  (1969) Dispute Settlement without Courts. In L. Nader *Law in Culture and Society*. Chicago: Aldine.
  (1971) *Neighbours and Networks: The Idiom of Kinship in Social Action among the Ndendeuli of Tanzania*. Berkeley: University of California Press.
  (1974) Political Evolution in the Songea Ngoni Chiefdoms, 1850–1905. *Bulletin of SOAS* 37.
  (1978) Networks and Factions. In M. Silverman and R. Salisbury *A House Divided?* St John's, Newfoundland Institute of Social and Economic Research.
3. (1957) Nyakyusa Labour Migration; *Rhodes-Livingstone Journal* 21.
4. (1958) *Land Tenure and Social Change among the Nyakyusa*. East African Studies 11, East African Institute of Social Research.
  (1961) Land Shortage, Social Change and Social Conflict. *Journal of Conflict Resolution* 5.

6. (1960) The Population of the Arusha Chiefdom. *Rhodes-Livingstone Journal* 28.
   (1961) Structural Dichotomy and Jural Processes among the Arusha. *Africa* 31.
   (1963) The Evolution of Arusha Trade. In P. Bohannon *Markets in Africa*. Evanston: Northwestern University Press.
   (1963) *Social Control in an African Society*. London: Routledge.
   (1964) The Arusha Family: In R. Gray and P. Gulliver *The Family Estate in Africa*. London, Routledge and Berkeley: University of California Press.
   (1969) An Arusha Land Dispute. In M. Karp *African Perspectives*. Boston: Boston University African Studies Program.
   (1979) *Disputes and Negotiations*. New York: Academic Press.

Notes

1. In Nigeria, Northcote Thomas was appointed in 1906. Like Talbot and Meek later in that colony, he was a seconded administrative officer, as was Rattray in the Gold Coast. The South African government employed permanent ethnologists from 1925. Nadel was probably the first professional social anthropologist employed by an African colonial government: in the Sudan and later in the British Military Administration in Eritrea. Evans-Pritchard was Tribal Affairs Officer with the British Military Administration in Cyrenaica during World War II.

2. The study of labour migration, its causes and consequences, had been given first priority in the anthropological research requirements for Tanganyika by W. H. Stanner in 1950: *Research Needs in Uganda and Tanganyika*, a report prepared for and circulated by the Colonial Office, London. (This was one of several such survey reports made by senior anthropologists in British colonial regions after World War II.) The Southern Province, and Songea District in particular, were areas from which there had been extensive labour migration since early in the century.

3. For example, the failure of tobacco-growing in some localities; persisting factionalism in a particular sub-chiefdom; the relative ineffectiveness of a local co-operative.

4. My decision was influenced by the fact that the Nyakyusa were already well described anthropologically (e.g. Wilson 1951), thus making it easier and quicker to obtain research results.

5. Although individually known by my own name, or some sobriquet, my usual title was the local equivalent of 'the man of customs'. Colonial officials were asked to refer to me as *Bwana wa Desturi*, the Swahili version.

6. Very few Africans at that time, in the areas in which I worked, were proficient enough in English to read my reports, but copies were made available when this was possible and Swahili versions of some shorter reports were circulated.

7. For the record, but also as a comment on being an applied anthropologist, I should explain why I voluntarily resigned from my appointment, since I believed that my work was positively successful. Some reasons were personal, such as the desire to live where my children could have a more stable life, and the desire to have access to Western culture. Besides these, however, one was particularly pertinent to the job of an applied anthropologist on a long-term basis. For nearly six years I had been engaged in what was almost continuous fieldwork in different areas, punctuated by brief periods of necessarily hasty writing up of my materials. There was no time to deliberate carefully over the data, nor opportunity to engage in library research. Increasingly I desired a break in which to consider the deeper implications of my research, as a theoretical rather than as an applied anthropologist.

8. Represented, for example, by contributions to the *Current Anthropology* symposium (1968) and to Asad's symposium (1973). It is not worthwhile attending to the occasional critics who seem to have thought that scholarly standards and the theoretical goals of social science would necessarily be debased by a professional's involvement in practical affairs and the application of academic knowledge and methods.

References

APTHORPE, R. (1961) Introduction in R. Apthorpe *Social Research and Community Development*. Lusaka: Rhodes-Livingstone Institute.

ASAD, T. (1973) *Anthropology and the Colonial Enounter*. London: Ithaca Press.

BROKENSHA, D. (1966) *Applied Anthropology in English-speaking Africa*. Lexington, Kentucky: Society for Applied Anthropology Monograph 8.

EVANS-PRITCHARD, E. E. (1946) Applied Anthropology. *Africa* 16 (1): 92–8.

FARIS, J. C. (1973) Pax Britannica and the Sudan: S. F. Nadel. In T. Asad. (ed.) *Anthropology and the Colonial Encounter*. London: Ithaca Press.

JAMES, W. (1973) The Anthropologist as Reluctant Imperialist. In T. Asad (ed.) *Anthropology and the Colonial Encounter*. London: Ithaca Press.

MAIR, L. (1969) *Anthropology and Social Change*. London: LSE Monographs on Social Anthropology, Athlone Press.

MEMMI, A. (1965) *The Colonizer and the Colonized*. Willows, CA: Orion Press.

WILSON, M. (1951) *Good Company*. London: Oxford University Press.

A. P. Cheater*

3 Anthropologists and Policy in Zimbabwe:

design at the centre and
reactions on the periphery

Anthropological Involvement in Zimbabwean Policy

Let me begin by isolating various referents of the term 'policy'. Policy is essentially a process of making decisions, while planning concerns their specification for implementation. At the national level, policy is distinct from planning. Below this level, the one shades into the other and the reason for the overlap in their dictionary meanings is plain. In independent Zimbabwe, policy making is ostensibly the prerogative of central government. In central government's view, decisions made by municipal or other forms of local government are thus 'planning' rather than 'policy', or what might be termed 'reactive' rather than 'independent' policy. In this chapter, therefore, I restrict myself to considering only central government policy at the national level and the local reactions which it may generate; and in *Table 1* I have summarized the various influences that may affect such policy at different levels, in order to indicate what *institutional* niches exist for the anthropologist to participate in such influence, ignoring informal channels of personal influence.

The determination of policy at the national level is unequivocally a political process. When a country decides on a broadly 'socialist' policy, this is a political decision, made at party and cabinet levels. Unless they wear the relevant political hat as well as formal academic dress, anthropologists cannot hope to participate directly in the formulation of policy at this level. As *Table 1* shows, however, in Zimbabwe there is some scope among citizens for indirect participation by serving on governmental commissions of inquiry whose terms of reference have very broad policy implications.[1]

* I am most grateful to Michael Bourdillon, Gordon Chavunduka, and Paul Devitt for their comments on an early draft of this chapter.

Table 3.1   Sources of influence on public policy in Zimbabwe

level of policy determination	institutions influencing policy determination directly	indirectly
national	Cabinet; Central Committee of ZANU(PF)	government commissions of inquiry of a general nature (e.g. Riddell Commission)
intermediate: translation of national policy into specific policies by ministries	Ministers; public servants of decision making rank	commissions of inquiry of a specific or sectoral nature; lobbies/pressure groups (e.g. farming unions); external advisers/consultants to ministries; private consultants attached to aid agencies and funding institutions, including foreign governments
local: implementation and evaluation of policies through specific projects	public servants, including professionally qualified not of decision making rank; professionally qualified consultants	local and expatriate consultants

Second, there is the translation of broad political directives into more detailed options for later implementation. Part-policy, part-planning, this process is the responsibility of individual ministries. At this level, anthropologists may participate in policy-cum-planning directly or indirectly. The direct route requires employment as a public servant of decision making rank. Indirectly, however, anthropological influence on decisions may occur through commissions of inquiry having fairly specific terms of reference and through consultancy, and in the latter case it may come from local or expatriate anthropologists.[2]

Finally, there is the practical implementation of specific projects, including feasibility studies which may recommend among different alternatives, and their later evaluation to assess the extent to which policy objectives have actually been achieved. Here potential anthropological involvement lies overwhelmingly in the field of consultancy, with a very limited opportunity for professional employment in certain ministries, such as Lands, Resettlement and Rural Development.

Opportunities for consultancy have expanded very dramatically since Zimbabwe became independent in April 1980, and they involve both local and foreign anthropologists. The opportunities for expatriate anthropologists lie primarily in the aid programmes to Zimbabwe, which are funded mainly by Western governments and non-governmental agencies, such as Oxfam, together with USAID and the World Bank. Very occasionally, individual anthropologists have been employed as consultants by ministries, but this is not the common pattern.[3] The relationships of expatriate anthropologists to the policy makers of Zimbabwe are thus mediated through foreign governments or foreign aid programmes. Such anthropologists contribute, not to Zimbabwean policy, but to policy made for Zimbabwe by external organizations. In future, such policy will have to take cognizance of internal government policy. Rumours have been current for some time that the Ministry of Finance, Economic Planning and Development will in future require that *all* aid money be channelled through itself, to control the local operations of foreign organizations which are deemed to be potentially contrary to government's broadest policy objectives. Already, certain public servants insist that anthropological advice to central government come from local citizens or those who have had past fieldwork experience in Zimbabwe.[4] The scope for expatriate anthropological influence on policy in Zimbabwe is thus perhaps diminishing, even as the demand for consultancy services, by government, continues to rise. Zimbabwe wishes to control its own policy, and that implies using advisers over whom it has some degree of control, even when it cannot assume their complete identification with governmental interests.

Which brings us to Zimbabwean anthropologists, whose future involvement in public policy is likely to rest heavily on their individual relationships with government. In this respect, those of us at the University of Zimbabwe suffer from the general stigma of the colonial association (Asad 1973), by virtue of having been 'inherited' by independent Zimbabwe.[5] Furthermore, the specific colonial history of social anthropology in Zimbabwe includes the employment of certain anthropologists unsympathetic to nationalist aspirations in the former Ministry of Internal Affairs (earlier the Department of Native Affairs), which was the effective organ of racial segregation in Southern Rhodesia under colonial governments. *NADA*, the annual publication of this ministry, largely propagated what has been criticized as the 'antiquarian' tradition (Ranger 1979) of anthropological endeavour, and it is this tradition which informs government's perspective on anthropology, overriding the counter-image presented by liberal anthropologists employed outside government during the colonial period.[6] Indeed, the radical image of anthropology during the 1960s, arising from the departure in 1967 of Mitchell, van Velsen, and others from the country's only university in protest against white racial politics, has been entirely submerged. Their successors have been regarded by definition as collaborators with the racism of the Rhodesian Front regime, partly through the influence of certain intellectuals associated directly with the liberation struggle.[7]

There are good reasons for government's suspicion of local anthropologists. We have distanced ourselves symbolically from the ruling party, as part of our attempt to maintain the ostensible objectivity associated with academic autonomy. At the same time, our graduates have tended to avoid employment in the public service, partly because there are few professional openings for them. But our graduates' scepticism of government employment is also an attitudinal response to our commitment to maintaining the distance between university and government. As researchers, we are aware of the negative reactions of our respondents to central government policy, past and present. As teachers, we try to sensitize our students to the intricacies of national problems. Inevitably, this orientation is seen as potentially threatening by the political policy makers, whose public rhetoric offers simple solutions to such problems. High-status intellectuals refusing to endorse policy publicly are a particular problem in countries where the population accords exaggerated and undeserved respect to 'the educated'. Our relations with political government are accordingly rather poor.

Yet, despite its reservations, government recognizes that it cannot wholly dispense with our services. In the context of cultural nationalism,[8] anthropologists hold valuable information, historical and contemporary, which Western-educated politicians lack but need. For example, in the recent institution of primary courts and the current examination of the role of customary law, the work of local anthropologists (Chavunduka 1979; Cheater, in press) has apparently been useful in the formulation of legal policy, although neither research project was undertaken with policy goals prominently in mind and neither anthropologist acted as a consultant.

One should note, too, that those policy areas in which anthropologists have a specific cultural expertise, may be extremely sensitive to the self-image of Third World politicians who see themselves as comprising the vanguard of modernization in their societies. Chavunduka's attempt shortly after independence to sensitize the Zimbabwean law-makers to the practical realities of our inherited colonial legislation on witchcraft, for example, was received with outright hostility by those who argued either that the belief in witchcraft is false or that it is wholly evil, and that either way the existing legislation is appropriate to independent Zimbabwe. More recently, government has undertaken to re-examine this issue, as a result of continued pressure from Professor Chavunduka,[9] perhaps because of the usefulness of Chavunduka's academic work in other areas of policy, namely law and medicine (see Chavunduka 1978).

In contrast to such ambivalent relations with government as politics, local anthropologists experience fewer problems with administrative government, or the public service. In this relationship, what mutual suspicion exists has a disciplinary rather than a political basis. Natural scientists in professional posts sometimes express their dismay at the involvement of 'soft' academics as consultants, in the practical implementation of development projects based on 'hard' techno-scientific skills. In contrast, those administrators who have already discovered the capacity of ordinary people to subvert tightly drawn plans, and who are responsible for implementing change in accordance with national policy, welcome local anthropological advice.

In Zimbabwe, then, there is a wide range of governmental opinion regarding the involvement of local anthropologists in policy and/or its implementation, from well developed political resistance to administrative insistence on their inclusion in policy making teams. To some extent these reactions depend on individual relationships and personal reputations. Contrary to what might be expected, however, they do not at present divide along racial lines. In general, these reactions indicate the complexity of the micro-political background to the involvement of anthropologists in policy and planning in any Third World country. It is in the context of this micro-political complexity that I would like to discuss one particular problem area, using a Zimbabwean example to illustrate local reactions to central government policy.

The articulation between national and local levels of government, as one specific aspect of the centre–periphery relationship *within* Third World states, has been of past interest to anthropologists. The concern with intercalation and its problems, arising from the policy of 'indirect rule', is inextricably part of British colonial anthropology (see Gluckman 1949; and with specific reference to Zimbabwe, Garbett 1966; Holleman 1969; Weinrich 1971). In independent Third World states, however, the study of national–local relationships appears largely to have been abandoned to political scientists (e.g. Lamb 1974; Miller 1968, 1970), although Bond (1975) and Kuper (1970; also Kuper and Gillett 1970) have worked in this area. Perhaps the abandonment of this area by anthropologists reflects its sensitivity, or perhaps it is simply that anthropologists have always been more concerned with the local level *per se*, than with the integration of part-societies into larger systems. Whatever the cause, there have been no dramatic developments in political anthropology in the past decade, notwithstanding Marxist pressure to address such issues.

But if we are to become involved in public policy in developing countries, this area is critically important. First, for the *academic* anthropologist acting as consultant, it represents one field in which his or her ethical unease in any working relationship with government will surface. Second, any distance between central and local government has major implications for the viability of implementing in rural areas policy which has been formulated at the urban centre. Third, in theoretical terms, as the centre impinges more and more heavily on local communities, we have to understand their modes of articulation in order to interpret the behaviour both of administrators and of ordinary people. Finally, from this relationship we may learn more of the singular significance of symbolism in the process of development in the Third World.

These points will be examined in some detail later, as they are generated by the history of the relationship between local and central government in one freehold area in central Zimbabwe. I first studied Msengezi in 1973–74, re-studied it in 1980–81, and have maintained continuous contact with the area in the intervening periods (Cheater 1984). In the conflict that is described here, I should note that I was never asked to involve myself by either of the parties concerned, but notwithstanding my links with Msengezi, was treated as a detached and neutral observer, having the right to enquire on the basis of my previous work. Any assistance that I might have been able to offer was regarded as irrelevant, for Msengezi people regarded themselves as perfectly capable of defending their own interests in their own way.

Local Government Policy: A Case Study

The black freehold areas in Zimbabwe were established in 1930, under the original Land Apportionment Act. The problem of administering local affairs surfaced shortly thereafter, as individual landowners sought mechanisms of decision making regarding collective interests in roads, schools, dipping services, marketing arrangements and so on. By the mid-1930s, such matters were being handled, in a number of areas, by farmers' associations, the fore-runners of the black freeholders' national union. By this time, too, certain black political associations had begun to recommend the formation of co-operatives in the freehold areas as a solution to the problems affecting farmers collectively. In Msengezi, an extension of the model of chiefly authority was sought, unsuccessfully, on an elective basis.[10] In some other areas, landowners apparently continued to accept the authority of neighbouring chiefs, from whose areas they had moved *en masse* (Weinrich 1975).

None of these solutions was favoured by the colonial government which, in 1937, made slightly belated provision for this problem in passing the Native Councils Act.[11] During the 1930s and 1940s, most of the early-established 'native purchase areas', including Msengezi, formed councils under the pro-visions of this Act. Councillors were elected by rate-paying landowners from among their own number.

Notwithstanding their legal validity, however, it would seem that not all Native Commissioners approved of the freeholders' rights to govern their own affairs. In Msengezi, for example, it took nearly two years for the Commissioner to accept the concept of a council. In 1942, with the encourage-ment of the Southern Rhodesia Native Farmers' Conference which backed this policy, Msengezi farmers raised the question of forming a council. The Native Commissioner, on his own admission, deliberately delayed the issue for over a year, ostensibly in order to give people time to reflect on all the possible consequences of such action.[12] Finally, in March 1944, the Msengezi and Kutama Council was gazetted.

By the mid-1970s this Council controlled a six-figure annual budget, more than half of which came from central government sources. In February 1979, under pressure from ZIPRA guerillas, who set up base in the general area for a short period towards the end of the liberation war, it deconstituted itself and left the running of local services to the permanent staff under the direct control of the District Commissioner. Following a protracted disagreement with Zimbabwe's newly independent and nominally socialist government, dominated by ZANU(PF), the Msengezi Rural Council was finally reconstituted on 1 December, 1981, this time including the Marshall Hartley mission estate as well as Msengezi and Kutama purchase lands, between which the mission is physically located.

At certain points in this history, freeholders in Msengezi found themselves in open conflict with the policies of central government, colonial and independent. The first major disagreement centred on the problems of representing local interests to central government and organizing the administration of collective services in the area. Central government finally introduced the institutional representation of local interests, under the direct control of its own representative (the Native Commissioner). The landowners accepted this solution and spent the next two decades familiarizing themselves with its operation, including the limits to their own decision making capacity. In the early 1950s, for example, Msengezi farmers protested to the Native Commissioner against the appointment of an additional Schools Superintendent by him, on the grounds that the Council, which ostensibly controlled the schools, had not been consulted about the appointment: 'We are all of the opinion that an act of appointing a School Superintendent, without the knowledge of the members of the Council and the School Council, reflects that the Council has less powers in dealing with its own rites [sic].' This protest elicited a sharp reaction from the subject of the rebuke: 'I consider your letter on the above subject an impertinence. I have already pointed out to your Council that there are certain matters which lie beyond their jurisdiction. . . I would advise you and your Council to be sure of their facts before being offensively insolent.'[13]

In the early 1960s, during a period of heightened nationalist political activity, the next major dispute arose, concerning the control of the Council itself. In terms of the African Councils Act of 1957, which replaced the Native Councils Act, Msengezi councillors demanded that the Commissioner relinquish chairmanship of the Council to one of the elected representatives of the farmers themselves: 'The Chairman was asked if it was not time that an African chairman be appointed. As an illustration he asked each member to read section 33 (which was chosen at random) and then asked each councillor to explain what it meant. None were able to do so. However, he undertook to enquire into the matter.'[14] In 1961, the Native Commissioner agreed that a Vice-chairman should be elected from among the councillors. Two years later, the chairmanship passed uneventfully into local hands, under the supervision of a new District Commissioner. The representative of central government became President of the council, an honorary and advisory position nominally lacking any decision-making capacity, which position was maintained in Msengezi. In practice, however, covert pressure was exerted using the leverage of central government grants, on which the council has always been crucially dependent for more than half of its total income. Without these grants, the maintenance of public roads and water supplies, dipping services, health care and education would not be possible. Nonetheless, the public interface between local and central administration in Msengezi appeared to be controlled by the local councillors, and it was on this premise of local control that much of the council's prestige and legitimacy rested. 'This is our council, not the government's' was the way in which people perceived their capacity to control their own society and its future development, notwithstanding their financial dependence on central government.

Thus when the council was forced to deconstitute itself late in the liberation war, people were unhappy. Their unhappiness increased following the electoral victory of ZANU(PF) in February 1980, after the Lancaster House Agreement of 1979, and the announcement of the new socialist policy of unified district administration a few months later. Originally this policy was designed to remove the inherited racial and class inequities between (white) Rural and (black) Local Councils, by creating District Councils which were to cover both commercial and peasant farming areas. In practice, this objective rapidly became subordinated to the amalgamation of previously autonomous black Local Councils, from both freehold and peasant areas, into larger units.[15] With past negative experience of what such amalgamation in the co-operative unions had meant for the class interests of freeholders (see Cheater 1976), landowners – spearheaded by those owning farms in Msengezi – fought this new policy. To a commission sent by the Minister of Local Government and Housing to explain the new policy, Msengezi farmers politely but firmly rejected the proposals. Their lead was followed by freeholders in other areas. Central government then attempted to pressurize them into accepting an enlarged District Council, *inter alia* by using the services of a Deputy Cabinet Minister from the dominant party (ZANU(PF)), who is 'a son of Msengezi'. He was told to convey to the appropriate places Msengezi's continued rejection of the new policy. On a subsequent visit to the area, when he attempted to 'blackmail' 'his own people' using the grants issue, this man was threatened publicly with physical violence.

In the meantime, support from opposition parties[16] was mobilized in the national political arena for Msengezi's opposition to the new policy. At one point, the effectiveness of this mobilization was reflected in the public denunciation in the national press, of opposition politics in the province in which Msengezi is located, by the Deputy Minister referred to above.[17]

In this last conflict, symbolic identity and the manipulation of political symbols were important. The man who was finally elected chairman of the Msengezi Rural Council early in December 1981, had held this position before fleeing Msengezi during the war. Neither he nor his fellow councillors had previously affiliated themselves to any political party. However, at the insistence of party commissars, they did agree to adopt the ZANU(PF) label for the purpose of the local elections, and did not dispute this public identification in the national press reportage of the election results, resting such proxy identity on their flight from ZIPRA control during the war, and conveniently ignoring Msengezi's overwhelming support, in the elections held in April 1979, for the UANC, in preference to ZANU under the leadership of Ndabaningi Sithole. Having won their battle over *material* interests, which they did not wish to jeopardize in the future by alienating the ruling party too badly, they were prepared to close the *symbolic* distance separating them from the ruling party. These councillors, together with other refugees who fled Msengezi during the war, also developed some degree of estrangement from those who remained and developed a PF identity during the 1979 ZIPRA 'occupation' of Msengezi. Yet such symbolic identities, including ethnicity, in no way hindered the collaboration of those who held them in pursuing *all* channels of opposition to central government policy in the field of local government.

'Non-political' channels of opposition included the use of bureaucratic delaying tactics. The conflict was also taken to the national executive of the Zimbabwe National Farmers' Union (the black freeholders' union), which carefully refrained from placing any such complaints on the agenda for its annual conference in 1981, but instead invited Ministers from all the Ministries involved in the purchase lands to address the delegates on their specific policies. The Ministry of Local Government and Housing was then castigated *from the floor* for having misled freeholders about the practical implications of the policy of unified district administration.[18] The union thus expressed the collective opposition of the freeholders to amalgamation with peasant areas, in a manner that did not associate this opposition with particular individuals; and those purchase lands which had entered District Councils, as an initial gesture of support for the new government, pleaded to be allowed to leave them.

Notwithstanding the Ministry's threat to end financial assistance from central government to 'unviable' small councils, the freeholders in Msengezi eventually won.[19] While the District Commissioner continued to administer services using central grants, the farmers' delaying tactics had bought them enough time to mobilize sufficient support at the *national* level successfully to defend their own *local* interests.

A final irony of the farmers' victory over central government, is that their contemporary form of local government, far from aligning them with the peasantry, is now identical with the local government of predominantly white, large scale, commercial farming interests. Rural Councils are governed by legislation passed in 1966 (the Rural Councils Act), which the District Councils Act (1980) was originally intended to supersede. The class interests and consciousness of freeholders have thus subverted socialist national policy. Indeed, this particular conflict, focusing on the control of infra-structure critical to continued development, was crucial in causing free-holders in Msengezi explicitly to acknowledge their separation, in class terms, from the peasantry. 'We have got our well-looked-after infrastructure – schools, the clinic, our tractor, roads, etc. Do they [peasants in areas of communal landholding] have the same? We don't want to have a situation whereby our tractor goes to serve in Mhondoro where it may stay for six months before it comes back.' 'We commercial farmers are few. We do not wish to be dominated by the many in the Tribal Trust Lands. . . We farmers will have to fight it, or we will be oppressed by them.'[20]

Yet in the longer term, the very success of the freeholders' defence of their class interests has further jeopardized these interests by drawing them to the attention of government. In May 1983, the Prime Minister again called for a unified system of local government in the countryside: 'The present system reflects a clear class differentiation with the rich commercial farmers on one hand and poor peasant farmers on the other. The sooner a more acceptable uniform system is established, the better.'[21]

Ethical and Theoretical Problems

I have outlined this Zimbabwean example of the ways in which central policy may be subverted locally, without anthropological or other external assist-ance, for a number of reasons.

Firstly, when talking of anthropological inputs to the development of public policy, we might ask: *whose* policy? That determined by central government and other official organizations; or the 'counter-policy' – which, as this example shows, may be successful – generated by local societies in their opposition to central control? This question is particularly important to the anthropologist hired to advise foreign governments. Should he be plaintiff or policeman? If hired as policeman, is the plaintiff role ruled out? What of his responsibility to those who make his advisory job possible by providing information, that might be used against their own definition of their own best interests?

Secondly, we might enquire whether the anthropologist as adviser on policy in the Third World may not already be redundant? If ordinary farmers have the capacity to manipulate central policy and policy makers with the skill shown in my example, might not the policy influencing anthropologist have all of his or her time cut out simply trying to keep informants in sight, so to speak? What is actually meant by 'central policy' under such circumstances? And how is the anthropologist going to be able to influence or 'develop' it, except perhaps as 'squealer' or hired hit man? The anthropologist's colonial role as mediator between government and people has already given way to the ability of wealthier people to negotiate directly with their popularly elected, but not always popularly supported governments. If this is the view of the people in the Third World, then as development proceeds we should expect our former colonial role of policy broker to decline in importance.

Finally, then, we must face reality. The policy making organization that employs the anthropologist will expect to call the tune. If that organization is part of the First World aid effort, it may well find itself in conflict with the governments of Third World states. If the employer is a Third World government, the anthropologist must expect to assist in the imposition of centrally defined policy on unwilling local recipients. (Current interest in the concept of an 'uncaptured peasantry' would appear to be related to this point.) In both cases, the anthropologist stands a good chance of coming into conflict with people who may believe that they have some right to direct and manage their own affairs in their own interests in their own country, and on whose co-operation his or her own position, status and salary depend. For the anthropologist seeking to influence public policy in the Third World, the ethical conflicts are serious.

These ethical problems are exacerbated by our current state of theoretical ignorance concerning the penetration of the state, rather than capital, into rural peripheries. This penetration affects not merely revised access to the means of production (for example, through land reform or redistribution, or changes in systems of tenure). Even more critically, state penetration also affects marketing possibilities; communications and transport; the administration of resources for collective welfare facilities; commodity pricing and returns to agricultural producers – in short, all those aspects of distribution and consumption that are not confined to individual households producing or exchanging their own requirements.

Another aspect of the penetration of the state into rural societies concerns the politically symbolic in policy formulation. We are aware of the gulf between 'theory' and 'practice', and that 'policy' is a type of 'theory'. Those responsible for making policy must publicly be seen to have, or to be acquiring, such policy.[22] Once policy is acquired, however, it may be forgotten or ignored by those who find it constraining. Moreover, in countries like Zimbabwe, where the public expression of policy is itself a form of symbolic behaviour, the subversion of policy must be achieved while continuing to extol it publicly. Those involved in the political process of policy making even at the local level are keenly aware of this requirement, and will maintain 'face' for government (or the ruling party) even while upending the implementation of a policy they reject.

This division between the symbolic and practical aspects of policy is very much part of the growing concern with the articulation of centre and periphery in Third World states, for it reflects an empirical separation of the ideological and the material in rural development. Symbolic policy is one means of mystifying what is actually happening (or, more likely, not happening) on the periphery. It is equally a means whereby politicians or their civil servants may reiterate a commitment to a particular set of policy objectives while implementing a contrary line. Local people, such as the Msengezi farmers, may be slightly more honest in quietly rejecting both policy and its implementation, but may nevertheless acquiesce in gestures of symbolic reconciliation that leave intact the public image of the policy. All of these procedures influence the process of class formation within Third World states, as an inextricable part of the process of rural development. They are all part of the mechanisms whereby the state establishes new relationships with the rural periphery. They all contribute to the growth of pressure groups within the national economy which affect policy and its implementation, and they all contribute to the problems of advisers on policy. It is in this context that local anthropologists in Third World countries may fear to enter the policy arena at all; whereas expatriate advisers, normally shielded from governmental infighting by aid agencies or foreign governments, may regard this attitude as both timorous and against the interests of 'development' and 'the people'.

And so I would make the following points regarding the role of anthropologists in the formulation of public policy in the Third World. First, anthropological involvement cannot be disinterested and objective, a purely advisory role. Especially for local anthropologists in the Third World, academic detachment is illusory. In reality the anthropologist is entering the political domain of decision making, which should be recognized for what it is.

Second, by training, the anthropologist is poorly equipped to cope with this situation. As Robertson (1981) points out, our knowledge of disciplines that are technically critical to rural development is scanty. Our specialist techniques of investigation and analysis are largely irrelevant. Our professional ability to survive in the corridors of power is questionable. Belshaw has already warned that 'the advice of social science, and especially of anthropology, can be wrong-headed, falsely founded and improperly motivated' (1976: xv). More recently, Fuller (1982) has questioned the capacity of anthropologists actually to produce the policy goods that we sometimes claim to be able to. In such circumstances, it is all the more important that we do not land ourselves in situations that we cannot handle, such as factioning within a national cabinet over policy issues.

Here I am not referring simply to individuals, but third and finally to the impact of individual actions on the viability of anthropology as an international profession seeking to expand its image of relevance at a time of shrinking opportunities for academic employment. For Zimbabwe, I have already detailed the causes of governmental suspicion of anthropologists.

Any instance of 'failure' or incompetence on the part of anthropological advisers to the government of Zimbabwe would be enough to prejudice the future of all, including future graduates of the local university seeking employment in government. And yet, in the literature concerning anthropology and policy, I see little indication that the profession has recognized that it is venturing into highly reactive areas, especially in Third World policy, ill-equipped and poorly protected.

Does the anthropologist really have a role in the formulation or development of public policy, especially in the Third World? Or is this wishful thinking in the context of international economic crisis?

Notes

1. The opportunities for direct and indirect participation by anthropologists are almost equally limited, although Dr Weinrich did sit on the Commission of Enquiry into Incomes, Prices and Conditions of Service (the Riddell Commission) in 1980–81.
2. In the early 1960s, Professor Holleman served on the commission investigating 'unrest' in one of the communal lands (see Holleman 1969). More recently, Professor Chavunduka has chaired the Commission of Enquiry into the Agricultural Industry, which reported in 1982.
3. Dr Alice Morton has advised USAID, Dr Walton Johnson Oxfam (USA), and Professor Michael Horowitz has acted as consultant to the IBRD, while Dr Peter Ucko has recently advised the Ministry of Education and Culture in an individual capacity.
4. Personal interview with Mr R. Mupawose, then Permanent Secretary in the Ministry of Lands, Resettlement and Rural Development, and now Permanent Secretary in the Ministry of Agriculture (November 1981).
5. All six members of the permanent teaching staff of this department in 1983 had been appointed before Zimbabwe became independent.
6. For example, by those employed in municipal government, in which capacity their planning sometimes contradicted the intent of colonial policy. Dr Hugh Ashton, for example, was the prime reason for the reputation enjoyed by the City of Bulawayo as particularly 'enlightened' regarding black urban housing.
7. Shortly after independence, the entire Department of Sociology at the University of Zimbabwe was publicly pilloried by the then Minister of Manpower Planning and Development. His speech is widely believed to have been instigated, and possibly written, by one of his senior public servants, himself a graduate of our university, whose experience in the Department of Sociology as an undergraduate student was somewhat unsatisfactory to all concerned. This incident should also be seen in the context of the desire of certain 'radical' politicians to transform this university itself. I mention these details because they indicate the importance, in a small developing country, of individuals and their specific experiences as part of the micro-politics of policy determination.
8. Belshaw (1976: xiv) draws attention to the importance of nationalism of all kinds in policy formulation, and rightly castigates anthropologists for ignoring it, noting that it becomes more and more important as the anthropologist moves conceptually or empirically 'from the village to the wider world'.
9. See Chavunduka (1980), which was delivered as his inaugural lecture in the Chair

of Sociology at the University of Zimbabwe in October 1980. The Witchcraft Suppression Act was defended by the then Deputy Minister for Home Affairs, who argued: 'It is not a new law in Zimbabwe. Neither is it a white man's law, nor a colonialist law,' notwithstanding its original enactment at the close of the nineteenth century! (*Sunday Mail* 28 June, 1981: 1.) The re-examination has been promised by the Minister of Legal and Parliamentary Affairs (*Herald* 1 May, 1982: 3), with the support of the Minister of Home Affairs, who controls the police, who in turn have experienced some difficulty in implementing the existing legislation (*Sunday Mail* 20 June, 1982).

10. See *Bantu Mirror* 6 February, 1937: 6; and 10 December, 1938: 4. A letter signed by P. Mtatabikwa gives details of the Msengezi farmers' desire to elect a 'chief farmer', and the quashing of this suggestion by the Hartley Native Commissioner.

11. This act was passed while Charles Bullock, an administrator with a considerable interest in anthropology, and great sympathy with the needs and wants of those he called 'advanced natives', was Chief Native Commissioner.

12. Native Commissioner Hartley (now renamed Chegutu) to Chief Native Commissioner, Salisbury (now renamed Harare) 1 November, 1943. The impetus towards the Native Commissioner's final acceptance of the Council may well have been the memorandum from his assistant, dated 25 October, 1943, which noted that all landowners at a special meeting had voted in favour of forming a council. The memorandum added, rather pointedly: 'To my mind it is very desirable that the council should be established as soon as possible. The matter has been under discussion for over a year and any delay at this juncture would induce a feeling of hopeless frustration' (File S 1033/2, Zimbabwe National Archives, Harare).

13. S. B. Magorimbo, Secretary, Msengezi and Kutama Council, to Native Commissioner, Hartley (Chegutu) 4 January, 1951; and N. C. Hartley (Chegutu) to Secretary, Msengezi and Kutama Council, 11 January, 1951 (File S 1033/2. ZNA, Harare).

14. See the Minutes of the 38th meeting of the Msengezi and Kutama Council, held on 17 February, 1960 (p. 3).

15. By July 1981, the then Minister of Local Government and Housing, Dr E. Zvobgo, had admitted publicly that the amalgamation of Rural and District Councils was a 'political hot potato', impossible under the 1980 Lancaster House Constitution, and unlikely to be achieved 'in the foreseeable future' (*Herald* 28 July, 1981: 1).

16. The United African National Council and ZAPU (Patriotic Front).

17. 'The Deputy Minister of Labour and Social Services, Mr Robson Manyika, yesterday lashed out at the UANC and the Patriotic Front, accusing them of subverting the government's development programmes in Mashonaland West' (*Herald* 24 September, 1981: 5).

18. 'The Ministry of Local Government and Housing was accused of misleading small scale farmers, and commissioners sent out to explain the new set-up were alleged to have dabbled in politics' (*Herald* 7 August, 1981: 16).

19. The decision to permit certain freehold areas to establish or continue independent local government was taken in September 1981 (*Herald* 26 September, 1981: 3).

20. Quotations from field notes of interviews with farmers in Msengezi. (December 1980; February 1981.)

21. *Herald* 17 May, 1983: 1.

22. This necessity to acquire policy may in practice grant policy consultants a surprising measure of freedom. An internationally known agricultural economist, for example, found himself virtually in a position to write his own terms of reference for his consultancy on livestock policy in this country (conversation with Dr Stephen Sandford, 21 May, 1982). Few anthropologists can expect such latitude, however!

72   A. P. Cheater

References

ASAD, T. (ed.) (1973) *Anthropology and the Colonial Encounter.* London: Ithaca Press.
BELSHAW, C. S. (1976) *The Sorcerer's Apprentice: An Anthropology of Public Policy.* New York: Pergamon Press.
BOND, C. G. (1975) New Coalitions and Traditional Chieftainship in Northern Zambia: The Politics of Local Government in Uyombe. *Africa* 45 (4): 348–62.
CHAVUNDUKA, G. L. (1978) *Traditional Healers and the Shona Patient.* Gwelo: Mambo Press.
— (1979) A Shona Urban Court. Gwelo: Mambo Press.
— (1980) Witchcraft and the Law in Zimbabwe. *Zambezia* 8 (2): 129–47. Also published as *Witches, Witchcraft and the Law in Zimbabwe.* Harare: ZINATHA (1982).
CHEATER, A. P. (1976) Co-operative Marketing among African Producers in Rhodesia. *Rhodesian Journal of Economics* 10 (1): 45–57.
— (1984) *Idioms of Accumulation: Rural Development and Class Formation among Freeholders in Zimbabwe.* Gweru: Mambo Press.
— (in press) Fighting over Property: The Articulation of Dominant and Subordinate Legal Systems Governing the Inheritance of Immovable Property among Blacks in Zimbabwe. *Zimbabwe Law Review.*
FULLER, C. J. (1982) Is Anthropology Special? *Rain* 48: 16–17.
GARBETT, G. K. (1966) The Rhodesian Chief's Dilemma: Government Officer or Tribal Leader? *Race* 8 (2): 113–28.
GLUCKMAN, M. (1949) The Village Headman in British Central Africa. *Africa* 19 (2): 89–106.
HOLLEMAN, J. F. (1969) *Chief, Council and Commissioner.* Assen: Royal vanGorcum.
KUPER, A. (1970) *Kalahari Village Politics.* Cambridge: Cambridge University Press.
KUPER, A. and GILLETT, S. (1970) Aspects of Administration in Western Botswana. *African Studies* 29 (3): 169–82.
LAMB, G. (1974) *Peasant Politics.* Lewes, Sussex: Julian Friedmann.
MARX, K. (1976, 1978) *Capital* (vols. 1 and 2). Harmondsworth: Penguin.
MILLER, N. (1968) The Political Survival of Traditional Leadership. *Journal of Modern African Studies* 6 (2): 183–98.
— (1970) The Rural African Party: Political Participation in Tanzania. *American Political Science Review* 64 (2): 548–71.
RANGER, T. O. (1979) The Mobilization of Labour and the Production of Knowledge: The Antiquarian Tradition in Rhodesia. *Journal of African History* 20 (3): 507–24.
ROBERTSON, A. F. (1981) Uncomfortable Anthropologists. *Rain* 45: 4–6.
WEINRICH, A. K. H. (1971) *Chiefs and Councils in Rhodesia.* London: Heinemann.
— (1975) *African Farmers in Rhodesia.* London: Oxford University Press.

S. Conlin

4 Anthropological Advice in a Government Context

Purpose

This chapter is concerned with the governmental setting of anthropological advice. It is the intention that, by explicating something of the ethnography of a particular organizational context, recommendations can be made for the practice of anthropology.

Background

Interest in anthropology outside the university has been growing of late since it has become clear that many anthropologists trained in universities in the UK will not be able to develop careers within the university structure. On 22 January, 1983, a forum on the employment of anthropologists was held under the auspices of the Group for Anthropology in Policy and Practice (GAPP) (Stirling 1983). Recently a report to the SSRC has been submitted by Clarke and Gowler (1983) concerning the same subject. The present chapter is therefore a contribution to this subject.

In the 1970s anthropologists who had acted occasionally as consultants in development projects, were often frustrated in their attempts to influence the technocratic decisions which were central to the planning process. Although the situation was very little changed by the start of the 1980s, anthropologists began to look at this in a different way; it was noticeable that, for example, agricultural economists were making the same points but were learning strategies to become more effective, and some anthropologists were starting to do the same. The problem for anthropologists is to know how to become effective in a context outside the university. The first step is to learn the ethnography as Hoben (1980) points out in his description of the process of decision making within the US AID agency. The present chapter attempts to do the same with regard to the UK Overseas Development Administration; it is first of all a description of certain aspects of the organization which bear on the practice of social anthropology, and there are many similarities with Hoben's description. Hoben's ultimate concern is to 'identify the best points to introduce new ideas and information' (Hoben 1980: 341), whilst the present chapter is also concerned with *how* to present those ideas effectively.

The views expressed here are the personal ones of the author, based on the experience in only one area of the work of the ODA and should not be taken to represent the official policy of the ODA.

Organizational Context

THE AGENCY

The Overseas Development Administration is part of the British government. It is a functional wing of the Foreign and Commonwealth Office: the Minister for Overseas Development is a Minister of State in the FCO. In the past it has been a separate Ministry, once briefly with its own Minister in Cabinet.

Whether the agency is an Administration or a Ministry, the general structure has been fairly consistent, with an administrative centre in London and various, mainly scientific, units outside. The scientific units are available to give specialist advice on topics such as crop storage, land resources, etc. Some of the units are wholly part of the ODA but others have associate status. There are also a number of individual advisers in the administrative headquarters.

Since most of the work of the agency concerns overseas countries there are also administrators and advisers working in other countries. Some of these are attached to British embassies and high commissions to administer country programmes, and others are concerned with certain regions of the world and are based on Development Divisions. There are presently five such DevDivs.

OBJECTIVES

The agency is involved in the promotion of economic and social development in Third World countries. There are a number of different interpretations of what constitutes 'development' and the precise policy objectives of the agency have changed over time. The present policy was defined by the then Secretary of State for Foreign and Commonwealth Affairs in a statement to Parliament in February 1980. Aid to the poorer countries is a primary focus of aid policy but the 'objectives are not confined to promoting the economic development of the poorest countries, though that is of course vital. Aid is also an arm of foreign policy in both the political and economic senses. It serves the diplomatic purpose of promoting better relations. It promotes commercial interests.' (Pym 1982: 5.)

Such macro-political concerns obviously influence the shape of the aid programme and determine the overall demand for various specializations, including social anthropology. However, they have very little direct relevance for a social anthropologist working for the agency; of much more importance in this respect are certain institutional objectives which are less prone to changing political emphasis. Of fundamental importance in the ODA is the need to disburse funds, to ensure their effective use and to account for these to Parliament. Much of the decision making process can be understood in respect of these three requirements: disbursements, effective use, and accountability.

DISBURSEMENTS AND ACCOUNTABILITY

The ODA is responsible to Parliament, through the Minister, for the way in which it uses the funds which are allocated for the development programme. The total funds are currently over £1,000 million per year. Parliament approves the Estimates and exercises control or influence in three other visible ways: the Select Committee on Foreign Affairs conducts inquiries from time to time on specific topics in the field of aid and development; debates are held on the subject, and individual MPs ask questions. Such inquiries, debates and questions are generally about the way in which the funds are being used in relation to the objectives, and providing answers to them takes precedence over all other business. Administrators and advisers in the ODA are involved in the process of advising the Minister so that these responsibilities to Parliament can be fulfilled.

Funds are disbursed in a number of ways. One way to disburse money in large quantities would be to give it to another agency to spend. Some degree of oversight is still required, of course, through participation on Boards, project reviews etc. Multilateral agencies, such as the World Bank and the Development Fund of the European Community, presently spend about 40 per cent of the funds allocated to the ODA. Whilst there are some advantages to the ODA in disbursing funds through these agencies in that most of the work of utilizing the funds is done by the other agency, there is a major disadvantage, since administrators who are responsible for allocating the funds in this manner do not have complete control over their use. So accountability suffers in the sense that the ODA cannot ensure that the funds are effectively managed in line with their intentions.

In contrast, bilateral aid, in which ODA deals directly with another country, ensures that there is greater accountability, but at the cost of greater effort in considering the most appropriate ways to spend the money and implement programmes. There are different categories of funds at the disposal of the ODA: capital funds are for the purchase of capital items, while Technical Co-operation (TC) funds are to provide expertise, and for training staff from overseas organizations in the UK. Functional TC funds are typically provided to other bodies in this country which are interested in development and with whom the ODA has close relations, such as the volunteer agencies.

In projects, the use of these funds can be combined. There are a number of advantages in allocating funds for projects: the costs and the benefits of the investment can normally be ascertained relatively easily since they are a discrete entity; technical inputs can be focused on specific objectives; the use of the funds can be clearly visible; depending on the scale of the project it is possible to disburse large quantities of funds; and British goods are purchased and British firms favoured etc. Clearly a number of the policy and institutional objectives of aid can be met through projects. There are, however, a number of disadvantages since it is often quite difficult to define a discrete entity out of a complex environment, at least on the scale required to have a substantial impact on development, and this is especially the case with regard to projects aimed at the rural poor. Projects also require staff and management structures and transport arrangements, which might prove to be a burden on the often rudimentary institutional provisions of underdeveloped countries. The advantages and disadvantages of projects have recently been the subject of academic discussion (Honadle and Rosengard 1983). Nonetheless, project aid accounted for 81 per cent of bilateral aid in 1981 (ODA 1982) and is likely to remain a major concern of the agency for the future.

An alternative method of disbursing aid funds is known as programme aid or balance of payments support and is used in particular economic circumstances. Instead of trying to support projects, funds are given to support a country's development programme. In 1981 this form of aid was 13 per cent of the bilateral programme. Recently there has been interest in improving procedures, and therefore effectiveness, by identifying *sectors* of the economy where support can be given through a mixture of project and programme aid.

Another category of funds is used in conjunction with commercial credit to enable British firms to compete on equal terms with foreign competitors on projects which have a developmental value. Usually a project is identified in which a commercial firm will be able to participate if given government financial support. Such projects are usually directed at overall economic growth and the creation of large scale economic infrastructure. Another category of funds is allocated to non-governmental agencies to disburse. The voluntary bodies identify projects, often small scale, and apply to the ODA for a matching grant. These projects are usually directed at the very poorest people, and potentially have a great impact.

The above commentary is not intended to be a comprehensive description of the ODA programme! Rather the intention is to demonstrate that there are a number of ways of achieving the institutional objectives of disbursing funds effectively and maintaining accountability, but that with each method there are a number of problems which must be overcome. In the event the ODA programme is a mixture of different means, though the main thrust has been through bilateral project aid.

The next two sections will deal with the way in which project aid is administered. In the first place it is necessary to consider the personnel involved – desk officers and advisers – and then to look at the stages through which a project passes.

DESK OFFICERS AND ADVISERS

In common with most large organizations ODA has a number of staff engaged in personnel functions, office procedures and organization etc., but for the actual programme of bilateral aid, the key personnel are the geographical Desk Officers. These are divided into two main divisions: Africa, and Asia and Oceans. The head of each division is an Under-Secretary. Within each division there are a number of regional departments headed by an Assistant Secretary; Asia and Oceans has four Departments, for South Asia, East Asia, Latin America, Caribbean and Pacific, and the South Atlantic. Within each regional department there are Desk Officers, normally at Principal level, who are responsible for a group of countries or, as in the case of India, more than one desk for one country. The Desk Officer will be assisted by a number of junior staff.

Desk Officers are responsible for the aid programme in a particular country on a day-to-day basis; they are in charge of the implementation of projects and for the accounting of disbursements that have been made. In order to carry out their duties, Desk Officers must maintain contact with, and seek advice from, a number of different people: Aid Secretaries posted to high commissions and embassies, staff in development divisions, project leaders in the field, and professional advisers. The Desk Officers are therefore responsible for the administration of the bilateral programme.

Professional advisers are divided into four main functional specialisms – Engineering, Education, Natural Resources, and Health and Population – in addition to the Economic Service which is part of the government-wide economic service. There are also a number of minority specialisms, such as the Legal Advisers, and the Social Development Advisers, of which there are two in the head office in London and one in the Caribbean Development Division.

Apart from having functional specialisms, the Advisers are also 'brigaded' into the geographical divisions as far as possible. Thus one Social Development Adviser is brigaded to Africa and the other to Asia and Oceans. This ensures that as close contact as possible is maintained between the Advisers and the Desk Officers. It is the responsibility of the latter to call for the advice of the professional advisers whenever this might be required. In order to assist Desk Officers in this task there is internal guidance about the roles of different advisers.

The advice of the Social Development Advisers is required, for example, where a project is aimed at the rural poor, since an understanding of sociological constraints is necessary to make the project effective. The advice becomes crucial in situations where investments in development could be jeopardized if the assumptions in project plans are sociologically unsound – for example, where indigenous land tenure systems or water rights might be misunderstood. The Adviser is therefore responsible for pointing out where professional concerns bear on project objectives and investment decisions.

In order to understand how Advisers offer advice it is first of all necessary to outline the project cycle.

PROJECT CYCLE AND ADVICE

Projects are identified in a number of different ways and involve negotiations between the ODA and the recipient country. Depending on their scale and complexity, projects are subject to different procedures. A small project involving, for example, the placing of one Technical Co-operation Officer in an agency of some overseas government, and perhaps a modest amount of equipment might be appraised and approved with the minimum of administrative and advisory effort. A large project involving, for example, expenditure of £5 million over five years has to follow a particular procedure. It is the project cycle involved for these large projects which is considered here.

Large projects must be considered by the Projects and Evaluation Committee (PEC) which will advise the Minister whether or not to approve a project, or what conditions should be met for the project to be acceptable. Following such approval there might still need to be further studies, either before the implementation of the project is begun or, in the case of certain projects, action research during the implementation phase.

The PEC is made up of senior management (including both administrators and professional advisers). The projects are submitted to the Committee in a particular format which details the objectives, technical commentary, economic justification, finance and management structure. There is also a requirement for consideration of social and environmental aspects. This is not a legal requirement, as in the case of AID mentioned by Hoben, but is a convention.

Project Submissions are drafted mainly by the staff of Development Divisions and Desk Officers on the basis of various contributions received from different sources (including Advisers). Once a submission has been drafted it will be distributed to various Advisers for comment. Once comments have been received and the submission re-drafted, it will be tabled before a committee which is charged with determining whether the project should be submitted for approval. The procedure leading up to submission allows the first opportunity for anthropological advice to be offered.

During the life of the project, Advisers make monitoring visits to the project with the prime intention of ensuring that it is running according to the objectives that were set. A Social Development Adviser might be one of the team of advisers and administrators, though involvement in such a team depends on how the Desk Officer assesses the priorities for advice in any particular project. Finally, after the project has been completed, it might be considered for evaluation. Depending on the focus of the evaluation, a Social Development Adviser might also be involved in defining the study and, occasionally, in participating in it.

From the above outline it is clear that during the project cycle the involvement of Advisers depends mainly on the Desk Officers. (There is a difference with regard to evaluation at the end of a project's life since that is undertaken by a special Evaluation Department.) The Desk Officers are unlikely to try to administer a project completely alone: there is no binding rule that Advisers must be consulted but there is a strong convention that Desk Officers should seek appropriate advice where possible. The Desk Officers look to the Advisers to warn them of possible professional pitfalls in the way of successful project implementation. This is important to keep the project on a sound footing, for the Desk Officer is ultimately responsible, at his level, for the effective use of aid funds on the project. Everyone is concerned, therefore, to ensure that decisions are taken on the best advice available.

Although the Desk Officer requires the best advice available, and so would wish to ensure that Advisers are aware of the situation surrounding a project, decisions regarding which particular Advisers will visit the project for monitoring and review purposes must be taken with a number of constraints in mind. Uppermost here is cost, which ensures that Desk Officers have to be very aware of priorities. These are often determined in consultation with a lead Adviser (in a health project this would be a Medical Adviser). Only where sociological issues are considered sufficiently central to the success of the project would it be likely that a Social Development Adviser be asked to visit. The case for this has to be made first of all to the geographical Desk Officers. In the event that a strong argument is, for some reason, not heeded, Social Development Advisers can argue the case for a sociological input through other channels, since Advisers are not directly responsible to geographical departments. This is a major difference from the system described by Hoben with US AID.

There is a growing awareness of the contribution that anthropological advice can make to a project but clearly this cannot be taken for granted; Advisers have to be concerned with the effectiveness of their advice so that there is often a tactical rationale in being positive and constructive in advising Desk Officers. There are, however, occasions when more fundamental criticisms of projects must be made. Decisions regarding the way in which advice can be made effective depend on the nature of the project and on the stage in the project cycle.

Offering Anthropological Advice

STAGES OF ADVICE

The kind of advice that is effective is determined in large measure by the administrative requirements of the project cycle. This is because Desk Officers are expecting to take some action on the basis of advice but the actions possible at any time are limited by previous actions and commitments. This is often not appreciated by an anthropologist engaged in a project and constrains the activities of the anthropologist; this is the source, I think, of much of the frustration felt by anthropologists involved in development projects. This is clearly a problem which concerns the relationship between field anthropologist, adviser, and administrator.

Stage 1

After initial identification of a project, the detailed preparation work leads up to a submission to the PEC. During this work, the desk which is preparing the project will normally consider the social aspects of the proposal. In cases where social aspects are of special importance, a Social Development Adviser will be invited to make a contribution to project preparation. At this stage a number of options are open in theory. The project is:

1 impossible or has massive adverse effects and ought to be abandoned;
2 sociologically complex or might have adverse effects, but with radical changes can be supported;
3 sociologically complex but adjustments cannot be specified without further study by a social scientist;
4 fairly straightforward but one or two sociological issues need to be considered – perhaps by the agricultural economist or extensionist;
5 not thought to have sociological problems.

These options will be considered in more detail later, but here it is worth noting that only options (2) and (3) will be likely to lead to having an anthropologist working in the field.

If option 2 is accepted then a feasibility study will be mounted. Here an anthropologist will be able to specify the problem and make a judgement as to whether the project is viable, perhaps with adjustments, or is simply 'not a starter'. Such conclusions involve micro-political as well as professional judgements.

If option 3 is favoured and the agency is expecting only minor adjustments, the anthropologist who, having just stepped off the plane, makes major criticisms, may face a hostile reception. Nonetheless, if a sociologist came up with a really deep-rooted criticism of project design, which had a bearing on the ability of the project to achieve its objectives or suggested an unforeseen adverse impact, the Social Development Adviser would have to probe this and argue out the position with the Desk Officers and others concerned. Obviously such a process would delay a project and the anthropologist might wish to be positive and recommend adjustments while alerting the organization to fundamental criticisms which can be taken up at the next stage. This might be a more effective way of introducing criticism at this stage.

The first lesson for anthropologists to learn is therefore at which stage they are operating, and what sort of comment the organization can act upon effectively. Much of the irritation *with* anthropologists comes because they assume they are working for option (2) when option (3) is the rule. Much of the frustration *of* anthropologists comes because they can see that there are major problems. The second lesson is that there is a chance to outline these problems in the next stage.

Stage 2

Assuming that the Minister has approved the project on the PEC's recommendation, there will be a regular process of monitoring progress as it is implemented. This process may include a major Project Review after a certain period. At this stage, in addition to the routine monitoring visits from the official (administrator or adviser) who has lead responsibility for the project, a larger team of advisers and administrators will visit the project to consider problems that may have arisen. There are a number of options. The project is:

1 not going to achieve its objectives and should be terminated;
2 not going to achieve its objectives without major revision;
3 in need of minor adjustments;
4 progressing well and should continue as before.

This process of review allows the anthropologist in the field to discuss with the Social Development Adviser the major problems in the project. It will also be necessary to discuss what action ought to be taken to resolve the difficulties; the Social Development Adviser would then be responsible for offering advice to the Desk Officer on these matters. Clearly anthropologists cannot expect action to be taken unless they are willing to make recommendations.

Stage 3

Finally in an evaluation there is a great deal of scope for an anthropologist to make fundamental criticisms about a project. Recommendations arising should be fed back into the process of project approval, because it is the same committee which considers the lessons of experience gained in evaluation studies.

COMMITMENTS AND CONSTRAINTS

In the above description it is clear that there are moments in the project cycle when anthropological advice can be offered most effectively, and a number of broad options are open at each stage. However, these options might not all be open to the Adviser. The process by which options are closed or made more open involves complex interactions between Desk Officers and Advisers, and involves the silent participation of professional colleagues outside the office.

At the stage of a PEC submission the Desk Officer or Development Division, in collaboration with lead Advisers in mainstream disciplines, will have drafted a project format which is already quite set. Often the draft reaches other Advisers with a request for suggestions for amendments but these are expected to be of a 'fine tuning' nature, not radical revisions. This is understandable in view of the amount of staff time, and perhaps negotiations with other agencies such as the World Bank, which have already been invested in the project. By the stage of a PEC submission there is already a great deal of institutional commitment to the project, and indeed a great measure of emotional investment by other Advisers and Desk Officers.

The presentation of comments by other Advisers is therefore constrained by this process of evolving commitment. Advisers are engaged in making judgements about the most effective way to offer advice: to be too negative could jeopardize relations with others who are important in maintaining information flow; to be too positive in the face of doubts would undermine one's professional credibility as an Adviser. The different tactics are partly a matter of Advisers' personal style but they are also partly calculated on the basis that Desk Officers and other Advisers must be kept aware that the advice can be useful and practical and also might indicate problems which would be expected to be avoided.

Discussion of the project is not just conducted by Desk Officers and Advisers, since the PEC submission procedure means that these professional perspectives on the project are evaluated by senior management. The PEC is concerned, apart from with the funding arrangements and management of the project, with the effectiveness of the use of the aid in question. It is important that the project in which scarce aid funds are being invested should have a satisfactory rate of return in developmental terms, i.e. that it should show a favourable cost benefit ratio. It is unlikely that a sociological commentary would lead to an abandonment of a project at this stage, but the committee might well ask for strict conditions to be met or for an anthropologist to study certain problems further. This can obviously lead to an anthropologist working on a project about which there are doubts concerning sociological soundness.

The Terms of Reference for a study reflect the nature of discussions within the ODA regarding the anthropological problems expected to be encountered. These would normally have been drafted in collaboration with a Social Development Adviser and should therefore be meaningful to the anthropologist and lead to conclusions useful to the planning process. The field anthropologist is operating in an organizational context which has been determined by the process of negotiations involving Desk Officers, Development Divisions, Advisers and the PEC. However, the field anthropologist is often unaware of the inbuilt commitments to the project and constraints on the anthropological advice that should emanate from the studies. Here the anthropologist needs to be briefed by the Social Development Advisers.

ADVISERS AND ANTHROPOLOGISTS

The anthropologist might be engaged in one of two ways: directly employed by the ODA as a TCO or indirectly as a member of a firm of consultants. The following comments formally concern TCOs, though a consultant might wish to make contact with the Adviser informally.

At the initial stages the Adviser must be able to brief the anthropologist about the constraints on the work. During the course of fieldwork the TCO anthropologist should be reporting to the Adviser on professional aspects of the project. This is important in order to provide professional support. It is also useful to the anthropologist in other ways: concern about the project can be expressed since it is the responsibility of the Adviser to feed such concerns into the monitoring and review procedures. In this way the anthropologist's comments can be effectively used in decision making. As mentioned previously for the Adviser, an anthropologist also has to make judgements about tactics and strategies in trying to be effective in project discussions.

Of course, the Adviser is not in a position only to correct errors in a project, but the continuing links of anthropologist and Adviser are important in making the best possible use of anthropological advice in the whole decision making context.

Clearly, the Adviser's effectiveness becomes very dependent on the performance of the field anthropologist. Consideration must now turn to effectiveness in presenting anthropological field data. This is done first by pointing out some negative aspects which can undermine effectiveness. Fortunately, there are anthropologists who avoid these problems and who promote anthropology's strengths.

Conclusions: Effective Presentation

PROBLEMS IN PERFORMANCE

Moral issues

Anthropologists often seem to think that they are the 'keepers of morality' and assume that no-one else working in the field possesses the same fine moral sense. Apart from being very irritating to others, this attitude is often adopted even in the face of moral dilemmas which development poses. The anthropologist is often labelled as the person who is *more* concerned with the fate of fifteen hunter-gatherers than with the benefits which will accrue to the two thousand sedentary agriculturalists who are to displace them. Rather than being accused of unrealistic conservationism it seems perfectly valid to ask whether the supposed benefits will actually materialize, to consider what provision has been made for the minority group, and what consultation there has been with either group. Such 'technical' considerations, however effective a strategy, seem often to be considered improper by anthropologists, who at all times favour the moral over the technical. For this reason the anthropologist is in danger of becoming considered as an ideologue rather than as a professional.

Poor teamwork

Perhaps because of the attitudes mentioned above, the anthropologist often finds it difficult to work in a team with other disciplines. The main identification is with the 'people' rather than with the other members of the team. As a result little time is given to work with the team, perhaps in the office or on the site, so that the anthropologist can soon be regarded as an outsider and thus becomes marginal to the decision making process.

Reports providing a poor basis for action

Perhaps the most serious weakness of the anthropologist is the lack of understanding of how to write a report of the studies conducted. This is partly a matter of style; anthropologists tend to be discursive when reports ought to be concise. However, this is merely a symptom of more basic inadequacies – the anthropologist seems not to know what the report is for, how it will be used, and what the key points for which answers are sought might be. Reports are often long discourses on abstruse exotica, and marginal notes by administrators and other professionals are often, 'fascinating – but so what?' This is really the key issue to which anthropologists seem unable to address themselves: what are the implications for action of the studies that have been conducted? Ideally the report would consist of conclusions and recommendations with some supporting statements; all the background material and detailed evidence can be consigned to Appendices to be read by other professionals.

STRENGTHS OF SOCIAL ANTHROPOLOGY

Social anthropologists have a number of strengths which could be used to good effect in overcoming the rather negative impression given in the last section.

Ethnography

To be effective it is necessary to understand the ethnography of a particular project. This involves an understanding not just of the local people but also of the other members of the team, and relations between the team and the local and national political structures. Anthropologists, if they realized the importance of addressing themselves to the ethnography of projects in this sense, could become especially effective practitioners. Fortunately, there are some excellent examples.

Methodology

There is growing disillusion with large survey techniques of data collection and interest in 'rapid rural appraisal' and case studies as an alternative methodology. To all intents and purposes these are the methods of social anthropology which are being colonized by other professionals and adapted to the requirements of the project cycle. Anthropologists are well fitted to undertake this kind of fieldwork which generates data in a timely and cost-effective manner.

Theoretical basis

The holistic perspective evident in case studies has enabled anthropologists to point out relations between events and situations which previously were not fully recognized. In project appraisals it is possible to point out the likely consequences of certain actions and to examine critically the social assumptions on which project planning is based by comparing with other known cases. Such comparisons are still a matter of judgement in many cases, since anthropologists have not formulated precise models for predictive purposes which are quantifiable. Nonetheless, judgements are solidly based on case study evidence and can therefore be sufficiently convincing to have an effect on planning.

Evaluation

The anthropologist is often highly effective in evaluation projects. This is one of the areas of greatest demand for services since the question to be answered is often, 'why did things not work out as intended?' Such evaluations are steadily strengthening the case study literature on which it is possible to build predictive judgements. There is, however, a need to systematize our understandings from evaluation case studies to formulate a structured set of questions to be addressed in appraisals.

The right place at the right time

Finally, there is a growing awareness that development is not just a technical problem of the best way to transfer skills and knowledge. Indeed, many engineers and agronomists recognize this as 'the easy bit'; the major problems are socio-economic. There is therefore a growing awareness that social anthropologists are in a position to contribute to an understanding of these problems. This has not yet become an effective demand since the central output is still a technical one and people are not clear quite how the anthropologist will be able to contribute. Nonetheless, it is possible to demonstrate that, alongside the economists, we offer a very useful support service. This impression can quickly be lost, however, unless anthropology responds to the needs of organizations such as the ODA, and this has implications for the discipline and the training of anthropologists.

IMPLICATIONS

Anthropologists need to be able to operate outside the university environment. Part of their training must involve knowledge of other organizational contexts and this chapter is a contribution to this. Another part of the training involves shifting attitudes about anthropology; because everything has a social aspect it is considered a central issue, but in terms of a project this is the 'software' which complements the 'hardware' of the technical disciplines, and we must recognize the need for co-operation and mutual support.

Of course, it is also clear that for anthropological advice to be effective Advisers have to be involved earlier in discussions about projects. Recent changes making the Social Development Advisers responsible to the Under-Secretary in charge of the Economic Service are expected to make a contribution to this. The involvement of anthropologists in evaluation and the successful feedback of results via the PEC will also help to create a climate in which Desk Officers recognize the usefulness of anthropological advice. There are other changes planned in the ODA's procedures which might be helpful (and no doubt others which are not) so that the context of advice is not static; it is the concern of Advisers to make the best use of changes and to work to increase the effectiveness of their advice.

Not all the work to be done involves the practitioners (or those who are potentially so). The climate in which the role of anthropology is viewed depends crucially on University-based anthropologists who must start work on systematic comparisons of projects, place more emphasis on policy-oriented research, be willing to undertake consultancy work where possible, and try to create opportunities for students to be involved in this kind of activity.

References

CLARKE, G. and GOWLER, D. (1983) *The Employment and Training of British Social Anthropologists*. Report to SSRC Oxford Centre for Management Studies.

CONLIN, S. (1981) *Questioning the Benefits: Anthropology in Planning*. Paper for 'Re-thinking Applied Anthropology', SfAA Conference, Edinburgh: LRDC Paper 239.

HOBEN, A. (1980) Agricultural Decision Making in Foreign Assistance: An Anthropological Analysis. In P. Barlett (ed.) *Agricultural Decision Making: Anthropological Contributions to Rural Development*. London: Academic Press.

HONADLE, G. H. and ROSENGARD, J. K. (1983) Putting 'Projectized' Development in Perspective. *Public Administration and Development* 3 (4) October–December 1983.

ODA (1982) *British Aid in Figures*. London: Government Statistical Service.

PYM, F. (1982) *Britain's Contribution to the Development of the Third World. Speech to the Royal Commonwealth Society*. London: FCO.

REW, A. (1981) *A Matrix for Anthropology and Development Studies*. Paper for 'Re-thinking Applied Anthropology', SfAA Conference, Edinburgh: Atkins Research and Development.

STIRLING, P. (1983) Employment in social anthropology. *RAIN* 55 April 1983.

Raymond Apthorpe*

5 Pleading and Reading Agricultural Development Policy:

small farm, big state, and 'the case of Taiwan'

This exercise in cultural anthropology and development studies argues that the semiotic avenue into cultural analysis of policy has an original contribution to make to the study of development. This avenue may, as yet, be relatively unexplored by anthropology, but it is unlikely to be explored at all by other disciplines in the development field. Recent work in political science and public administration by the late Bernard Schaffer is a notable exception.

It will be obvious that the approach taken in this paper owes much to the so-called 'post-structuralist' orientation in social and literary studies associated primarily with the late Michel Foucault and Roland Barthes (see Sturrock 1979; Culler 1983; Hirsch 1983). It is a semiotic approach through which policy, and the language of policy, 'policyspeak', is treated as institutionally sited 'discourse'. Offered by way of illustration is a critical review of the way in which a model of what is called 'small farmer' rural development policy and strategy – 'the case of Taiwan' – has been promoted. This chapter also examines some aspects of what might be termed the 'prescription–description tension' in development anthropology, and that is where it begins.

Anthropology and Policy Studies

It is a paradox: social studies of rural development policy, while aiming to be instrumental and practical, largely remain, in their prescriptions and de-

*The writer carried out United Nations' research, teaching and other assignments in Taiwan between 1970 and 1972, returning in 1975 for a further period with the UK Social Science Research Council, the aid of which is gratefully acknowledged. His field research in Taiwan owed very much indeed to the limitless generosity of Wang Sung-hsing and Chiu Wan-tuo. The present chapter is an expanded version of remarks set down for the ASA 1983 Decennial Conference, this time round mainly on 'applied anthropology'; I am most grateful to friends who urged an expanded version, above all Ralph Grillo, disappointed though they may be with the result of their kind efforts.

scriptions alike, in the realms of models and deals. This is so even in respect of 'cases': learn, the injunctions go, from Tachai, Anand, Comilla. Both socialist and non-socialist rural development literature has rallied of late to the 'case of Taiwan'. Modernization and dependency schools alike affirm this as a 'model' of prosperity which has been achieved through a 'small farm' (or 'small farmer' or 'family farm') policy and strategy. In such policy discourse a model is meant to serve as a practical lesson for development planning (see Chakravarty 1980), as a cutting edge to be honed, and as a strategy to be applied. Believe it or not, such models can be, and often are, recommended even as 'miracles' to be replicated elsewhere.

In anthropology, most explanatory models are meant to serve mainly heuristic purposes, heuristic that is for theoretical purposes internal to the profession. The discipline's principal elective affinity is for description rather than prescription. Consonantly with this, even development anthropology is often content to accept merely the dependent and contingent roles assigned to it by development economics.

Such passivity can to an extent have two unfortunately restrictive effects. One has to do with the condoning of a categorical pure/applied distinction, a sort of ideas/action discrimination, as if pure ideas were denotative only, and applied action solely operative. The other is the condemning of development anthropology to a virtual casuism in the area of policy studies.

The academic debates in anthropology which reject even the possibility of generalization about development (or other) policy, or those which seek to contrast this discipline's pure versus applied forms, are not in the least focal for this paper. Nonetheless, it should be said that some pure and indeed classically structural anthropology can, and does, address development and policy issues: some applied work does not and cannot. The latter may be too purist in its professional and single disciplinary focus to give it much chance of achieving what nevertheless it says it sets out to do. The former may be sufficiently 'post', or in Victor Turner's term (1969) 'anti', structural as to make it as able as it is willing, in its own way and language, to address policy.

Like other social studies, anthropology may be explicitly or implicitly addressed to policy. Some anthropological studies are only implicitly concerned with application and do not overtly claim to be contributions to development studies as conventionally understood. Nevertheless, covertly they may consider themselves to be even more apposite than explicit attempts to grapple with, perchance to solve, public issues. For instance, and as commonly expressed in their subtitles, social anthropological monographs often deal not with change *or* continuity, but change *and* continuity (and schism *and* continuity, conflict *and* co-operation, and so forth). Their very starting-point is that a society's status quo is a principal problematic, something which is very far from what could be taken as a given, as non-problematic. This being so, how very much *more* problematic must any proposed change of it be, especially structural change.

What is crucial for the present exercise is the premise that policy oriented study does not necessarily have to go so far as actually to recommend a course of policy before it could qualify as being such (Apthorpe and Gasper 1982). For example, 'evaluative' studies do not also have to be prescriptive before they could be judged applied, and 'diagnostic' work does not have to be 'prognostic' as well, either in aim or implication, before it could make an important contribution. However, one present tendency in the ethos of institutes of development studies and the like puts such strong emphasis on just the one kind and form of policy orientedness, prescription, as to relegate all others if not to oblivion, then at least to residual marginality. Alas nothing could be less conducive to either understanding or changing institutions and livelihoods, whether 'theirs' or 'ours'. It is equally unfortunate that so much debate about pure and applied in British anthropology, and for that matter in economics, has been so sterile, because, for example, it does not go into matters of different sorts of policy orientedness. One task is for criticism to consider a whole range of different sorts of such policy orientednesses. Both analysing policy models and advocating them have their own place, though perhaps to begin with they may seem to be mutually exclusive, even contradictory, forms of inquiry and activity.

Policy Studies and Policy Discourse

Anthropology which says it deals explicitly with development and policy includes a corpus of studies on selected 'social factors' deemed, echoing the language of development economics, to be either 'obstructing' or 'facilitating' change. As, now, is commonly remarked, this is true generally of work of the modernization persuasion. However, while much dependency literature tends as a rule to conceptualize the social in terms of 'formations' rather than 'factors', as for instance when writing of 'modes of production' and their 'articulations', this latter literature is also much exercised by 'obstacles' and 'prerequisites' of a pseudo-mechanist sort.

Modernization studies are not necessarily always either liberal, conservative or populist. Dependency positions are not always necessarily Marxist, Darwinist or radical. In their actual working out and applications, contrasting schools have similarities as well as differences (and in any event there are unorthdoox forms of both schools). What, for example, do the modernization and dependency schools have in common? That each claims to hold the whole truth, the complete truth, and not the partial truth, is one thing. Another is the strong tendency, which follows from this, of each to utopianism. There is also the extent to which each says that only *structural* change and development could be *significant*, without having worked out quite what is meant by such utterance. Other common areas are the ways in which virtually all doctrinal positions of a general sort in development studies exaggerate the First and Second World determinisms over those of the Third and Fourth Worlds, and the extent to which planning is always treated as exogenous to economic and socio-political organization and planned structure (Apthorpe 1982; Apthorpe and Krahl 1984).

Another similarity is that few explicitly applied studies, whether of function or policy, go so far as to consider the operative languages of research and of policy as being themselves problematic. Most tend to proceed as if cultural theory were either the enemy of practice or policy, or else altogether irrelevant for practical purposes.

It was suggested earlier that a semiotic approach to the cultural analysis of policy could be rewarding. In development studies it would represent a somewhat novel kind of inquiry into policy orientedness. Immediately, there are two points about such an approach which might be noted. First, those who would follow this approach must go to great lengths to distinguish one mode of thinking-wording-willing, and of strategy, from another, notwithstanding that their ultimate aim by so doing is so to concentrate the mind that all can be brought together again. Otherwise issues may simply escape identification or, for the purposes of a particular debate, have been wrongly or insufficiently identified. The language of policy in political and other practice, and that of criticism of policy in social and other science, are largely coincident. In particular instances recourse is to one language rather than another, but the range, the repertoire, tends to be the same for both. Behaviouralist, institutionalist, materialist, physicalist, or instrumentalist theories and methods are at the same time behaviouralist, institutionalist, materialist, physicalist, or instrumentalist *discourses* (Apthorpe 1984). Discourse, like other analysis of idiom and style which takes itself too literally, may take too typological a stance. Purportedly clear cut contrasts may provide convenient starting-points for criticism, but in the end, cultural no less than political analysis of discourse, as of institutions, must be conditional, about stronger or weaker forms of combinations – emphases here, de-emphases or other issues altogether there. As Geertz put it, self-referential theory 'is not its own master . . . what generality cultural theory can contrive to achieve . . . grows out of the delicacy of its distinctions not the sweep of its abstractions' (Geertz 1975: 26).

The second point is that, for anthropology, semiotics has as much to do with institutions as with discourses and communication. All is *not* reduced to text alone. By contrast, most policy studies appear to assume that the intellectual devices on which criticism turns in effect devise and reproduce themselves. Yet where an approach has become institutionalized in one pattern and language rather than, or as well as, another, this is never, patently, because it has or could have institutionalized itself. This implies that for the analytical task involved the best method would be dialogical. Inquiring into discourses interpenetrating institutions, and institutions interpenetrating discourses, for example, we would ask: how could the latent actually happen without becoming manifest in thought and word as well as in strategy, and how could the manifest actually persist if nothing were latent? The simultaneity – or perhaps better 'instantaneity' – of functions, purposes, meanings, policies, effects, actions, discourses and institutions is a principal datum and issue.

The Perennial Speech of Policy

Whether the purpose is to prescribe or to describe, to plead or to read, on the one hand there are some common semiotics such as those of language that orders and organizes, that induces people to do: to do, to accept. This is a language which abridges and condenses in such a way as to repel demonstration, qualification, or negation of its codified and declared meaning. Even fundamental contradictions may be welded together into units of language that repel criticism – 'a clean bomb' (Knights 1971, reporting and discussing Marcuse, cf. Draper 1982); 'policy evaluation' as in policyspeak; 'structural change' as in development-speak. On the other hand there are patterns of thinking, wording and willing about policy and strategy which emphasize difference, which identify their own enemies.

One task for cultural anthropology and policy analysis is to identify, as a matter for further investigation, the particularity of the promotional mode of policy commendations, as in prescriptions about models proposed for adoption and implementation elsewhere.

To begin with, this is, as a rule, speech which says it is 'macro'. This is a convenient term with which to take the politics out of policy, to replace politics with semiotics. As thus policy becomes semiotic, so, too, does semiology become as necessary for policy analysis as is political economy, political sociology, or political anthropology.

A step towards a first approximation of the semiotic particularity of prescriptive policy discourse might look to its doubly 'would-be' character. It is would-be persuasive recommendation, of would-be action. It is discourse which says it has to do with praxis, and undoubtedly it does seek to be distinctively action-oriented in this way. But this verbalized degree of will and intent and engagement in strategy notwithstanding, the words chosen should not be mistaken, by actor or audience, for what they recommend so stridently. Policy statements are not necessarily policies as well as statements, not necessarily the policies they state.

What then could be the perennial speech, the *parole*, of policy? Because its primary purpose *is* persuasion, it seeks first of all a style, a sound and an audience best suited to obtain this effect. So its first principle must be so to announce itself as to avoid sowing any seed of doubt. It must be seen to be resolute and firm, as entertaining not even any possibility of any doubt about its would-be effectiveness. Sloganizing is one expression of, and instrument for, this kind of resolve. This is one sign of 'permanent intent to persuade' about which surely no one would disagree.

Second, policy, as prescription, unlike planning or programming, is safest said when and by saying nothing at all about implementation. This makes it unnecessary to defend itself against doubts or charges with regard to its implementation, its implementability even. Prescription is thus best restricted to the enunciation of ideas that are to be valued in and for themselves. It follows that it will be greatly formalized (Bloch 1975), highly inclusive-exclusive (Clay and Schaffer 1984). It is laid down, judgemental, and not logical or scientific in style. It hopes thereby not even to be open to being faulted on logical or scientific grounds. Best of all, if it gives no contingent reasons for itself, or courts no qualifying proof, it can pretend to stand for all seasons, and therefore remain constantly aloof.

Thirdly, and unlike ideology in some views, as well as plan and programme in others (on plan, programme and ideology see, building on Bailey 1969; Parkin 1975), policy as prescription seeks to realize its aim to persuade principally by denying that there is or could be any alternative to what it announces. Any other way only disaster lies. What is made out in this way as being necessary is therefore at the same time made out to be perfectly necessary, perfect necessity even. Pronouncing necessity to be perfect is meant, in this message, to mean that there should not, indeed cannot, be any ground for worrisome argument about it. Nothing more can remain to be said.

By this semiotic as well as politic device and task, policy aims to distinguish itself from both theory and practice, as if there were only one kind and form of policy orientedness, namely prescription orientedness. All other kinds and forms of policy orientedness, including diagnosis and prognosis, are distanced as far as possible in this speech from its principal burden, which is prescription. Ideally they would be best left out altogether. The policy game is to prohibit even the possibility of relevant doubt. The issues which the policy says speak for themselves – even do not need speaking for – are unveiled, tabled, as the only issues. Attention can thus at a stroke be deflected *both* from the diagnosis which may have led to them *and* prognosis about what might happen if, if . . . if say what is proposed were actually to be implemented and institutionalized. There must be nothing iffy, nothing politicy, nothing ordinary and exceptional to complicate the extraordinary and unexceptionable.

As for description, prescriptive discourse may want you to believe prescription is even a substitute for description, and a better substitute at that.

Summing up, prescriptive policy discourse talks action, that is would-be action, sets out to manage crises in calls for agendas for action, yet is not itself that type of action. Words about deeds, we must remember, remain, all said, words: words about deeds though they may be, they are not themselves (other than verbal) deeds, however loudly and resolutely they insist deeds, not words, are necessary: 'deeds speak louder than words' (A. P. Herbert, discussed by Stebbing 1939). This is a perfect illustration of the power of wording over deeding to go much further by far than no matter how many irreproachable deeds (see also Brenneis 1980). Policy comes in this way to be treated, whether offensively or defensively, as if it were cultural property 'owned' by the agent or agency uttering it.

Awkward history, imperfect geography, in this particular recurring pattern of perennial speech are given little play. Certainly they are not permitted to interfere with the charmed life that models of 'the case of Taiwan' sort lead in it. Yet some distinctions, of course, are necessary. Positions must be upheld and replaced. For example, policy which says its primary purpose is to uphold the status quo of a power regime will, for that reason alone, be likely to tend to prefer institutionalist over distributionalist prescription (Apthorpe 1984). The former can more readily and much more conveniently invoke 'general will' rather than 'political will' in its characteristic appeal to the 'wisdom' of 'inherent' and 'essential' values and the like which they embody. Holding that such values are perfectly well known to people inspired and committed enough to know them, it can hold equally that no further justification for them is needed. It is distributionalist, that is, redistributionalist, discourse with its instrumentalist not essentialist leanings which tends to pervade policy aiming to replace the status quo.

Small farm strategy is proclaimed by the state or parastate – by which is meant here and throughout this chapter what more ordinarily would be called 'government' – engaged, it will be said, in the best interests of national as well as rural development. In true institutionalist fashion it can and will be given more a cultural than a political rationale, be said to build on 'family farms' or just 'families' as 'the common basic units' of 'our society' which is 'our heritage' and so on. Evaluations of the performance in actual practice of small farm strategies which share this cultural orientation, will, in various ways, seek to preserve this 'policy itself'. For instance, they will blame difficulties on to 'implementation' in particular, if not 'the human factor' (Apthorpe 1970; Ortiz 1970) in general, and various other 'escape hatches' (Clay and Schaffer 1984).

Admittedly distributionalist criticism in policy studies may aim to achieve the same thing. However, whether it comes from what standard British political language calls opposition not government, or from self-saying 'neutral' third party professionals, either institutionalist or distributionalist discourse may, in an effort to clinch matters, have recourse to physicalist inevitability idiom of the 'dictates of nature' sort. Again, the aim is to make 'necessary' the meaning of nature, and 'perfection' the meaning of necessity. Thus may new constructions be made and put upon actions and things – but be said to reside, forever to have resided, *in* actions and things which are therefore as they can only be.

Scale Internal, Scale External

It is as a type case of rural prosperity achieved through what is said to be 'small' farmer development that 'the case of Taiwan' figures most prominently in the rural (and other) development literature. The agencies which advocate and provide financial and other assistance for this policy and strategy are many. Of course at the same time there are as many critiques as advocacies. It is, as Michel Foucault wrote of prisons in *Discipline and Punish* (1977), the irony of reform that 'the movement for reforming the prison, for controlling its functioning, is not a recent phenomenon. It does not even seem to have originated in failure. Prison reform is virtually contemporary with the prison itself: it constitutes its programme.'

Now it is certainly beyond dispute that farms in Taiwan *are* small. With this there is no quarrel. In cadastral terms they are on average of less than one hectare. Farms are small (so to say 'weak') also in another 'internal' regard of scale: in some critical areas conventionally called 'decision making' farmers have little scope or control over their farming in respect, for example, of what, or what not, to grow, rice included. However in some key 'external' regards of scale, rice farming is *not* small scale. For example, the regional physical irrigation and the infrastructure involved, the mountains always excluded, is virtually island-wide. Various socio-economic kinds and dimensions of rural–urban relations, forces and communications are similarly virtually co-extensive with whole regions, if not the entire island. For instance the town in Taiwan could be described as being nowhere distant from contact with the countryside; the countryside nowhere isolated from the town; the town not cut off from the city. People constantly travel from place to place. Under such conditions 'external' links of all kinds are part and parcel of 'internal' links in local communities, those of both continuity and change.

It follows that societies and cultures as economies and polities are small scale and large scale simultaneously, without contradiction. 'Smallness' in one regard is not necessarily diminished – and perhaps not affected at all – by 'largeness' in another. Neither is any practical, for example economic, advantage necessarily linked to a particular scale as a property of organization, whether private or public (Kaldor 1976). Even evolutionary and functional description in which change and development are represented always as a matter of passage from just one scale or organization to just one other, or as a matter of voluting pattern in just one, must in this connection be considered to be untrue to its own convictions.

If Taiwan's Provincial Food Bureau's compulsory rice collection system, and the rice-fertilizer barter-exchange, put farmers in a 'forced savings' dependency on the government in classic 'squeeze agriculture' fashion, this if nothing else is a strategy which 'presupposes the existence of strong state power as well as an effective administration organization' (Sasamoto 1968).

But our small farm slogan does not mention that the 'public' agricultural and marketing services and supplies which every 'private' rice farmer requires are, in principle or practice in Taiwan, available to every farm. Whether in this regard small farmers in Taiwan are or are not comparatively better off relative to otherwise similar small farmers elsewhere, an investigation could show.

Now just as our policy voices and justifies small farm strategies as small farm strategies *tout court*, so criticisms of their outcomes or effects are similarly expressed as for example when their burden is to the effect that it may be 'big', or 'middle', but in all events not 'small' farmers who are served by them. Unvoiced, unremarked, in such justifications and rejections alike of these strategies is their 'big state' side. Yet only if the state and parastate were big – meaning here perhaps 'strong' or effective – enough actually to reach the small farms could they be supplied with the inputs which the uttered strategy requires and promises.

Metaphorically and meta-organizationally but nonetheless realistically, our island could be described as being among other things one big farm:

'when . . . a wide variety of basic conditions of Taiwanese agriculture (in general) and rice farming in particular are considered together it becomes evident that the conventional "intensive small scale" categorization as in agricultural economics and human geography only inadequately describes farming in Taiwan. The physical extent, the average spatial size, of farms is small-scale but from ordinary administrative or sociological viewpoints there is a large-scale aspect as well because the socio-political organization of agriculture is . . . the mountainous zone excluded . . . effectively even island-wide.'

(Apthorpe 1974)

Benedict Stavis' concise overview of local governance and agricultural development agreed with this: government policy's aim in rural matters is that rural institutions should be

'characterized by firm centralization, strict central regulations and guidelines (coupled though these were) with some flexibility at local levels and a great deal of communication up and down the administration (so that) the central political authorities (could) implement their vision . . . in the final analysis the central authorities carried out the policies they wanted to.'

(Stavis 1975)

The outcome could be said to be like one big private-public farm. No patronage without clientage, no process of co-optation of, without also a process of co-optation by. No government without grain, no grain without government. Chinese economic and political organization proceeds not least by a double process of mutual accommodation (Willmott 1972), not merely the single process of incorporation, whether of 'private' into 'public' or 'public' into 'private' (Wang and Apthorpe 1974). However, rural development studies, particularly in the modernization mode, vary in the way and extent to which they address state and governmental issues if, that is, they address these directly at all. Now they 'assume' state power and its effects; now they 'lose' any such orientation; now they 'find' governmental intervention as such again and do not take as resolved even the smallest questions which political and other analysis outside development studies traditionally asks about such intervention (for a critique of 'as resolved' questions see Miliband 1973). Research in the dependency idiom may be less inconsistent in this regard, but this too is seldom in practice completely constant or uniform.

Descriptive Muddles in the Prescriptive Model

The omission of all 'statery' from depictions as it were of 'peasantry' in our small farm literature is compounded by some descriptive muddles of commission. For instance, this literature portrays farmers in Taiwan as rice farmers. A majority of farmers, and farm families, most definitely customarily does grow rice. But to focus on this one crop alone is to leave out, among other things, sugar and banana farming. For many reasons this is a serious omission. Sugar and bananas are economically and therefore politically important crops, and their relations of production are those of plantations and partnerships, not family farms.

Another descriptive muddle in the prescriptive model is with regard to its over-selection of land, as if land, here farmers' own land, were their principal resource base, and even the principal resource base of farming. Modelling-in land in this primordial way in effect models-out labour, capital and perhaps, above all, water, as primordial resources and constraints in production bases. Yet paddy rice depends, obviously, on water no less basically than it does on land, not to mention labour, management and so on. In Taiwan irrigation and water is state owned and directly controlled through various channels. And, while it is logical is one sense that along with its focus on land should go this model's recourse to the degree and extent of multiple cropping of land as an agricultural development index, this includes of course not only rice but other crops as well.

A third problem is with the high rural household income (rather than, say, allocative or technical efficiency) that is held to be the manifest and direct evidence of 'the success' and 'prosperity' of small farming. Not only does total rural household income in Taiwan come significantly from non-agriculture as well as agriculture: total income comes *principally* from non-agriculture. On average something of the order of around only one third of rural household income on the island comes from farming (Wang and Apthorpe 1974, cited and discussed by Griffin 1973).

In holding this 'success story of rural development' to be particularly a post-1953 one, because of the land-to-the-tiller programme of that year, in the fourth place our literature again makes the single factor of land bear the principal 'explanatory' weight. Undoubtedly the 1953 land reform did practically eliminate the upper tail of the distribution of private tenanted paddy land. But this is not all that must be said. It is also significant (a) that private tenanted paddy land does not equal all land, even all rice land. Further (b) it is very much open to interpretation both precisely what that 'upper tail' was, quantitatively, in 1953, and what its role was, not least in rice production. One must take note, for instance, that the 1960 *Rural Progress Survey* by Taiwan's Joint Commission on Rural Reconstruction, did not claim more than that 52 per cent of the household heads interviewed had improved their position (35 per cent could make no comment, 4 per cent said their position had not improved as a result of it). And again (c) it remains debatable whether this reform either aimed at, or achieved, exactly the 'structural change' effect which virtually all rural (and other) development literature on the island attributes to it, the exceptions including Apthorpe 1979; Ranis 1978; Myint 1981.

Fifthly comes a problem with areas of inconsistency, or possibly contradiction. If, as the model holds, the Taiwan success story is one specifically of peaceful, nationalist, *institutionalist* policy, how can this same story at the same time be read or pleaded as one exclusively of *technological* 'high yielding varieties' reform, nay 'revolution'? If the island's rural and agricultural story is '*despite* [its] *small farm problem* [my italics] because the ideal size of a family farm in Taiwan should be about three hectares' (Joint Commission on Rural Reconstruction 1975), how could it also be advocated as a small farm strategy?

A more detailed study of rural development in Taiwan than is required for the very limited and illustrative purposes of this chapter might at this point go on to look into some of the remedies proposed for this 'problem', including 'joint farming' and increased use of fertilizer. Leaving such rural organizations and formations out of prescriptive or descriptive account means, for example, that interconnections with them of the 'basic unit' which is noticed are also neglected. Additionally, leaving the one selected institution as it were internally unanalysed, has the limitation that this neglects the extent to which even its defining characteristics may vary, independently of one another. At all events, what, sufficiently for present purposes, this exercise has shown is that, all in all, in Taiwan, rural does not equal agricultural, agricultural does not equal small farm, small farm does not equal rice, and rice does not equal livelihood. The substance of the island's considerable rural achievements deserves better representation.

Not to Make a Model of Muddle

Would-be persuasive pleading of would-be action has, as presented in an earlier section, requisites of its own: sloganatic brevity, seemingly firm resolution, little if anything to do with either abstract theory or troublesome practice. What, for the purposes of this chapter, has been called an emphasis on description, and contrasted with prescription, description that is as is familiar in, indeed characteristic of, anthropological monographs, has, in turn, canons of *its* own: denotation, illustration, selection for instance.

Any polemic runs the risk of making a model, that is to say, another model, of muddle, and of replacing an innocent victim by a guilty one. The discussion in the preceding section is no exception. For example, it has not avoided taking over some of the features of the perceived other which surely it should have sought to reject. So let us not undo by overdoing the project, not make a model of muddle. The limitations of both special and general cases are to be kept in mind.

Principally, our polemic has identified a convergence in three or four regards. First there is the matter of period-frame and time-intervals. Both model and muddle are presented ahistorically and apolitically as if 'the story' told were one with only setbacks or advances, only costs or benefits. Convenient though such a perspective may be for both promotional and critical purposes alike at the moment, it is distinctly inconvenient for intelligibility, let alone credibility, over time. Difference is reduced to deviation, dynamics to comparative statics. Events have been willed to stop so as to exclude what happened before, to foreclose on what happens after. But of what value could a timeless and indeed spaceless model or other presentation be for action-oriented concern with timely steering of events? The most basic of all basic tenets for rural and agricultural development studies must be: 'the roles of government, farmers, rural organizations and market price mechanisms in determining agricultural development . . . differ from period to period' (Lee 1970).

Second, somewhat separate from that of 'the qualifying conditions under which' just discussed, is the area of bias in which intended outcomes are brought into what are supposed to be simply ostensive definitions. Hoped-for results may be brought into either model or muddle, into either pleading or reading. Conversely, either may find additional, even unexpected, outcomes to be beneficial even if they are contrary or contradictory, as well as untoward. Both are manoeuvred to include the vices of a system among with its virtues, as for example when distributive – that is re-distributive – policy is found to have failed to bring about its stated redistributional objective but nevertheless and notwithstanding this to have succeeded in having induced, or at least not diminished, growth.

Third, and somewhat separate from 'but nevertheless' convenience, is another model-muddle tendency: the countering as well as the encountered position may encapsulate extraneous events provided only that fit can be found for them.

This could be called the area of absorptive capacity for boundary conditions. Extraneous factors and forces can be encapsulated in this way no matter how independent in their actual occurrence they may be from the ideal forms at issue. It is not just that their independence of provenance does not disqualify them. It is rather that their independence left alone spells danger. So whether or not prescription or description 'gets its facts right' about boundary (or for that matter pivotal) conditions either may nonetheless, and whether by accident or design, come mischievously to magnify or minimize or otherwise misinform. Other policy orientednesses, especially diagnosis, is not well served by bias of this type.

Finally, a fourth area. Closely related to the other areas indicated briefly above is that of the 'one best solution' which may be built into model and muddle alike, say positively in the former, negatively in the latter.

In conclusion, both the received prescription reviewed and the elements of description offered in this exercise have to do with matters of replication only, not explication. For explication would be, for instance, exploitative of other dependent relationships in the 'small farm: big state' situation, indeterminate or independent links, fields of competition and conflict and their outcomes, and so on. Such explication has been left outside the scope of the present paper, not because the problems that have been taken up here are more crucial or intractable than others. Rather it is because they tend to pass unnoticed, and tend therefore to remain unanalysed altogether. Finally, it has to be said that all kinds of policy orientedness, not just prescription, are idiomatic and emblematic and therefore problematic for development studies to explore. Nothing in policy is innocent, least of all innocence.

References

APTHORPE, R. (1970) African Rural Development Planning and Conceptions of the 'Human Factor'. *Journal of Development Studies* VI (7): 140–51.
— (1974). In S. H. Wang and R. Apthorpe, *Rice Farming in Taiwan: Three Village Studies*. Taiwan: Institute of Ethnology, Academia Sinica.
— (1979) An Asian Model Land Reform Re-analysed: The Burden of Land Reform in Taiwan. *World Development* 7: 519–30.
— (1982) Historical and Ahistorical Perspectives in Development Studies: Modernization Discourse. *Proceedings of the Development Policy Seminar for Senior UNDP Executives*, 15–26 November 1982. The Hague: Institute of Social Studies Advisory Service.
— (1984) Agricultures and strategies. In E. J. Clay and B. B. Schaffer (eds) *Room for Manoeuvre: An Exploration of Public Policy for Rural Development*. London: Heinemann-Gower.
— and GASPER, D. R. (1982) Policy Evaluation and Meta-evaluation: The Case of Rural Co-operatives. *World Development* 10 (8): 651–68.
— and KRAHL, A. (1984) Researching for development. In R. Apthorpe and A. Krahl (eds) *Development Studies: Critique and Renewal*. The Hague: Institute of Social Studies. Leiden: Brill.
BAILEY, F. G. (1969) Political Statements. *Contributions to Indian Sociology* New Series 3 (December): 1–16.
BLOCH, M. (ed.) (1975) Introduction to *Political Language and Oratory in Traditional Societies*. London: Academic Press.

BRENNEIS, D. (1980) Fighting Words. In J. Cherfas and R. Lewin (eds) *Not Work Alone*. London: Temple Smith.

CHAKRAVARTY, S. (1980) Relevance of Growth Models to Development Planning. *Pakistan Development Review* XXI (2): 101–12.

CLAY, E. J. and SCHAFFER, B. B. (eds) (1984) *Room for Manoeuvre: An Exploration of Public Policy for Rural Development*. London: Heinemann.

CULLER, J. (1983) *On 'Deconstruction': Theory and Criticism after Structuralism*. London: Routledge & Kegan Paul.

DRAPER, T. (1982) How Not to Think about Nuclear War. *New York Review of Books* XXIX (12) 15 July, 1982.

FOUCAULT, M. (1979) *Discipline and Punish: the Birth of the Prison*. London: Penguin Books.

GEERTZ, C. (1975) *The Interpretation of Cultures. Selected Essays*. New York: Basic Books.

GRIFFIN, K. (1973) An Assessment of Development in Taiwan. *World Development* 1 (6).

HIRSCH, E. D. Jr (1983) Derrida's Axioms. *London Review of Books* 21 July–3 August.

Joint Commission on Rural Reconstruction (1960) *Rural Progress Survey*. Taipei: Joint Commission on Rural Reconstruction.

— (1975) *31st General Report*. Taipei: Joint Commission on Rural Reconstruction.

KALDOR, N. (1976) Public and Private Enterprise: The Issues to be Considered. In W. G. Shepherd (ed.) *Public Enterprise: Economic Theory and Practice*. Lexington: Lexington Books.

KNIGHTS, L. C. (1971) *Public Voices: Literature and Politics with Special Reference to the Seventeenth Century* (The Clark Lectures for 1970–71). London: Chatto & Windus.

LEE, T. H. (1970) *Process and Pattern of Growth in Agricultural Production in Taiwan*. Economic Essays 1, Graduate Institute of Economics, National Taiwan University.

MILIBAND, R. (1973) *The State in Capitalist Society*. London: Quartet Books.

MYINT, H. (1981) Comparative Analysis of Taiwan's Economic Development with Other Countries. From *Conference on 'Experiences and Lessons of Economic Development in Taiwan'*. Nankang, Taipei: Institute of Economics, Academia Sinica.

ORTIZ, S. (1970) 'The Human Factor' in Social Planning in Latin America. *Journal of Development Studies* VI (4): 152–62.

PARKIN, D. J. (1975) The Rhetoric of Responsibility: Bureaucratic Communications in a Kenya Farming Area. In M. Bloch (ed.) *Political Language and Oratory in Traditional Societies*. London: Academic Press.

RANIS, G. (1978) Equity with Growth in Taiwan: How 'Special' is the 'Special Case'? *World Development* 6 (3): 397–409.

SASAMOTO, T. (1968) A Salient Feature of Capital Accumulation in Taiwan: The System of Rice Collection by the Taiwan Food Bureau. *The Developing Economies* VI (1).

STAVIS, B. (1975) *Rural Local Governance and Agricultural Development in Taiwan*. Ithaca, New York: Rural Development Committee, Center for International Studies, Cornell.

STEBBING, S. (1939) *Thinking to Some Purpose*. London: Penguin Books.

STURROCK, J. (ed.) (1979) *Structuralism and Since: From Lévi-Strauss to Derrida*. Oxford: Oxford University Press.

TURNER, V. W. (1969) *The Ritual Process: Structure and Anti-Structure*. London: Penguin Books.

WANG, S. H. and APTHORPE, R. (1974) *Rice Farming in Taiwan: Three Village Studies*. Taiwan: Institute of Ethnology, Academia Sinica.

WILLMOTT, W. E. (ed.) (1972) Introduction to *Economic Organization in Chinese Society*. Stanford: Stanford University Press.

Donald Curtis*

6 Anthropology in Project Management:

on being useful to those who must design and operate rural water supplies

It may appear to be a contradiction that a paper with 'useful' in the title turns out to be mostly about questions of method. Yet the main contention in what follows is that while it is possible and desirable to be useful, so far social anthropology has had little impact upon the practice of project management. The main reasons for this failure lie in the difference between the organization and presentation of knowledge in the anthropological tradition and the knowledge requirements of the project management trade.

These differences, which are spelt out and justified below, would suggest that anthropology has small part to play in development work and that anthropologists, to be employable, should rapidly convert themselves into something else. Yet, as someone with a background in anthropology/sociology, called upon sometimes to give a hand in development project work, I find that many projects work badly and have unforeseen consequences, at least in part because they are conceived in a socially naïve manner. Faced with the requirement to say something useful, one can sometimes do so since many of the problems are predictable and can be analysed in terms of generalized expectations of cause and effect that can be derived directly or indirectly from anthropological studies. I also find that I cannot point to a text book that sets out these generalizations in a consistent way. There appears to be something about the anthropological tradition that militates against the development of an applied anthropology.

In this chapter I explore some of these issues as they have arisen in my own attempts to apply anthropological or sociological concepts in relation to domestic water supply programmes. I do not set it out in terms of a case study as such because I regard the case study approach as symptomatic of the limitations of the anthropological method. I attempt instead to illustrate what

*I would like to thank Paul Stirling, John Stewart and Richard Batley for useful comments on this chapter in an earlier draft.

is involved in drawing upon the strengths of observation and explanation in the anthropological/sociological tradition in a manner which will be of value to project management.

Project management is usually discussed in terms either of a linear programme or of a cycle of activities that include identification, appraisal, planning, implementation, operation and maintenance, and evaluation. In the cyclical model, evaluation leads once again into the preparation of new projects. Anthropologists could be useful to any of these phases but historically they have most often been called upon in the early phases to provide background information on the people involved or to identify the nature of social problems (e.g. Barnett 1956). This is perhaps the role in which anthropologists have generally been happiest because their instructions have basically been to go out and observe. In this case there have been few restrictions upon their liberty to range widely in the search for linkages and to indulge in that favoured discovery: 'that all is not as it seems'. At best the results of such pre-project studies will make intelligible to the authorities what was previously unintelligible and problematic and thus encourage authorities to conceive projects that are closer to the values and interests of their client population. But there is no necessary correlation between more information and better or more humane administration, and at worst these studies have enabled administrators to be more sure-footed in imposition of their prejudices. However, to be fair to the administrator, it is also true that anthropological studies have scarcely ever been conceived within a framework that would enable authorities to predict what would be the effect of changing any of the relationships so elaborately described, or at what point an intervention might be effective in producing changes of a specified variety (Mair 1969: 5).

Anthropologists can also take part in the ex-post evaluation of projects that has recently become popular. Here the attempt should be to find out how they deviated from their objectives and what unforeseen consequences there were. This is a more narrowly project-centred activity than the pre-project study, but here the anthropologists' (or sociologists') propensity to look for the unexpected can come in useful. For instance, the discovery that toilets could be offensive in a Muslim country if inappropriately oriented towards Mecca (Goyder 1977) is an observation which, if it has to be discovered by external observers, relies upon some ability to note the linkages between the secular and the religious.

Cochrane (1979) illustrates the way in which anthropologists can find a whole range of linkages that may have an effect upon projects. But in spite of his attempt to relate anthropological research activity to the different stages of the project management cycle, the illustrative examples appear to be anecdotal: a string of exotic features of societies which in particular cases could arguably have had an impact upon project outcomes. This boils down to an attempt to show the limitations of the application of economic models in project planning: the identification of 'common errors due to cultural variation'

(p. 11). This is no doubt valuable in relation to the particular projects (if heeded) but is often less than persuasive unless clearly related to some broader understanding of the forces of social change. Because they are presented as particular phenomena the discovery of such 'errors' condemns anthropologists to a perpetual 'trouble shooting' role in the project management process.

There is value in attempts to tune projects more closely to the particular environment in which they operate (Nicholson 1981). The weakness of this approach lies in its propensity to find particular problems of cultural variance where there are more important structural regularities in the project management business which are not predicted or planned for. The main challenge for anthropologists who have some notion of what these regular problems are is to be able to influence the project planning and design stage of the project management cycle. For that one has not only to develop a set of common understandings of how projects work in different social environments, but also to turn these into a conventional wisdom about information requirements, modes of analysis and decision rules that is widely available within the development industry; the best word that I can find for this kind of conceptual apparatus is *praxis*. So far anthropologists and indeed sociologists have not made much contribution to management praxis and in consequence have made little impact upon project planning.

If one produced a glossary of the specialized language of 'development', increasingly shared amongst the national and international experts and within the many specialized institutions that make up the development industry, few of the words it contained would have their origins in anthropological (or indeed sociological) usage. Much of this language is founded in economics: 'capital', 'labour', 'returns to investment', 'elasticity', etc. – indicating the utility of that discipline. Some, however, encapsulate a broader social meaning such as 'mobilization', 'basic needs' 'participation', 'land reform', and 'the poor'. Few of these words are in current usage in theoretical social science as such, yet there is an evident need for concepts of this kind. This is an indication of the failure of the social sciences other than economics to develop an adequate conceptual apparatus in the applied as distinct from the theoretical field.

If the most likely avenue for the development of an applied anthropology is in the search for structural regularities in project management, this should be simplified by the fact that development projects share many features and could, without difficulty, be arranged into a number of common types. At the broadest they all involve government agencies and members of the public as participants or clients, opening up questions about the values and interests of the actors in the agencies themselves, for which organization theory in its various manifestations has some appeal (cf. Leonard 1977); questions about the relationships between agencies and their clients (for which access studies, drawing considerably upon concepts of patron-clientage and dependency, provide a beginning); and questions about the behaviour of individuals, groups and communities as they respond to development projects. It is with one aspect of this last that I am particularly concerned in this chapter.

The difficulty in developing an applied anthropology lies in the contrast between the typical methods of anthropological field studies and the requirements of project management information. To simplify the presentation let me try to summarize the contrast as I see it here (*Table 1*) and build in some justification for the summary as I proceed:

Table 6.1 Anthropological field studies contrasted with project management information

	anthropological studies	project information
focus	community	project
location	local	area or nationwide; only occasionally site-bounded and local
depth	in-depth analysis	economy of information essential
models of causality	'everything relates to everything'	'what will happen if': (x causes y or x constrains y or without x no y)
duration	long term (not implying longitudinal)	time phased inputs to the project (before, during or after)
action orientation	contemplation: 'all is not as it seems'	action: 'it may not be right but it's good enough to act upon'

The contrast is presented in terms which are in some cases polar opposites yet in some aspects at least this represents the transition that has to be made in any discipline between the theoretical and the applied, the positive and the normative or between science and engineering.[1]

A problem that arises in the search for an applied social anthropology (that would not arise quite the same way in the wider field of sociology) is that of the level of generality. The 'aggressively empirical' approach of the anthropologist in his field studies (Kuper 1970: 1) militates against the kind of generalization that carries over easily from one study to another, or from these studies to text books, or from text books into the field of the applied. Whereas the sociologist can sometimes be accused of trying to see the typical class formations of capitalist society in the most unlikely places, the anthropologist might with an equal level of justification be accused of finding unique social configurations in the most ordinary places.[2] Both may lead to their own kinds of blindness, but of the two the sociologists' presuppositions could be more easily incorporated into an applied praxis because the elements of a model are clearly articulated, and the implications for policy could be deduced.[3]

Nevertheless, anthropology could not really be about uniqueness otherwise we would have even more difficulty in communication than we do. The particular features of a people under study have to be explained in terms of more general propositions (even if the first chapter of every dissertation is about redefining one's predecessors' terms for one's own convenience). Let me illustrate the problem by reference to an example: one which came to mind when I was asked to take part in an evaluation of a village water supply programme in Lesotho. This was Adam Kuper's account of the dispute over a bore-hole (tubewell – even engineers have problems with language), in Kuli village in the Western Kalahari desert in Botswana. This dispute in Kuli centred around the need for the village to employ a pumper to operate and maintain the diesel pump that provided the main source of drinking water in the settlement. The job changed hands several times between members of different factions in the village. Kuper summarizes the case as follows, and I will quote the summary in full in order to be able to make some comments on the language later on:

'The first round began when Morimonongwe left Kuli and his son, Sekoma, took over his job as pumper without the consent of the headman or *lekgota* (village assembly). A crisis was precipitated when Morimonongwe returned to Kuli and Sekoma went on strike, putting the bore-hole out of action, and demanded his wages. The headman, with the support of the Silebe, [one faction] ignored Sekoma's demands and in-stalled his own candidate (one Merahe) as pumper.

The headman's victory was not decisive. Several citizens indicated that they were withholding public approval of the appointment, and were therefore not committed to recognizing the pumper. Round two followed swiftly. Mabote (leader of the faction supporting Morimonongwe) and his supporters withheld their contributions to Merahe's wages, and Merahe went on strike and hid the crank to the bore-hole. When the issue came before the lekgota, the Silebe and several influential neutrals supported the headman. Mabote's attempts to raise Sekoma's case once more were defeated. The headman then clinched his (temporary) victory by manoeuvring the District Commissioner into recognizing Merahe as the official pumper, and ordering that all users of the bore-hole should con-tribute towards his wages.

Far from resolving the matter, this crisis led to an extension of the area of conflict. All co-operation, even on the purchase of fuel, ceased. Small groups operated the bore-hole for themselves, and when the headman's family-group was suspected of asserting a special right to the use of the bore-hole, Mabote's son detonated the third crisis by hiding the crank once more. This time the District Councillor intervened, and a possible resol-ution was attempted through the transfer of control over the bore-hole to external authorities.'

(Kuper 1970: 123–4)

This is a summary of some five pages of description of the dispute. His detail is laudable and his quotes from speeches in the village assembly have a ring of authenticity which enables one to judge for oneself. For a general analysis, however, one has to wait until the concluding chapter of the book where the relevant section is sufficiently brief to be able again to quote in full. These paragraphs form part of a general analysis of the way in which the lekgota functions under differing circumstances. Kuper finds that as a court, the membership is generally cohesive during the judicial process. As a body representing the village over and against external authority the different sections of the village generally unite in their demands but a third category of behaviour is evident in the case of internal disputes such as that over the bore-hole pump:

'The third set of issues concern internal policy, a category which covers matters of internal administration, jobs and authority. In dealing with matters of this sort the lekgota is often split into factions. A temporary resolution may be reached if two factions combine against a third, particularly if the majority successfully invokes the support of external authorities. . .

In internal policy matters, however, the demands come from a section of the [village] authorities, supported by their factions, and are directed against other factions. Support is segmentary, and unless one faction can gain the backing of external authorities it is extremely difficult to get an effective decision to take positive action.'

(Kuper 1970: 174–5)

This kind of analysis gets us somewhere, but a higher level of generalization is necessary before one can have a convincing set of expectations to bring to bear on a national rural water supply programme or before one can make much impression upon a project planning or evaluation process where one's colleagues are engineers or economists, who are characteristically armed with a rather firm ability to diagnose, and a willingness to prescribe. What one would like to be able to offer in this context is an equally firm contribution to planning praxis setting out the likely organizational forms or conditions for favourable installation and operation of rural water supplies, and possible social constraints upon design of the system.

In Kuper's second passage we find statements of the general which can be used to explain a particular case cited in the early part of his text, and by implication which purport to explain what is likely to happen to other judicial, representative, and internal issues in the village. This becomes a model which, in a sociological as against anthropological dissertation, would have been spelt out at the beginning and then used to illumine what follows.

Now the 'aggressive empiricist' denies the legitimacy of the sociological propensity to produce models first and observe afterwards because the observations may be unduly shaped by the model constructed. The complacent model builder, on the other hand, points to the impossibility of observing anything without some set of concepts to frame reality and claims that if an observer lacks good models he will perforce be guided by bad ones (Rex 1961). However, I doubt if anything except the middle ground between these positions is either theoretically possible or practically useful. Both extremes seem to rest upon an unnecessary level of self-assurance. But whatever the case, from the project planning point of view *explicit suppositions* about cause and effect are essential.

Although the term 'aggressive empiricist' is Kuper's, and in his book he purports to describe first and analyse afterwards, in fact it is clear that the intellectual baggage which he brings to the field is founded upon that 'assumption derived from "naïve introspection"' as Lucy Mair has it, 'that most men aspire to some level of material wealth and comfort, that all care for the esteem of their fellows, that many compete for power and prestige' (Mair 1969: 5), and furthermore, that his description implicitly contains the model of the game or the play in which actors move for advantage, one against others (often to the cost of the advantage of the group as a whole), but with reasonably predictable outcomes.

The words 'co-operation, conflict, resolution, allies, and rounds', are all Kuper's rather than the Kuli villagers', and derive from the model he very sensibly brings to bear. Nothing would be lost in Kuper's exposition if this model had been outlined first, and then tested against the facts discovered. The point is that the contrast between the anthropological and the sociological procedure is one of style more than substance. However, we are left with the question of how typical these conflict and co-operation situations are: in other words can one take the model further and use it to anticipate moves and outcomes in other kinds of disputes in Kuli or, more importantly, to the social engineering of water supplies in other villages?

It can be said immediately that two of the situations that Kuper identifies in Kuli where the villagers unite to face outside challenges but tend to divide over internal issues fit the picture for a wide range of 'self-help' type activities where governments challenge villages into undertaking village development projects. On the basis of the model it can be predicted that the *initiation* of projects will be relatively straightforward from the village point of view because the villagers will tend to unite to request additional resources from outside. Equally it can be predicted that operation and maintenance will be difficult if left to the village as a community because this then becomes an internal issue (cost or resource) over which the segmentarily divided village will tend to split. This was indeed one finding of the evaluation of village water supplies in Lesotho (Feachem *et al.* 1978).

To be really useful in project management terms the model needs to be extended to cover a wider range of situations than the village studied by Kuper or indeed the similarly Sotho-speaking villages elsewhere in Botswana or in Lesotho where I have worked. Kuper of course makes no claim that his generalization would apply elsewhere, and since his study is not explicitly comparative there is no sustained attempt to state what the limiting or governing conditions for these patterns of interaction might be. Governing conditions I take to be those which pertain in Botswana but which could be different in other village water supply situations. To derive them one must make some generalizations about what these differences are likely to be. Kuper does provide hints but I have had to extend his argument in the diagrammatic presentation of the model in *Figure 6.1*. In it I set out the two responses noted by Kuper, 'plus' signs indicating attempts to achieve solidarity or co-operation, 'minus' signs indicating probability of divisions or conflict. I then indicate the associated moves in relation to community projects and list what I see to be the governing conditions of the case:

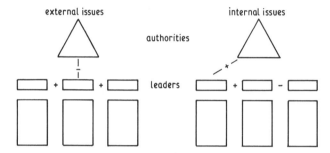

Figure 6.1   Limiting or governing conditions for patterns of interaction situations

moves

villagers conceive of a need	leader initiates
village leader solicits and receives support from different sections of the village in an appeal or challenge to government for resources	other leaders tend to oppose
	one or other appeals to authorities for support

governing conditions

(1) where government does not exercise direct control
(2) where unitary resource, that is, one that cannot be subdivided, is in dispute
(3) where leaders lack authority to enforce sanctions
(4) where villages divide segmentarily or (to change the metaphor) vertically

To attempt a model of greater general applicability one can start by changing some of these governing conditions. This is not quite such an innocent procedure as it appears since the identification of governing conditions assumes that the alternative situations which, it is implied, might exist else-where are those which may be found in practice. It also implies that these variables rather than others are open to manipulation for the better management of water supplies. The adequacy of the scheme cannot be fully tested in this paper but its plausibility can be assessed in the following sections. By setting out different conditions one may hope both to consider what is attainable by authorities (or by other public action) and also to consider what the effects of these changes might be:

Condition 1   no direct government control ⟶ direct government control

If government does exert direct control over village water supplies so that no management functions remain with the village this alters the picture completely. As before, a village wanting a supply would unite to demand it. Once they got it, it would probably break down occasionally due to poor maintenance. Since the villagers are not responsible, their role would again be to demand repairs and this they should not find difficult to do. How effective their demands would be depends upon the sanctions available to them. If, for example, they were able to withhold payments for water, or votes for their representative, this might constitute an effective incentive to managerial efficiency on the part of the authorities, and an instrument around which the village could unite. However, this is a minimal role for the village and we cease to be concerned in this case with the practicality of local level control (moving instead into the range of access theory).

Condition 2   unitary resources ⟶ multiple resources

The problem with the single resource, like the bore-hole, is, as we argued in Lesotho, that it creates 'winner takes all' or 'zero sum' game situations. This applies to both social as well as material resources; for instance, competition over water supply committee chairmanship as well as over the pump handle. Our response to this situation in Lesotho was to argue that authorities should, when possible, create multiple resources. This could, in part, be a question of technology choice. For instance it could be shown in Lesotho that the cost of several handpumps each on its own bore-hole, compared favourably with the cost of one bore-hole with engine, storage and reticulation, and even with the more common boxed spring with storage and reticulation to standpipes (Feachem *et al.* 1978: 39–41). With separate handpump, each section of a segmentarily divided village could have organized its own supply, thus avoiding the effects of competitive leadership in one community organization. However, even in circumstances where the technology is indivisible it is still possible, viewing the village activities as a whole, to envisage a situation where there are several organizations around different activities which would enable different segments of the village to have some influence. This led us to the recommendation in Lesotho that single-purpose committees for the water supply, the communal garden, and so on, be favoured over the multi-purpose village development committees which could so easily be captured by one village faction (Feachem *et al.* 1978: 73–7).

Condition 3   village leaders lack authority ———→ authoritative leaders

For governments to use this variable manipulatively would involve a degree of decentralization that is not often undertaken in the developing world except perhaps in one or two of the more experimentally oriented socialist regimes. In Kuli, as elsewhere in Botswana, as my own studies into community development-type activities showed (Curtis 1977) and in Lesotho (Feachem *et al.* 1978) the growing weakness of traditional leaders was apparent. This is a trend in many parts of the world and is associated as much with the declining significance of the village arena as the locale in which men see their destiny being shaped, as with specific moves to weaken the authority of the leaders themselves.

However, decentralization of authority can take many forms. In Lesotho where, as is often the case, villagers were *de facto* given responsibility for management of domestic water supplies (amongst other projects) without any authoritative structures being established, we found two different attempts by leaders to claim powers which they did not actually possess. Neither worked very well but they were indicative both of the quandary which leaders faced, and of possible lines of devolution.

In some cases villagers attempted to exclude non-contributors to the water supply construction or maintenance fund from the use of the service. Non-contributors sometimes saw the justice of this move but, in general, it proved difficult to enforce this ban, since informal sanctions had to be relied upon. Furthermore, since a single village supply was created by the chosen technology (in most cases a boxed spring above the village leading to a gravity-fed reticulation system), the excluded had no opportunity to create an alternative supply and had to rely upon unprotected sources.

The other response to the dilemma was to pretend, and to appeal to the Community Development authorities to back up the pretence, that the village development committee or water supply committee did have powers of enforcement. The signs were that in most cases recalcitrant villagers were prepared to call the bluff of both the leader and the authority, but again this indicates a possible line of development. If village committees were granted powers of enforcement this would be a true form of devolution. So authoritative leadership might find expression through two different forms of local organization, a voluntary association or a village level water authority. As institutional forms the former would have the disadvantage that non-contributors would be excluded. The latter could introduce an element of monopoly power into the arena of local politics. This could be controlled constitutionally through limiting the tenure of the leadership or by ensuring that other leadership were present elsewhere in the local economy.

Condition 4   Vertical (or segmentary) divisions and horizontal (caste or class) divisions

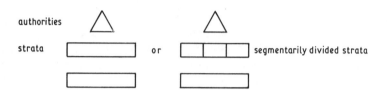

Where villagers are divided vertically along caste or class lines with different levels of access to resources then we can expect a rather different kind of interaction between local groups and the authorities. The picture is complicated by the fact that this situation is not likely to be a true alternative to the vertically divided village, since the dominant structure may well be divided internally into factions. Under some circumstances it may be in the interests of one faction or another to ally itself with the dominated strata. A successful alliance of this type might lead to a 'pay off' to the dominated groups taking the form of a new well or other welfare provision (because it does not damage long-term class interests of the dominant group). However this is not a reliable means of getting access to village water supplies for the 'weaker sections' (to use Indian parlance). If that is seriously expected one could envisage:

1. a plural solution in which strata are treated separately as often happens in *caste* divided villages in India (but to be effective each should be provided with an authoritative governing body), or
2. where a unitary supply is necessary the dominated strata must take or be given means of organizing themselves to ensure access to the supply. This would take the form of statutory representation on local water supply organizations and perhaps a solidarity group of some kind (probably a union having other explicit functions as well) recognized by the authorities.

At this point it may be noted that I am able to provide rather few examples of organizations of the varieties indicated in the previous paragraphs. Perhaps this is because effective *locally* managed water supplies or other community services are in any case the exceptions to the rule and the many examples of badly managed and ineffective projects are evidence of the need for a more systematic approach.

It remains now to take this analytic scheme through to the point at which it is expressed in terms of operational guidelines and information requirements. This also serves as a summary. What a water supply planner is presumably looking for is some guidance in choosing a reliable form of local organization to complement technically proficient plumbing. At the least, such an organization should be such as to avoid internal disputes that lead to breakdowns of routine functions and disappearing pump handles.

More demanding may be the specific responsibilities of water management that are to be left to local organization, such as reporting faults, carrying out repairs or collecting dues, or those which they take upon themselves such as campaigning for improvements or organizing labour for 'self-help' activities. In line with the analysis above I divide these into *representational responsibilities*, which highlight 'external' relationships with the authorities and *operational responsibilities*, which, for a local body raise the strains and stresses of 'internal' relationships.

The technology choice open to a water authority: mechanically operated bore-holes with storage and reticulation; gravity-fed supplies, major reticulation schemes with standpipe access, dispersed tubewells with hand pumps, or open wells, and so on, can be reduced, in terms of its various demands upon local management, to *unitary resources* which must be dealt with on a community-wide basis, and *multiple resources* to which smaller social units can respond.

Guidance to the water supply planner on how his technology choice and his allocations of responsibility relate to features of social structure and appropriate local organization, is summarized diagrammatically in *Table 2*. From this it can be seen that the necessary information takes the form of basic data on social structure, for the collection of which guidelines can be provided (Cairncross *et al.* 1980).

The foregoing has traced the development of an attempted anthropological contribution to management praxis in the form of a middle level theory of an applicable kind derived from observation, from logical extension from the observed, but also from the hidden hand of higher level theory of social change. To be useful, this kind of understanding should enter the consciousness of planners and administrators. It is recognized, however, that these understandings may contradict all kinds of morally comfortable generalization in the development trade which hold sway for want of the challenge of ideas that are better founded upon some interpretation of cause and effect in society. For example, the above model contradicts the dicta that one can find scattered through planning or project documents, that one should work through traditional bodies or use existing institutions because they are familiar to the people, or that if people contribute to the construction of a project they will look after it because they feel that it is theirs.

Table 6.2   Appropriate forms of local organization

	type of responsibility	*for local representational responsibilities* e.g. participation in planning raising 'matching' funds extracting improvements or maintenance from government	*for local operational responsibilities* e.g. collecting regular subscriptions operation and maintenance
type of resource in relation to social structure			
unitary resources	services in segmentarily divided communities	(1) local organizations on a community or area wide basis to act as a pressure group.	(2) management responsibility lies with either a water users' association with powers of exclusion or, a village level water supply authority with powers of levy
	services in stratified communities	(3) stratum-based forms of organization to represent the interests of poorer strata at least	(4) management responsibility given to village level water authority but with statutory representation of lower strata; preferably safeguarded by area wide representative organizations
multiple resources	services for each segment or strata within localities	(5) loose federation or joint action by representative organizations of segments or strata to pressurize authorities	(6) single service based associations with rights of ownership, control and exclusion of non contributors

Hopefully, 'the applied' will reflect the generalized set of expectations or models that anthropologists carry with them to the field but tend to hide beneath the ideology of aggressive empiricism and participant observation. Like any body of applied knowledge these will be limited truths, the strengths of which are that they improve thinking about a wide range of cases and suggest something to do. Generalizations here can afford to be crude because they must deal practically with the worst case, and because they do not pretend to be the ultimate in analysis but rather a set of working ideas.

The weakness of such bodies of ideas is that they can come to dominate thinking to the exclusion of alternative interpretations. However, any good anthropologist dealing with what would hopefully become a new conventional interpretation, like any good economist dealing with the conventional calculus of costs and benefits, would know the limitations of current formulations and have ideas on how to find exceptions to the rule or to abandon the convention and produce something else. In other words, the establishment of a convention does not deny all opportunities to observe and find 'that all is not as it seems'.

Notes

1. In this paper I do not consider the moral problems associated with the concept of social engineering. To many people the concept stinks, since it reminds them of episodes like the involvement of the social sciences in the American endeavour to pacify Vietnam. However, if one takes the view that all project management entails social engineering then it becomes a matter of urgency to get in there and do something about it. In this chapter I adopt the perhaps morally naïve position that anthropology or sociology has something to contribute to the design of things like rural water supplies to make them serve the interests of rural people rather better than they would if they were left purely in the hands of engineers and economists and politicians.
2. This is the entry point of the formalist–substantivist debate, which I rather dismiss here as a matter of style of writing. Whatever position one may wish to take up in relation to the requirements of analytical anthropology, a move towards the formal seems to be necessary in management praxis.
3. Curiously, even sociologists have little impact. Recent concern in the development industry with poverty, for example, is scarcely informed by any concept of class or of the 'causal components of life chances' which characterize these classes, let alone any judgement as to which of these causal components could be subject to manipulation by public authorities.

References

BARNETT, H. G. (1956) *Anthropology and Administration*. Evanston, Ill.: Row, Peterson.

CAIRNCROSS, S. *et al.* (1980) *Evaluation for Village Water Supply Planning*. Chichester: John Wiley & Sons.

COCHRANE, G. (1979) *The Cultural Appraisal of Development Projects*. New York: Praeger.

CURTIS, D. (1977) *Ideology and the Impact of Development Agency Activities*. Unpublished PhD thesis, University of Kent at Canterbury.

FEACHEM, R. *et al.* (1978) *Water, Health and Development*. London: TRI-MED Books.

GOYDER, C. (1977) Voluntary and Foremost Sanitation Programmes. Paper presented at the Conference on Sanitation in Developing Countries, Pembroke College, Oxford. Reproduced in part in A. Pacey (ed.) (1978) *Sanitation in Developing Countries*. Chichester: John Wiley & Sons.

KUPER, A. (1970) *Kalahari Village Politics*. Studies in Social Anthropology 3. Cambridge: Cambridge University Press.

LEONARD, D. K. (1977) *Reaching the Peasant Farmer: Organization Theory and Practice in Kenya*. Chicago: Chicago University Press.

MAIR, L. P. (1969) *Anthropology and Social Change*. London: LSE Monographs on Social Anthropology 38, Athlone Press.

NICHOLSON, K. N. (1981) Introduction to C. S. Russell and K. N. Nicholson (eds) *Public Choice and Rural Development: Resources for the Future*. Washington DC: United States Agency for International Development.

REX, J. (1961) *Key Problems in Sociological Theory*. London: Routledge & Kegan Paul.

Polly Hill

7 The Practical Need for a Socio-economic Classification of Tropical Agrarian Systems

The word *taxonomy*, which has to do with scientific classification in relation to general laws and principles, was not coined until 1813 (OED), although Linnaeus' *Species Plantarium*, which forms the basis of modern classification of plants and animals, had been published as early as 1753. We economic anthropologists have not only lacked a Linnaeus, but have also disdained scientific taxonomy – perhaps mainly because of its association with discredited evolutionary approaches. So it is that the idea of classifying tropical agrarian systems according to scientific principles has received no serious attention during the past forty years (or so) when 'tropical economic under-development' has become such a fashionable subject in academia[1] – even though, as I claim our understanding of the operation of tropical rural economies has hardly increased during this period, and may even have retrogressed.

Just as botanists and zoologists necessarily work within a framework of scientific taxonomy, and would make no progress otherwise, so the same ought to apply in our case – I speak all the time of the taxonomy of tropical agrarian systems, excluding 'exotic systems'[2] (Papua New Guinea, south-west Kerala, etc.) from my discussion. For if such a framework is lacking, one of two things happens: either we devote ourselves to the pursuit of enormous generalizations of very broad and vague application, but of no real practical utility; or we regard each rural economy as an interesting specimen in its own right. In a very general way it used to be true, in this context, that economists were the *macro* people, we the *micro* – but nowadays all has changed partly because many anthropologists have become contemptuous of empiricism. The two camps (the grand generalizers and those who are derogatorily supposed to pursue mere 'village studies') are at daggers drawn, the chief victims of this appalling state of affairs being the world's poorest people.

So that I shall not be accused of exaggerating the rigid posture of many economists, I now refer to a very 'respectable' and very recent book by two economists of high status (Bliss and Stern 1982) who undertook fieldwork for seven months in the Indian village of Palanpur[3] in 1974–75 for the purpose of testing certain theories they had in mind. When these authors go so far as to claim that: '. . . theories of development economics should have the power to explain what one finds in a village such as Palanpur' (p. 4), it is obvious that they are indifferent to the need for any taxonomy in our sense.

This is because the theories they are out to test are of an enormously generalized and all-too-familiar and time-worn character. Thus (p. 51), they contrast Schultz' view (Schultz 1964) that, given the constraints of knowledge, village economies make efficient use of their assets, with Hirschman's belief (Hirschman 1958) that 'entrepreneurial decision-making is in short supply'. In testing such theories they ignore at least two factors of supreme import-ance. Because they regard 'tropical underdevelopment' as a kind of standard condition (no taxonomy being required), they overlook the fact that Schultz might happen to provide a better (though necessarily inadequate) explan-ation of the workings of one type of agrarian system, Hirschman of another. Then, because they overlook the extreme significance of economic inequality in most tropical agrarian economies, they fail to realize that no theories relating to such general matters as the motivations of cultivators ever apply to rich and poor alike – that the economic behaviour of richer farmers may be the mirror image of that of poorer farmers.

As for the economic anthropologists, it was towards the end of the 1960s that so many of them lost all interest in empirical work, which they regarded as old-fashioned, both in aim and method (as indeed much of it was), and resorted instead to a theoretical approach which often *purported* to derive a good deal of support from various ahistorical variants of Marxism.[4] It was mainly, though not entirely, as a result of their highly motivated enthusiasm, that a kind of corpus of orthodox beliefs (received doctrine) took partial expression; most interestingly, this was acceptable to people of greatly varying political persuasions, owing to the lack of any serious or systematic alternative.

Now the curious thing about this 'body of orthodox beliefs' is that it both exists and does not exist: *it exists* because of the crying need to fill the vacuum in our knowledge of the workings of tropical agrarian systems (vacuums are abhorred to the point that they seem to be eliminated, without verification, by any vaguely familiar set of plausible suppositions); it *does not exist* because it is nowhere properly analysed as an organized, coherent system of wide application, but consists rather of a set of vaguely formulated or implicit assumptions. One knows that it *does exist* because of the commotion that is caused if one accidentally steps upon (appears to dismiss or question) any of these implicit assumptions:[5] one knows that it *does not exist* because of the lack of any reliable expositor of especial renown.

My three starting-points in this discussion are: (1) that generalizations of widespread (but not universal) application are very badly needed for all kinds of practical reasons; (2) that no useful set of generalizations is conceivably applicable to *all* tropical agrarian systems; and (3) that we should aim at establishing a taxonomy of agrarian systems, such that different sets of economic generalizations apply to each of them.

In my recent book (Hill 1982), I have sought, on the basis of detailed fieldwork in Katsina and Kano Emirates in Hausaland, northern Nigeria – (see Hill 1972, 1977), and in six small villages in Anekal Taluk in south-eastern Karnataka (south India),[6] to identify one of the important types of agrarian system in such a taxonomy. I have suggested, very tentatively, that it may be that the number of important types which require identification (important in terms of the sizes of the world populations involved) would not prove to be unmanageably large, say between ten and twenty. To my entire surprise[7] I had accidentally discovered that the rural economies of the two regions in the two continents had so much in common (despite one being Muslim and casteless, the other Hindu and caste-ridden) that a large number of really useful general conclusions applied to both of them. For the sake of convenience (*not* of provocation) I designated this particular world agrarian system, *a* (not *the*)[8] dry grain *mode*, dry grain being non-irrigated grain. Using my knowledge and judgement, after I had left the field, I compiled a list of variables identifying this particular dry grain mode.

Before discussing the categories of variable which might be regarded as identifying any particular agrarian mode – though I must insist at once that systems involving irrigation must never be bracketed with rainfed systems – I want to quote from a remarkable book for the general reader on Parkinson's disease (Sacks 1976). Sacks says (in a note on p. 20) that Parkinson, who first identified the disease: 'came to recognize that certain stars form a constellation, that many seemingly unrelated phenomena form a definite and constant "assemblage of systems"'.

This 'assemblage', he noted, 'seemed to have a coherent inner logic and order of its own', 'inspection at a distance' being insufficient for its nature to be understood: 'with this he adopted an entirely different stance and . . . a quite different language.' Having first established a genuine empiricism, he had then moved to an existential position. He saw Parkinsonism not as 'an assemblage of symptoms' but as a 'form of behaviour'. By analogy with this analysis, I regard the list of variables identifying a particular agrarian system as corresponding to the 'assemblage of symptoms', and the conclusions one was able to draw about the operation of the system, in each of the continents, as corresponding to the 'form of behaviour' involved in Parkinsonism.

I am only too well aware that critics of this chapter will be much more likely to decry the practical attempt I have made to identify one important agrarian system (this particular dry grain mode) than to condone it. I anticipate hostile criticism and expect to suffer severely under the whip of scorn. But my point is that someone has got to make a start somewhere – someone has got to blunder in. If we want our findings to be useful to decision takers, planners, administrators, etc. in the tropical world (and it is my firm insistence, as I shall later emphasize, that the function of an anthropologist like myself is to offer conclusions designed to be useful to such people when they take decisions, rather than to formulate recommendations ourselves), why then, we have got to plunge in and start making fools of ourselves in a good cause.

I am also aware that there are likely to be many who will object both to my belief that, as with Parkinsonism, a considerable number of variables may be required to identify a particular mode, and to the element of subjectivity involved in their selection. It is on the basis of my experience of over thirteen years' fieldwork in the rural tropics that I insist on the need for a multi-variate approach (one which should normally take account of at least one historical factor), though this is not to deny that many more variables may be required to identify some modes than others.

I know from an otherwise friendly review of my recent book (Byres 1983) that I shall be severely criticized for my reluctance, at this stage, to identify other regions to which this particular dry grain mode might apply. But such an investigation would have severely delayed publication. My main purpose is polemical and urgent: that of persuading others that an immediate start should be made in formulating a taxonomy of (non-exotic) tropical agrarian systems – a taxonomy which should be based both on existent publications and (let us hope) on fieldwork designed for the purpose.

The very act of embarking on such a project would be certain to do something to improve the very poor quality of official statistics relating to the rural tropical world. I shall take but a single example. The great bulk of Indian statistics relating to the size of farm-holdings by household do not distinguish irrigated and non-irrigated (dry) land. They relate to farmland as such. But in most circumstances, irrigated and dry land are effectively different factors of production owing to the much higher yield and price of the former;[9] so in localities where some land is irrigated and some is not, it makes little sense to bulk the figures, though this is the normal practice.

Therefore, my best hope is that you will feel that in embarking upon this unconventional work of identifying one of the common modes, I have made a fool of myself in a thought-provoking and reasonably responsible way, one which will encourage others to undertake superior work on other modes. *It is no good arguing that a multi-variate taxonomy would serve no useful purpose.*

The Dry Grain Mode

Before listing the variables defining this dry grain mode, I must make it clear that such lists emerge as a result of the fieldwork and necessarily involve some judgment. This means that my list would be bound to differ somewhat from any compiled by another worker in the same regions – although, as I insist, the lists would have much in common. The variables must be diverse in general character – sociological, demographic, agricultural, technological, and so forth.

The set of nine variables that I regarded as identifying this dry grain mode are summarized in Hill (1982: 50), the following list being even briefer:

1. *The population is so dense*[10] *that nearly all the available farmland is necessarily manured and cultivated every year* – and densities are increasing fast.
2. *Most farmland is used for cultivating basic food grains* (millets and sorghums in these regions) *without irrigation.* (Some grain is sold, some used for household consumption.)
3. *The farmland is effectively owned by individuals – being inherited by sons,* on, or before, their father's death.
4. *Cultivation is undertaken by household members,*[11] *with or without the help of daily-paid labourers.*
5. *Cultivators have for long been wont to buy and sell farmland for cash.*
6. However, land scarcity and rising land prices have *recently led to a much reduced incidence of land selling.*
7. *Grain yields per acre are very low on any standard*, two of many reasons for this being the common reliance on scarce organic manure and the fact that there is only one annual grain crop – despite the two monsoons in south India.
8. *Most farm tools and equipment*, which are of 'traditional design', *are made by local blacksmiths and carpenters.*
9. *Over the long term there has been much transfer of economic activity away from the countryside to urban areas* – the scale of actual outward migration being negligible in comparison. (The countryside having formerly been the matrix, within which most economic activity flourished, has now become a backwater.)

As I have already said, on the basis of my detailed field enquiries I have been able to formulate many conclusions regarding this dry grain mode in the two regions in the two continents. In the following list I concentrate on those of my findings which seem to be particularly at variance with 'prevailing general orthodoxy' as I have myself experienced it in the past decade or so.[12] (With considerable temerity, I deal further with this elusive 'orthodoxy' on pp. 125–26 below.)

SOME SPECIMEN CONCLUSIONS REGARDING THIS DRY GRAIN MODE
WHICH SEEM TO BE AT VARIANCE WITH 'ORTHODOXY'

a. Contemporary stagnation is due to a withdrawal of economic activity from the countryside rather than to urban 'capitalist intrusion', as is so commonly supposed. This stagnation is particularly expressed in terms of low grain yields and lack of occupational diversification, both agricultural and other.

b. Partly owing to the weakness of the centralized bureaucracies in relation to the countryside, hierarchical marketing structures, with their apices in the cities, which are often supposed to have been characteristic features of centralized states, were lacking in the old centralized states of Katsina, Kano and Karnataka (formerly Mysore). As a result, rural/urban marketing linkages are still poorly organized and the role of farmers in the marketing of their produce (and in their own provisioning) is very weak, especially in Karnataka,[13] where very few transport animals (and no lorries) are owned by villagers.

c. Agrestic servitude (farm-slavery in Hausaland and small-scale bonded labouring in south-eastern Karnataka) has given way to daily-paid farm labouring – the systems in the two continents are very similar, high proportions of labourers being smaller scale farmers or their sons. *The profound poverty of the masses*, rather than the diminutive incidence of adult bonded labouring in south-eastern Karnataka (where few farmers are, or were, rich enough to employ permanent men), *is, and was, the real problem.*[14]

d. The large estates have all been dissolved. In Hausaland this resulted from the effective abolition of farm-slavery about sixty years ago; in Karnataka prolonged political pressure led, fairly recently, to the legal dispossession of the large hereditary landlords – an ousting which preceded land reform proper. As for ordinary private farmers, hardly any of them nowadays would care to operate on a scale exceeding some thirty acres (even if they could), owing to the severe practical difficulties of supervising the work of numerous daily-paid labourers, who work in groups of constantly changing composition.

e. As there are no restrictions on the sale of the land pertaining to any village community to outsiders, it follows that there is a strong tendency for a considerable proportion of 'village land' to be owned by non-residents, most of them from nearby villages. This is one reason – and a very strong one – why *villages are not isolates but parts of a general matrix, the countryside.* (Another reason is the high propensity of women to marry outside their natal village.)

f. The *paradox of poverty* is such that the poorest farmers are often obliged to act in a way which is very adverse to their medium or longer term interests; thus, the poorest cultivators are those who sell grain immediately after harvest, when prices are lowest, not because it is surplus to their requirements but because they have urgent debts and consumption needs. *Grain sales should not be equated with grain surpluses*, as they invariably are in the literature.

g. It follows that insofar as supplies of grain consumed in the cities are drawn from very densely populated localities, they represent, to a large degree, a compulsory levy on hungry communities which cannot afford to 'import' sufficient replacement supplies at higher average seasonal prices than they have themselves received for their grain.

h. The only real 'subsistence farmers' (a misleading and ambiguous term which I never employ) are much richer cultivators than the average – most farmers would produce insufficient grain for their household needs, even if they sold none of it.

i. Because of the pronounced seasonality of economic life (owing to the long non-farming season), there is a special need for short and medium term credit, of a kind which would not normally be granted by banks or other official agencies, but which has to be rurally generated. One form of urban exploitation consists in the endeavour to suppress village-generated credit (which is all that is anyway available to poorer people), while providing no-one, not even the 'rich', with anything like sufficient non-village credit for their needs. Rurally generated credit is by no means necessarily exploitative and there are no specialist money-lenders – certainly not the shopkeepers, who are unimportant traders in both regions.

j. The volume of employment offered by richer farmers, *whose holdings are constantly diminishing in size*, is quite insufficient to meet the demand for daily-paid agricultural work. The labour market is in a chronic state of disequilibrium, the miserably low wage rates bearing no relationship either to minimum household needs or to the productivity of labour.

k. Contrary to general belief, there was an active market in farmland in the more densely populated localities in both regions a century or more ago; this meant that for many decades the richest households were able to buy land to compensate, at least in part, for the reduction in holding-size resulting from division between sons on inheritance. However, the recent rise in land prices has made everyone, including the poorest landowners, reluctant to sell their land.

l. Our detailed statistics show that the uneven distribution of farmland between households continues to be the fundamental basis of economic inequality; but, owing to (k), the pattern of land ownership has become more inflexible than at any time during the past century or longer.

m. The pattern of land *ownership* in fact corresponds very closely to that of land cultivation – this is because there is no share-cropping in either region[15] and tenancy is unimportant, being illegal[16] under Karnataka land reform and non-existent[17] in Katsina and Kano Emirates. (Mortgaging is effectively to be equated with enforced selling.)

n. Farmland is increasingly coveted, despite its very high price in relation to the yield of basic crops. Among the numerous reasons for this are: (i) that high status is achieved by no man who neglects or disdains farming as a way of life; (ii) the common desire to retire into farming (from other activities) in middle life; (iii) the fact that land is far and away the best form of security for raising loans from banks and other official agencies; (iv) the wish to cultivate sufficient land to retain the services of married sons (see (v) below).

o. The extent of the dependence of rural communities on arable farming is apt to be greatly exaggerated. On the one hand, farming *does* come first (there being no other occupation whose neglect automatically leads to loss of status); on the other hand, there are many households, from the richest to the poorest, which are more economically dependent on their non-farming occupations than on cultivation and/or labouring.

p. Unfortunately, however, the lack of lucrative economic opportunities (particularly such as involve trading in Karnataka) is a great problem, even for richer men, just as under-employment is for labourers in agriculture.

q. Richer households have a greatly superior capacity to diversify and intensify their economic activities of all types; all the really lucrative occupations are followed by the largest farmers only.

r. The belief in an inverse relationship between the scale of household farming and crop yield per acre used to be very strong indeed in relation to India, though some doubts are now being expressed.[18] However, this belief, which is belied by our research findings, remains part of *general* prevailing orthodoxy. Under our dry grain mode I would replace the 'inverse relationship law' with one stating that *poorer farmers usually receive a lower reward per unit of effort than richer men* – shortage of manure being one explanation.

s. The rural communities are, and have long been, *innately inegalitarian* in terms of the distribution of land and other types of property – and, contrary to general belief, *landlessness is nothing new*, the Karnataka Harijans, for instance, having owned hardly any land until very recently. Contrary to general orthodoxy, rural economic inequality does not derive from the outside world, thought it is often enhanced by it, richer villagers (for instance) being especially apt to be selected as agents by urban business men.

t. As for outward migration, this is not the automatic panacea it is often presumed to be, especially as the poorest people, notably the Harijans of south India, are those most strongly impeded from migrating by lack of finance. (As the great proportion of the population continues to live in the countryside, the very rapid expansion of city populations is entirely compatible with very low rates of outward migration from villages.)

u. Older men are much more apt to be 'rich' than younger men; on the other hand, the incidence of severe poverty shows little age variation. Poverty is the natural condition of most younger household heads.

v. Owing to increasing land scarcity, and reluctance to sell, married sons find it increasingly difficult to establish themselves as farmers on their own account, which may very well mean that the incidence of joint[19] (or extended) households is not decreasing, as is commonly supposed, but may even be increasing.

w. Most of the largest farmers owe their position to the accident of being brotherless, having thus inherited all their father's land. With the exception of the richest caste (the Reddy) in south-eastern Karnataka, the economic circumstances of brothers are notably unequal (particularly in polygynous[20] Hausaland), partly because land is apt to be divided in a very rough and ready way on, or before, death, this being one reason (*inter vivos* gifts being another) why prevailing notions of economic stratification are far too crude and mechanistic.

Such is my short list, a selection from a much longer set of conclusions applicable to both regions. At this point I can imagine many readers complaining that my findings are to a greater degree commonplace than I seem to think: 'Oh, but it's like that in my area', they will be saying. I must, therefore, reiterate that just as my *set* of nine variables identifying this dry grain mode must be taken as a whole (like the symptoms defining Parkinsonism), so my list of conclusions is a set, which *taken as a set* would apply to no other mode. Of course *many* of my individual findings will be found to apply to other modes, but not *all* of them – in other words, a tremor does not necessarily indicate Parkinsonism.

Many people have urged me to provide a list of other world regions to which this tropical dry grain mode might be expected to apply, but owing to lack of information I cannot oblige. However, I must emphasize that as population densities continue to increase, and as more and more land is manured and kept under regular cultivation with no fallow, there will be many tens of millions of people, in widely flung world regions, who will find themselves enduring conditions similar to those just described – unless, for example, the acreages under non-grain crops and/or irrigation systems are greatly extended, cheap supplies of chemical fertilizers are vastly increased, and/or much more serious efforts are made to introduce appropriate village industries.[21]

My chief difficulty is uncertainty as to the list of basic grains to which this mode might apply. I do not know whether there are any tropical regions which are as dependent on maize as south-eastern Karnataka is on a particular variety of millet (*ragi*);[22] if so, they are unlikely to conform to our mode since maize is one of the highest yielding of all grain crops. As for wheat, this is often considered to be a temperate crop,[23] although it is widely grown as the basic crop in much of north India. Areas of central India where, owing to high rainfall, rice grows well without irrigation,[24] do not conform to our mode, if only because grain yields are so relatively high.

Finally, I should add that I am well aware of my neglect of causal factors in this brief chapter, and I hope that readers will find my book more satisfactory in this respect.

Prevailing Orthodoxy

I must add some more brief remarks about my provocative notion of 'prevailing orthodoxy'. As I said earlier, it is to a large extent true that one only comes to know what is orthodox, when one finds that one's fieldwork has led one into paths which prove (unknown to oneself when one trod them) to be regarded as hopelessly heterodox. I say 'hopelessly heterodox' because I have found that so few people read the evidence justifying *heretical* ideas – it's no wonder I've accidentally changed my terminology here. I hope I shall be excused for offering a personal example.[25] When I went to Kano Emirate in 1971 I assumed that M. G. Smith's findings on farm-slavery[26] in part of Zaria Emirate (on the southern edge of Hausaland) would be certain to apply to Kano. When I found that they did not (and that there had not been, for instance, an intermediate status between a slave proper and a free man) I was very much surprised – which led me to collect and publish (Hill 1976, 1977) a great mass of statistical material in support of my findings. But these findings have been almost wholly ignored in the extensive and detailed literature on African slavery systems that has since appeared. My evidence remains unread, even though I was at pains to insist that Smith's findings were, presumably, entirely correct so far as his research area was involved.[27] The point was that Smith's findings fitted far better than mine into prevailing orthodoxy relating to the origins of economic stratification (and so forth) – so my findings *had* to be ignored.

Tentative Summary List of Aspects of 'Prevailing Orthodoxy' which do *not* Apply to this Dry Grain Mode

For the convenience of readers, though perhaps at the cost of my own reputation,[28] I now arbitrarily reiterate, in headline fashion, some of the features of 'prevailing orthodoxy' which do *not* apply to this dry grain mode. (The reference letters are those used in the list on pp. 121–24.)

(a) Rural stagnation is apt to be due to capitalist intrusion into the countryside.

(b) Hierarchical marketing structures, with their apices in the city, are characteristic of old centralized states.

(s), (j) Landlessness is a new phenomenon bound up with the development of daily-paid farm-labouring systems.

(e) Villagers are necessarily closely identified with *their* village land.

(d), (j) etc. As population densities increase, an increasing proportion of farmland tends to become concentrated in the ownership of the richest cultivators, which often results in the creation of systems of class stratification comparable with European types.

(f), (g) The grain sold by individual villagers is surplus to their requirements.

(h) The poorest cultivators are subsistence farmers.

(i) Village-generated credit is necessarily exploitative.

(l) Farmland was not sold on any scale until 'recently'.

(l) The incidence of farm-selling increases in response to increasing population pressure.

(m) Systems of tenancy and/or share-cropping necessarily existed in colonial times.

(s), (v) Questions of Indian caste apart, economic inequality in rural communities necessarily derives from the outside world.

(o) The proportion of income derived from arable farming is apt to be high.
(r) There is apt to be an inverse relationship between the scale of farming and yield per acre.
(w) In societies where farmland is divided between sons on, or before, death, great trouble is usually taken to achieve equal division.
(t) Extreme individual poverty is very commonly relieved by outward migration.
(v) Joint or extended households are everywhere rapidly disintegrating.
(n), (p) Richer men are apt to contract out of farming in favour of other occupations.

Conclusions

Finally, I revert to my insistence that our present ignorance is so great that, for the time being at least, the main function of field economic anthropologists should be to offer conclusions designed in a general way to be useful to policy makers, rather than to become involved in policy formulation themselves.

We cannot hope to be simultaneously iconoclastic and creative unless we are free to pursue our work in a manner dictated by our own research findings, as they gradually emerge. We must be iconoclastic because it is the old orthodox ideas, which have been eagerly absorbed by policy makers (who desperately need guidance), which stand in the way of sensible new policies; we must pursue our work as open-mindedly as possible (free from the influence of those who believe that we are already aware of the main gaps in our knowledge), because we know that we are all far more ignorant than we know – and that our ignorance is increasing over time.[29]

There must be division of labour. Unless we, the open-minded field-workers, are allowed to concentrate on our arduous and multifarious tasks, which include so much in the way of archival and library work, the collation of notes and statistics, the writing and re-writing of drafts (which are always blundering in the earlier stages), the quality of our work is bound to suffer. But at the same time I must insist that when writing our books and articles, *the requirements of the policy makers should always lie near the top of our minds*, for callous we are not, and we are all bound to hold strong views about many aspects of policy. (Nor should we keep quiet about the poor quality of many official socio-economic statistics (see Hill 1984), especially those relating to rural India.)

It is because we want to help the policy formulators that we have got to start classifying the agrarian systems: we cannot expect them to do it themselves because, like us, they are far too ignorant – and even more apt to be biased by conventional wisdom. The policy men, with their ignorance of the countryside, are not well qualified to identify the gaps in our knowledge; they are the last people with sound ideas on what research is likely to be particularly useful. We are the people whose job it is to ascertain the kinds of things we need to know, and we cannot function properly if our priorities are predetermined by others who are even more ignorant than ourselves.

I am told by some with a good general overview of the academic scene, that rural economic anthropology, as a discipline with any appeal to students, is on the verge of collapse in this country. Certainly, it is a most unfashionable subject in tropical countries – where, as we all know, the very word *anthropology* has such a colonial ring, that it is invariably replaced by *sociology*, which is nearly always urban in content. Of course I do not deny that there are times and circumstances when applied economic anthropologists ought to be concerned with policy formulation. But unless our discipline is constantly refreshed by free scientific investigation in the field, our advisory class will lose all academic identity. Since economic anthropology has a very poor reputation with 'experts' such as engineers, hydrologists, agronomists, etc. in general, as well as with administrators, so it is that our advisers are apt to be treated with scant respect. Only by undertaking fieldwork which is designed to be *fundamentally enlightening* (rather than problem solving), can we help to remedy this desperate situation.

Notes

1. A fashionableness which, as we shall later discuss, is now waning fast.
2. I am well aware of the impossibility of defining *exotic*, but fortunately the evidently 'non-exotic systems', such as the particular dry grain mode discussed in this paper, probably cover a very high proportion of the total population of the rural tropical world.
3. A village about 200 miles east of Delhi.
4. I am here ignoring the 'Polanyi debate' which seems to me a dead duck, and which ought never to have been born. In general I believe that the recent retreat from empiricism was triggered by the false belief that economics, in its application to tropical rural economies, is necessarily an arcane matter: in other words, anthropologists were so overawed by economists, that they lost sight of their own identity. (The theories which Bliss and Stern 1982 list in their Chapter 2, 'Theory and India', were all formulated by economists.)
5. This hostility is particularly apt to be expressed in book reviews. (See further discussion below.)
6. My 1982 book represents my only substantial contribution to south Indian ethnography.
7. I had not gone to India in 1977 with any idea of doing comparative work, but because immigration restrictions had prevented my going to Nigeria, as I had intended.
8. There are undoubtedly several other dry grain modes – a fact which reviewers of my book have, so far, overlooked.
9. In 1982 I observed the extraordinary fact that in coastal Kerala, in south-west India, the price of dry land was very much higher than that of irrigated paddy land – presumably because of the shortage of house sites in this desperately overpopulated region.

10. It is hard to provide meaningful statistics of population density, which varied within each of the regions. Average cultivated acreage per head of population varied between about 0.4 for Dorayi (Hill 1977), 0.7 for the Anekal villages (Hill 1982) and 0.9 (manured farmland only) for Batagarawa (Hill 1972).

11. Many of whom are women in Karnataka. But in most localities in Hausaland most women are in full Muslim seclusion within their houses and can do no farming.

12. I employ 'experience' to convey the fact that this amorphous body of received wisdom is nowhere systematically expounded as such, but is rather the atmosphere within which discussion commonly occurs, being the received wisdom of students, examiners, popular textbooks, lecturers on 'peasants' and *The Journal of Peasant Studies*. Not all the victims of this degenerative intellectual process are anthropologists: many are economists, historians and sociologists (see also n. 28).

13. It has to be admitted that an important difference between Hausaland and Karnataka relates to the great involvement of Hausa farmers in long distance trading caravans in former times: the Hausa farmers owned most of the long distance transport animals (mainly donkeys), whereas the south Indian farmers owned none.

14. Such was the high ratio of impoverished Harijans to reasonably prosperous farmers in the Anekal villages during the past century, that any notion that the *jajmani* system significantly alleviated the insecurity of most Harijans is sheer sentiment. Hill (1982: 265–7).

15. By which I mean share-cropping proper, which is such as necessarily involves the landlord in providing some inputs additional to land: the British, having no tradition of share-cropping in their own country, seldom define it correctly.

16. Even were it not illegal, there would be little tenancy as so few farmers have 'spare land'.

17. There is a Hausa system of 'land-borrowing' for a single season, which usually involves relatives and notional rents.

18. By Bliss and Stern (1982) among others.

19. Regarded simply as farming organizations, the Indian joint family and the Hausa system of *gandu* have much in common, both involving married sons working on their father's farms. (In neither research region was there any evidence of a weakening of the system.)

20. The Karnataka villages are basically (though not exclusively) monogamous.

21. With the exception of sericulture, which is an ideal domestic occupation, the common expression 'cottage industry' does not convey the type of modern enterprises that are required.

22. This finger millet (*Eleusine coracana*) has a greatly inferior yield of grain and straw compared with the bulrush millet (*Pennisetum*) of Hausaland, unless it is grown on irrigated land in place of paddy.

23. Its yield is necessarily so low in northern Nigeria that the current attempts to promote its cultivation are misguided.

24. Personal information from C. A. Gregory relating to his recent research in India.

25. Unfortunately, I could provide many others!

26. Reported in Smith (1960) and elsewhere.

27. The significant variation between Zaria and Kano involved land tenure.

28. Readers will find this list hilarious, if they fail to appreciate that it represents the kinds of assumptions commonly made, failing evidence to the contrary.

29. The reduced number of fieldworkers in regions like West Africa, and the inapplicability of so much prevailing orthodoxy to rapidly changing circumstances – are among the important reasons for our growing ignorance.

References

BLISS, C. J. and STERN, N. H. (1982) *Palanpur: The Economy of an Indian Village.* Oxford: Clarendon Press.

BYRES, T. J. (1983) Review of Hill (1982) in *British Book News* April.

HILL, P. (1972) *Rural Hausa: A Village and a Setting.* Cambridge: Cambridge University Press.

— (1976) From Slavery to Freedom: The Case of Farm-slavery in Nigerian Hausaland. *Comparative Studies in Society and History* 18 (3).

— (1977) *Population, Prosperity and Poverty: Rural Kano, 1900 and 1970.* Cambridge: Cambridge University Press.

— (1982) *Dry Grain Farming Families: Hausaland (Nigeria) and Karnataka (India) compared.* Cambridge: Cambridge University Press.

— (1984) The Poor Quality of Official Socio-Economic Statistics Relating to the Rural Tropical World. *Journal of Modern Asian Studies* 18 (3).

HIRSCHMAN, A. (1958) *The Strategy of Economic Development.* Newhaven: Yale University Press.

SACKS, O. W. (1976) *Awakening.* Harmondsworth: Penguin.

SCHULTZ, T. W. (1964) *Transforming Traditional Agriculture.* Newhaven: Yale University Press.

SMITH, M. G. (1960) *Government in Zazzau, 1800–1950.* London: Oxford University Press.

M. G. Whisson*

8 Advocates, Brokers, and Collaborators:

anthropologists in the real world

Conventional wisdom divides most sciences into pure and applied branches. Those disciplines whose ancestry pre-dates, or encompasses more than, the scientific method, like anatomy and physiology, have distinctive terms to describe their application. The more youthful human sciences, however, rarely do more than add the gerundive 'applied' to indicate that in addition to the inductive or deductive exercises being performed in order to establish elements and relationships in their data, *a priori* moral values are being incorporated with the intention of indicating or achieving certain identifiable goals. In this chapter I first question that conventional wisdom or way of seeing the discipline, and try to indicate how anthropologists actually relate to their human environment. The method adopted in the latter part of the exercise is frankly autobiographical, as it is difficult to find convincing accounts of how anthropologists have viewed the effects of their presence and their work upon their subjects, and I have been fortunate in being involved in a wide range of applied research projects in my career to date.

Intentions and Effects: Means and Ends

Since the time that L. H. Morgan wrote his *League of the Iroquois* with the intention of combining an understanding of the Indians with sympathy for their circumstances on the periphery of Morgan's own expanding society, anthropologists have usually worked in communities which form parts of larger social systems. The colonial flag, the missionary and the trader

*I acknowledge with appreciation the financial assistance afforded by Rhodes University and The Human Sciences Research Council of South Africa to enable me to attend the conference at which this paper was presented, and the helpful comments of my departmental colleagues on the initial draft.

generally preceded the social scientist, even if the subsequently published studies suggested that the writer had experienced the ideal, untouched and isolated society. This being the case, even the writers of the pure classics of social anthropology, like Malinowski (1922) and Evans-Pritchard (1940) contributed towards the process of interaction between the subjects of their studies and the rulers of those subjects. Their intentions may have been purely scientific, but their effects were applied.

Malinowski, as an outsider in relation to the rulers of the Trobriands, had little difficulty in adopting the role of the Trobrianders' unbriefed advocate. His passionate digression (1922: 464ff.) on the catastrophic impact of colonial administrators and missionaries, neither of whom grace his index, demonstrates his moral stance and spells out his prescription – indirect rule, and as little of it as possible. As Evans-Pritchard indicates (1940: 11) and Johnson (1979) describes more fully, the material for the Nuer corpus was collected by one who could be viewed, quite reasonably, as an enemy or spy by his subjects. Evans-Pritchard was there because he was asked to go by the Sudan government which had experienced problems in the administration of a people whose 'country and character are alike intractable' (1940: 8–9). By offering some scientific corroboration of the views held by experienced administrators about Nuer–Dinka relations (1940: 125), he made a contribution to the formation of the colonial government's policy. While his intention was to make 'a contribution to the ethnology of a particular area' (1940: 15), a pure scientific aim, the effect of his work on the peoples in the region may have been substantially more than that. Radcliffe-Brown was more explicit in his assessment of the anthropologist's role: 'A wise anthropologist will not try to tell an administrator what he ought to do; it is his special task to provide the scientifically collected and analysed knowledge that the administrator can use if he likes' (1950: 85). Malinowski, the advocate, and Radcliffe-Brown, the collaborator, thus recognized their involvement in the real world of their subjects, and the administrators who governed them. Evans-Pritchard, in the least propitious circumstances, implausibly suggests the possibility of evading the practical implications of published information.

Where the structure of control lay primarily through commissioners and missionaries to their governing bodies in London, collaboration between the anthropologists and the colonial rulers was relatively easy. As Kuper (1973: 123ff.) illustrates, some anthropologists were recruited by the colonial governments to carry out specific enquiries, and the work of all was available to those who trained officers or administered the fieldwork areas. Tensions existed between administrators and anthropologists in the field when the latter appeared to be 'going native', 'stirring trouble', or 'getting bush happy'. District officers showing symptoms of those conditions could be transferred to more urbane surroundings to facilitate recovery, but independent fieldworkers under the protection of distant institutes or universities were less easily controlled. But beyond those tensions there was the identification of the common British middle-class culture, in which conflicts about issues and even behaviour could be set aside over a sundowner and the patronage which those housed in permanent bungalows with hot running water exercise over dwellers in tents and mud huts.

Where permanent white settlers formed an influential element in the local body politic, which meant that labour recruitment might be added to the two primary duties of the commissioners (keeping the peace and maintaining the revenue), and land alienation was a constant threat or *fait accompli*, clashes of interest between the people studied (and their anthropologist) and the rulers were almost inevitable. It was not by chance that the African 'exceptions' to the collaborator role listed by Kuper (1973: 148) were working in settler dominated societies.

Outside the British functionalist school, South African scholars in the *volkekunde* tradition generally identified with the ruling Afrikaners and provided the rationale for the division of the country into ethnic communities, each one of which was destined to be given a measure of local autonomy on land officially designated 'homelands' or 'black states'. The Department of Co-operation and Development (formerly the Native Affairs Department) employs a number of ethnologists as advisers and research officers, most of whom were trained in the *volkekunde* tradition, summarized thus by one of its most powerful professors:[1]

'By nature man is also a social being and cannot survive by living alone. As ants and bees, for example, have their existence in natural, organic social entities, nests and hives respectively, so has man his existence in culturally determined, organic social entities, i.e. ethnies (sing. ethnos), whose structures and existential activities are culturally determined. Such units cannot be organized but originate organically as the outcome of the combined action of the forces controlling and determining human existence.

Ontologically speaking human existence is an existence within the framework of varying ethnical units, each having a separate corporate existence. This is man's normal existence, he cannot survive and lead a happy life in any other way.

The proper study of man as a comprehensive and general science of man, therefore must be a study of ethnies as ontical [sic], human, social units, being separate corporate bodies, each composed of separate but closely linked human units (members of one body), existing and surviving successfully through the continuous and combined creative activities of its members in a process of constantly changing environment.'

(Coertze 1978: 1)

Those who could affirm such an academic faith were more than collaborators and 'handmaidens' of the South African government as it sought to implement its policies of apartheid: they were the ideological spearhead and the theoreticians of the National Party prior to and during its first decades in power. Government ethnologists advised the Department and the Minister on such matters as which local communities should be allocated to each homeland, and which individuals possessed the right qualities in terms of traditional criteria of descent, and willingness to support the policy of the government to be chosen as the leaders of the reconstructed ethnic enclaves. The Minister of Co-operation and Development, who has presided over the implementation of the grand apartheid design for the blacks since 1978 was himself trained in the *volkekunde* tradition and, after a period in Oxford where he wrote his D.Phil., returned to take up a political career within the National Party.

In British colonial Africa, scholars such as Gulliver, Huntingford and Gordon Wilson were employed as government sociologists or anthropologists, apparently experiencing no great crises of conscience in their roles. Such men have been the target of vigorous criticism by writers such as Asad (1973) and Okot p'Bitek (1970), but the moral basis of their position is not hard to divine, whether or not they thought about it much at the time. Given the structures of power at the time of their employment; the alternatives which they might have perceived as being open to them; the policies of the colonial governments to promote development in the rural areas; and the access to men of power and influence which they gained from being within the colonial structure; participation in the system as government sociologists was probably the most rational and effective means whereby they could promote the sort of ideals which they had imbibed from Malinowski and his heirs.[2] Unlike the vulnerable, government appointed chiefs who endeavoured, as one explained to me, 'to represent my people to the government, and to represent the government to my people', the anthropologists only had to communicate the views and values of their people to the government – '*his* [the native's] vision of *his* world' in Malinowski's words (1922: 25). Further, they were in a position to press the interests of the communities which they studied from a position often stronger than that of outsiders. Their personal knowledge of the decision makers in the small colonial executive, their long periods of tenure in their jobs, their acknowledged expertise, and their assumed loyalty to the British crown by virtue of their appointments, added up to substantial resources in the long processes of negotiation and policy planning.

The disadvantages of their positions within governments increasingly at odds with rising nationalism were also serious. As support or staff officers outside the executive or line hierarchy, they were, *par excellence*, formally in the collaborator role to which Radcliffe-Brown assigned anthropologists, informing the decision makers but unable to control the use made of their reports. Also, if their masters thought fit, they could not make their material available to the opposition through publication.

The idea that applied anthropology is primarily a matter of anthropologists being employed by, or assisting, powerful bureaucracies to implement pro-

grammes 'believed to ameliorate contemporary social, economic, and technological problems' (Foster 1969: 54) was not limited to colonial or quasi-
colonial powers like Britain and South Africa, as Foster's standard introduction indicates. Malinowski's impassioned advocacy, like that of his pupil
Kenyatta (1938), would scarcely have fitted the definitions and assumptions of
Foster, yet each in his own way sought to 'ameliorate contemporary social
. . . problems' as he experienced them. The essential difference between
Foster on the one hand, and Kenyatta and Malinowski on the other, is not one
of goals (although there may be a difference about who can or should define
them) but of means, and that difference in turn stems from beliefs about the
character, motivation and pliability of those who hold power. The advocate
assumes no goodwill on the part of the authorities, only a concern to pursue
their own interests as they see them, and is but a short step from the activist
who seeks to mobilize forces to press his point of view, in effect raising the cost
of opposing him and his clients or subjects. The advocate reared in the
functionalist tradition will tend to see the removal of outside interference as
having merit, so that the target community can continue to develop the
institutions appropriate to its own perceived needs. The collaborator assumes
that goodhearted ignorance pervades the bureaucracy with which he works (if
it were not so, he would not work with it) so that his role is to lead a willing
horse to the waters of truth. For the advocate, desirable changes tend to come
through mobilized popular opinion and local action; for the collaborator such
changes come through the execution of policies formulated in the bureaucracies which he serves.

While ideally the roles are opposed, there will usually be pressure, in
varying degrees, on the researcher to fluctuate from one to the other, or to
endeavour to combine both. If the researcher has a strong interest in
remaining in, or returning to, the field, the pressure to collaborate with the
authorities as the price of continuing the research may be intense. The
collaborator role, effective in relatively homogeneous or peaceful societies,
becomes problematic as conflicts of interest between ruler and ruled, core and
periphery, or dominant and minority ethnic group, become serious. The role
of applied anthropologists in politically contentious situations, and
especially in a war which did not command much popular support among
academics led, in November 1970, to the publication of a set of 'Principles of
Professional Responsibility' (AAA 1970). Strictly followed, these would
make research virtually impossible, and would remove from applied
researchers what might well be their only valuable resource in transactions
with those in power – the possession of information. They would virtually
compel the anthropologist to adopt the advocate's role, since any other would
be likely to fall foul of the strictures on private dealing and confidential
reporting. Given the circumstances which faced the authors of the Principles,
the articulation of such counsels of perfection was understandable, but one
may reasonably question the universality of either circumstances or

prescription. Alinsky, a confessing and acknowledged 'radical', would seem to concur:

> 'I present here a series of rules pertaining to the ethics of means and ends: first, that *one's concern with the ethics of means and ends varies inversely with one's personal interest in the issue* [or] *with one's distance from the scene of conflict.*
>
> *The second rule of the ethics of means and ends is that the judgement of the ethics of means is dependent upon the political position of those sitting in judgement.*'
>
> (Alinsky 1972: 26, italics in original)

Alinsky does not present what Radcliffe-Brown would have considered 'scientifically collected and analysed knowledge' (1950: 79) in support of his 'rules', but several dramatic examples. The approach which he is suggesting for applied anthropologists or 'those who want to change the world from what it is to what they believe it should be' (1972: 2), which is a more spirited definition than Foster's, for all the questions that it begs, involves the utilization of skills, knowledge and ongoing research into the problems of communities large and small, in order to define or establish and achieve goals. F. G. Bailey suggests a similar approach in *Stratagems and Spoils* (1969) and *Morality and Expediency* (1979), and that there is a third role for the applied anthropologist, that of the broker, of whom he writes: 'There has existed for many years a category of men who make a profession of bridging this gap between peasants and the administrative and political élite. For the peasants these are the men who know where to get a licence for a shotgun, how to get a real injection in the hospital instead of distilled water' (1969: 41). The indigenous fixers to whom Bailey refers require payment in coin, or kind, or even in status: the exotic variant may be satisfied with a couple of learned articles and a book which can be used to obtain further research funds or tenure. Bailey describes 'middlemen' as 'roles which come into existence to bridge a gap in communications between the larger and the smaller structures' (1969: 167). Monica Wilson called them interpreters: 'I use *interpreter* for the man between, whose primary function is communication, and secondary function negotiation. Now interpreters, just because they are *men between*, are commonly distrusted. Where the groups between whom they interpret are in conflict they are likely to be distrusted by both sides because they are negotiators between opponents' (Wilson 1972: 20).

The 'pure' anthropologist will limit himself to Wilson's primary function, the 'applied' anthropologist be no less concerned with the secondary. In the case studies, or apologia, which follow, the essence of the argument is that if anthropology is to be applied, then the anthropologist himself must be committed to his task beyond the compilation of reports and the provision of knowledge 'that the administrator can use if he likes' (Radcliffe-Brown 1950: 85); beyond the constant display of academic virginity demanded by the AAA

Principles, and be ready to go into the real world of politics, power and persuasion. Martin Luther King urged his congregations to be 'wise as serpents and harmless as doves' (Matthew 10.16), which he glossed as combining 'a tough mind and a tender heart', the former characterized by 'incisive thinking, realistic appraisal, and decisive judgement' (King 1969).

Applied anthropologists could do worse than to start from that point, drawing the essential distinctions between intentions and effects, as well as between their possibly conflicting roles as advocates, brokers or collaborators (the tough minded element) whilst remaining sensitive to the needs of their subjects as their subjects themselves experience them (the tender hearted element).

Case Studies

LUOLAND RURAL DEVELOPMENT

From 1960 to 1962, I was sponsored by the Christian Council of Kenya to carry out research among the Kenya Luo, the purpose of which was to assist the former body in planning its priorities after independence. The report, written during my last month in the field, and published without amendment (or proof reading) two years later (Whisson 1964) caused a certain amount of irritation among some of the old Kenya missionary hands who saw it, but otherwise had no appreciable effect. With hindsight, it was easy to see the naïveté which characterized the entire exercise.

The promoters of the project were young men without mission station experience, who sought to eliminate the denominational and racial divisions which existed in Kenya, as one aspect of the church's adaptation to independence under black rule. The practical consequences of my research were to be another. Their position in an ecumenical body peripheral to the missionary and ecclesiastical hierarchies gave them little real influence with an establishment which had laboured long in tough conditions, through decades of political unrest which had culminated in Mau Mau and the constitutional struggle for independence. That establishment had serious reservations about the promoters' theology, politics and style.[3] However, since all concerned were devout Christians, among whom there should have been no divisions or factional politics, and who, like me, believed that 'truth' was both identifiable and irresistible, I learned of the factions only through the experience of being categorized as a part of the sponsors' faction. The report was seen as a creature of that faction and judged accordingly. I had failed to do what many preach but few practise (Foster 1969: Chapter 5) – to master the ethnography of the ruling group, of which the church hierarchies were integral parts, as thoroughly as I sought to understand the Luo community.

The recommendations included programmes to promote modest capital formation, a legal basis for land reform as and when the individual Luo and local communities wanted it, improved education and more effective church involvement, most changes requiring inexpensive modifications in organization rather than huge injections of capital and expertise. There was, however, little to benefit any of the existing interest groups very directly, apart from the largely inarticulate and generally less successful people who were the main subjects of the study. Once the researcher had left, there was little incentive for anyone to press the ideas presented in the report, if indeed anyone agreed with them, and whatever merit might have existed in the work was neither assessed nor its insights seriously considered for application.

The target community gained nothing from the research as far as its defined goals were concerned, although individuals did benefit from the presence of the researcher, mainly when he was doing things not directly a part of the research programme, such as teaching English, providing medical care or transport, or acting as a broker in various transactions with educational, ecclesiastical and other authorities.

The failure of the project to achieve the goals intended by the sponsors could be attributed in part to fundamental weaknesses in my own theoretical orientation, which directed me to look at the cultural or ethnic group as a functionally integrated whole, rather than as a part of the complex whole of Kenya (including Kenya's relationship to the metropolitan power). For the research to have succeeded, it would have been necessary for the part to be understood in terms of the very much larger whole, since it was from the controllers of that larger whole that substantial resources and the exercise of political power would have to be sought. A better understanding of the history of the fieldwork area itself could have provided the necessary insight, for the missionary of the previous generation had himself little hesitation in utilizing British Members of Parliament and the *Manchester Guardian* in the pursuit of what he saw as the best interests of his people (Whisson and Lonsdale 1975). Development, seen even from a traditional anthropological position of assisting people to achieve their own goals for themselves, involves endless transactions between the innovators in the community and the controllers of material resources and knowledge both inside and outside. My interpretation of my brief – to tell people of influence what ought to be done in the expectation that they, as people of goodwill and good sense, would act – was woefully inadequate, pure 'dove'. The serpentine element, of working on the strategies of implementation, cultivating the decision makers at every level from wary ploughman to the relevant ministers of state, was left to the sponsors to handle after the report was produced. By that time it was too late.

HEROIN IN HONG KONG

In 1964 I was sponsored by the Hong Kong Council of Social Service to carry out research into the causes of, and the cure for, the high incidence of heroin and opium addiction in Hong Kong. The initiative stemmed from the Discharged Prisoners' Aid Society, about 75 per cent of whose clients were, or had been, addicts at the time of their release from jail, and were far more difficult to rehabilitate than those who had not been addicted. The other welfare bodies co-ordinated by the Council shared the view that just about every form of social pathology which presented itself in the colony was associated either directly or indirectly with narcotics. As in Kenya, I found what appeared to be a united front of concerned citizens, churchmen and officials, all dedicated to the elimination of the opiates, the trade in which had been the *raison d'être* for the seizure of the colony in 1841. Experience, even without Bailey (1969) or Alinsky (1972) as interpreters, made me more wary, and the outcome may well have been marginally more effective. Certainly the press cover of the publication, and the subsequent debate, suggested that important people had read the report and were prepared to consider its recommendations seriously (*South China Morning Post* 9 August 1965; *Hong Kong Standard* 26 August 1965; *Far Eastern Economic Review* 28 July 1965 and 19 August 1965).

The main thrust of the analysis, that the provision of narcotics is a big and profitable business whose operators seek only to make profits and neither promote political goals nor pursue 'evil' for its own sake, made sense to men of influence in the showplace of capitalism. The prescriptions, of necessity compressed and hastily composed, touched raw nerves in several government departments, including some which featured in spectacular corruption exposés a few years later. Friendly correspondents, however, indicated that the combination of generally favourable press publicity and the quietly political activities of those sponsors who had been impressed with the report (Whisson 1965), moderated official opinion and contributed to the application of substantially more resources to tackling some aspects of the problem, and to greater co-operation between the various governmental and welfare agencies involved: 'Your efforts in Hong Kong raised some screams. One morning I received a very guarded phone call from somewhere in the Legal Department, wanting to know if we had printed your book and if I could tell them where the author was and where they could get copies' (A printer, 21 August 1965). 'I had lunch with Lord Jim [a departmental head] who was unspeakably angry. S [a very senior policeman] . . . felt you had got too much information from "lower levels" and if you had been "in on" higher counsels would have got a more balanced picture . . . In general, we are not talking about "Whisson" in committees, but "doing our homework"' (A sponsor, 9 August 1965). 'Les [a senior official and friend of the sponsor] says that reactions to "Under the Rug" are improving, after the first wave of anger (?) at reading their own bits, many govt. folk are apparently reading the book as a whole, and seeing there may be something in it' (Same sponsor, 28 October 1965).

The sponsor's view was that there were advantages to be gained from having the author of the book several thousand miles away, where he could be castigated for ignorance, immaturity, and any number of excesses, whilst the sponsors got on with the job of using his insights in their politically delicate negotiations. He was able to produce substantiation of that view in the form of resources which were being directed into welfare programmes and into the co-ordination of preventive work. A social worker outside the negotiations saw things differently: 'One of my first reactions, and still a strong one, is what a pity it is you couldn't stay here to defend, drive home and develop further the material in your book' (A Methodist relief official, 11 October 1965). The book was however prescribed for social work courses at the University of Hong Kong.

The experience, and the limited success of the study in the fields of education and welfare, if not in the central area of narcotics control, underlined three important elements which are necessary to even a modest achievement in the applied field. First, appropriate use of the mass media can be effective – politically, it is easier to ignore a brilliant article in *Nature* than a pungent editorial in *The Times*. Second, the personal commitment of individuals with access to the levers of power, even if only at second hand (two members of the sponsoring group were married to very influential officials) or through committees, is essential. In this case the sponsors had also spent a lot of money which had been given for welfare on a research project, expenditure which had to be justified to some extent by what they did with the results. Third, even in an apparently tightly knit colonial executive, made up of men whose backgrounds, working and residential circumstances, friendships and pleasures, would suggest amity and unity against the outside world, made up as it is of inscrutable colonial subjects and generally unwelcome intruders, there are conflicts of interest and personal fiefs which can be used by the well-informed agents of change. 'Divide and rule' is an adage as relevant to those who seek influence as it is to those who would exercise power.

DOMESTIC SERVANTS IN SOUTH AFRICA

In 1969 I initiated a piece of research whose effectiveness was closely related both to my continuing involvement with the results and to the use of various forms of communication of the findings. It stemmed, not from external perceptions of a problem and sponsorship by well-intentioned people outside the major decision making bodies, but from my own experience in the community where I studied, taught and lived.

There had been complaints in the Cape Town press about the behaviour of 'maids' and their 'boyfriends', particularly in the wealthy seaside suburbs. Some attempt had been made to provide social amenities for the domestics against a background of local prejudice and apartheid legislation which made the provision of a social centre almost impossible for 'blacks' in a 'white' area. Advertisements for domestics which specified a wage, ranged from about R20 to R40 per month, with or without food and accommodation, but such details were rarely mentioned (£1 = R1.70). We sought to explore the economics of domestic employment with the intention of improving wages and conditions, as the workers were excluded from all provisions of the Industrial Conciliation Acts, were subject to penal sanctions under the Masters and Servants Act of 1875, and had little bargaining power. Further, as the wages offered in advertisements and preliminary enquiries suggested, there appeared to be no established norms: a worker receiving R20 per month and working six twelve-hour days per week might have her room adjacent to that of a friend who worked forty hours per week for R40 per month in the same block of flats. In each case the employer claimed to be paying 'about the same as everybody else around here'.

The first step was to devise a scale which could claim some 'scientific' backing, and which could be translated simply into most forms of domestic labour 'contract', e.g. whether living in or out, paid by the hour, week or month, with or without meals etc. By using the locally well-known Poverty Datum Line and Effective Minimum Level of income (Batson 1968) – ostensibly objective and scientific measures of the cost of meeting minimal living requirements, which had been used to monitor the level of poverty for about twenty-five years – and a 'normal' situation of a servant supporting herself and two dependants on her income, we constructed a minimum basic wage which amounted to R40.20 for a living-in servant working 44 hours per week, or 27c per hour plus transport costs for those employed on a daily basis. The figures, though honestly calculated (Whisson 1969) had two virtues. First, although it was about double the average being paid in Cape Town at the time (and Cape Town paid better than any of the other major cities in South Africa), it was only marginally higher than the upper level of wages offered in newspaper advertisements (R40) and hence could not readily be dismissed as ridiculously high. Second, because it was not rounded off, it suggested a very precise, 'scientific' calculation, and even before the computer revolution had struck South Africa, there was some popular conflation of numbers, science and truth, which provided such a figure with an aura of authority.

The publication of the argument and recommended scale in the *South African Outlook*, a small Christian journal, had remarkable consequences. At least seven popular publications reprinted the recommendations, usually with the preliminary argument (Whisson and Weil 1971: 49). Letters appeared, lauding or condemning them, and I received a few rude letters and several invitations to speak on the subject at women's meetings. The official national figures for domestic wages showed a rise of 16.3 per cent in the year following publication, compared with a rise of 26 per cent in the previous *five*-year period, and the newspaper from which the advertisements had been monitored showed a rise of 13.8 per cent in the fifteen months following publication (p. 54). Over the next three years, the Anglican and Catholic churches produced their own scales which they recommended to their members; the South African Institute of Race Relations and the South African Council of Churches each initiated long term projects to provide relaxation facilities, training and bargaining assistance to workers, and in 1974 the Masters and Servants Acts were repealed.

It would be preposterous to suggest that all the developments outlined above flowed from the initial article and the more detailed research which followed, but scrutiny of the comprehensive *Review of Race Relations* (Horrell 1964–73) makes it clear that the research did constitute a watershed in public awareness and concern and, as the figures cited above suggest, had positive results. As applied anthropology, the exercise was unlike either of the two previous cases and unlike most of what is described as applied studies in the textbooks. There was no sponsor, no bureaucracy to, or through, whom reports could be made, only a few Rands in research expenses and voluntary labour whose sole reward was co-authorship of the research publication. The results were not published in what would normally pass as a learned journal and they were not directed at any particular group of policy makers. Rather, they were directed initially at people who would describe themselves as liberal and Christian, a somewhat unlikely leaven in the lumpen bourgeoisie of South Africa. However, the exercise bore the hallmarks of authentic applied anthropology. First, it was rooted in theory – the notion that where there are two models of the normal relationship available to the parties to a transaction (in this case the multiplex master–servant and the contractual employer–employee) there is scope for substantial negotiation and manipulation. Second, the data were collected in an orderly manner with the appropriate trappings of statistical and academic authority, which tends to lend compelling, if philosophically spurious, weight to the transformation of that data into normative prescriptions. Third, the data and recommendations were communicated in terms which all readers could both understand and apply, with little room for morally justifiable evasion, e.g. the argument that if one 'cannot afford to pay more' to a servant, one should buy less of her time at a fair rate (Whisson 1969). Fourth, the issue was kept in the public eye long enough to enable the growth of institutions designed to tackle the problems exposed by the research. Fifth, the issue came to be seen as one suitable to be pursued as a doctoral study by a specialist in an allied discipline (Cock 1980). Finally, its distinctive anthropological element was that it presented 'the natives' vision' (both employer and employee) across a cultural divide composed of an amalgam of class, ethnicity, language and fear within the context of the institutionalized relationship.

RESETTLEMENT IN SOUTH AFRICA

Subsequently I have had the opportunity to explore the problems of identifying and articulating the hurts and aspirations of several communities with minimal access to, or influence over, the authorities which decide where they should live, study, work and play (Whisson 1981a; 1982a; 1982b; *et al.* 1983). In most cases the temptation to act as advocate has been irresistible – for this is gratifying, socially acceptable among my peers and students, and consistent with the AAA *Principles*. However, in so far as I can point to any tangible results which have been to the benefit of the subjects of those studies, they have come about as much through unpublicized brokerage as through noisy advocacy.

At Glenmore, a farm bought by the South African government for incorporation into the Ciskei state, some 3,500 people were 'resettled', having been compelled to leave their peri-urban coastal homes as a part of government policy. They were given wooden sheds, clean water, a sewage removal service, a clinic and a primary school, but no means of generating an income from employment or craft work as they had done from their former homes. Information was collected systematically and used to press for attention to be paid to the people's articulated needs – work, food, blankets and pensions. The various hierarchies of officials were identified and the responsible minister solicited by letter and telephone. Voluntary agencies were recruited to provide short term relief and press publicity sought whenever progress on pensions and the proper administration of relief was blocked. The combination of incontrovertible data, understanding of the complex bureaucratic structures, a long term commitment to the area, and a free press proved effective in getting modest results for the specific community, if not for others in similar circumstances.

Conclusions

South Africa is often held up as an exception among states, and the rules that apply in dealings with or within that country inapplicable elsewhere. On that political and moral judgement I lack the comparable data to comment, although I have tried to indicate some of the problems of doing research there which may be compared with problems elsewhere (Whisson 1981b). But interesting parallels can be drawn between the strategies suggested here as being appropriate to applied anthropologists and the approaches adopted by black South Africans in relation to the white government (Whisson 1980). The parallels are not coincidental or particularly forced, but reflect the fact that applied anthropology is ultimately political and usually concerned with the interests of structurally subordinated groups.

Analogous to the advocate role is the approach of those who, to the best of their ability, have no dealings with the white government at all, but who proclaim, in various ways, that radical structural change, probably preceded by revolutionary war, is the only solution to the country's problems of social injustice. At the leadership level they include those who have left the country to organize an armed struggle, some labour organizers and intellectuals who remain in the country. Their organizations and some of their goals vary and conflict in certain respects e.g. in their commitment to violence and in their ideological positions, but their stance is essentially that of uncompromising advocacy. Their perception of what is right for the people is not subject to revision in the light of popular feeling, but a programme to be promoted through education and success in 'the struggle'. In this some clearly go beyond what I have earlier defined as the advocate role, which articulates the aspirations of the client, into the activist role, which attempts to educate the client into having certain aspirations which the activist deems worthy of advocacy.

Analogous to the brokers are many, often competing bodies, whose common element is their determination to make the present system unworkable and so compel change through negotiation. The most dramatic and successful examples of this approach have been *Inkatha*, the Zulu political movement, and the South African Labour Party, both of which have frustrated the grand apartheid plan by capturing institutions set up to implement it. Similar in its philosophy and approach has been part of the labour movement, whose unions have participated in negotiations at all levels without accepting the legitimacy of the existing economic order or the policies of the government. These bodies have been compelled to develop the organization and negotiating skills essential if one is to beat the system at its own game, but the application of those skills is less simple to explain to their potential followers. The justification of their specific actions tends to lie in their delivery of short term rewards or victories, such as an increase in wages or a paralysed council, rather than in terms of ultimate millenarian goals. They are the middlemen, the brokers, widely mistrusted and readily outflanked by the ideologues and advocates, but yet the people through whom peaceful change, if such be possible, may well be mediated.

Analogous to the collaborators and, indeed, generally so described with heavy pejorative gloss, are those who have been prepared to follow the path laid down for them by the government, utilizing the institutions available 'to take what we are given and use it to get what we want' (Whisson 1980: 14). Given a measure of administrative authority, they believe that they can use it to advance the interests of their people as well as their own personal interests, in part by making themselves indispensable to their powerful sponsors.

While these three broad categories, and the factions within them, campaign in their diverse ways for mass support, competing with and denouncing each other, it is easy for all concerned to miss the point that they differ far more about means than they do about most of their ends. Asked for a summary of what they seek to achieve in South Africa, Mandela, Buthelezi and Matanzima, respectively representing the three categories of approach, would probably give broadly similar answers, varying primarily in the relative weight to be given to the state and the private sector in economic activity. Similarly, whether applied anthropologists work outside, through or within the bureaucracies which rule 'their' people, they should be largely at one on their goals – if only because they seek to articulate the needs of their subjects, their prescriptions should be consistent with those of these subjects. This, of course, does not deny the value of the particular knowledge, skills and experience of the anthropologist as scholar in translating needs into prescriptions, and of the anthropologist as politician in ensuring that those prescriptions are filled. It is at the ideological level, where scholars may differ in their beliefs about the way that the world works, that irreconcilable conflicts over prescriptions may occur. But if their prescriptions are opposed to the interests of their subjects in the eyes of their academic colleagues and, more important, in the eyes of their subjects, then they are betraying their trust and the very basis of their professional calling.[4] However, that ultimate test of integrity and competence does not necessarily preclude the broker or collaborator roles – the researcher introduces his own insight and understanding which may not be readily understood by his subjects, just as a doctor or architect endeavours to execute his client's wishes through the often incomprehensible application of his skills.

Each role has its place, and the same scholar can fill all three, if not in the same transaction, then in respect of a single project or people. The right to publish, which should be built into every contract, will ensure that flexibility, even if the 'duty' to publish will be assessed in the light of circumstances. Rigid prescriptions can ensure only a safe retreat from one's critics, they cannot ensure competence, integrity, nor even the benefit of the target group. The genius of anthropology has rested in its ability to transform itself; in its exploration of the boundaries of mankind over time and space, and of the categories used to make sense of his world, and in continually returning to its living sources of inspiration and information. These qualities make the discipline uniquely applicable to the solution of apparently intractable problems in ways rooted in human experience, unfettered by obsessions with ideologies or the ethics of means and ends.

Notes

1. Coertze's orthodoxy no longer commands the respect of all *volkekunde* departments in South Africa. The University of South Africa and Stellenbosch University have long had heterodox elements, and the English summary of the inaugural lecture given by J. C. Kotze of the Randse Afrikaanse Universiteit begins, 'If ethnic units (or "volke") are to be the object of study or the starting point of explanation for everything else in the field of Anthropology nothing, man included, is explained.' (Kotze 1982: 3.)
2. Gulliver's chapter in this volume largely confirms these speculations.
3. One of the promoters was the founder and editor of the ecumenical newspaper *Rock*, whose very title (ostensibly a reference to the trusty leader of the apostles) smacked of Roman theology, degenerate music, and disturbing motion to conservative Protestants.

4. Conviction here is less simple than it may seem. Even in a small community, interests are rarely homogeneous, and a prescription in the interests of all may be impossible. Also, when a theoretical position is elevated into an ideological conviction (as happens most readily in applied exercises), then the perception of the researcher about the ultimate good for the subject community may be at odds with that of most of its members.

References

AAA (AMERICAN ANTHROPOLOGICAL ASSOCIATION) (1970) *Principles of Professional Responsibility*. In *AAA Newsletter* XI (9).

ALINSKY, S. (1972) *Rules for Radicals*. New York: Vintage Books.

ASAD, T. (ed.) (1973) *Anthropology and the Colonial Encounter*. London: Ithaca Press.

BAILEY, F. G. (1969) *Stratagems and Spoils*. Oxford: Blackwell.

— (1979) *Morality and Expediency*. Oxford: Blackwell.

BATSON, E. (1968) *Revision of Estimated Poverty Datum Line Factors (March 1968)*. Mimeographed, University of Cape Town.

COCK, J. (1980) *Maids and Madams*. Johannesburg: Ravan Press.

COERTZE, P. J. (1978) Volkekunde. *South African Journal of Ethnology* 1 (1).

EVANS-PRITCHARD, E. E. (1940) *The Nuer*. Oxford: Oxford University Press.

FOSTER, G. M. (1969) *Applied Anthropology*. Boston: Little Brown.

HORRELL, M. (ed.) (1964–73) *A Survey of Race Relations* (annual). Johannesburg: South African Institute of Race Relations.

JOHNSON, D. (1979) Colonial Policy and Prophets: The Nuer Settlement, 1929–30. *Journal of the Anthropological Society of Oxford* X (1).

KENYATTA, J. (1938) *Facing Mount Kenya*. London: Secker and Warburg.

KING, M. L. (1969) *Strength to Love*. London: Fontana.

KOTZE, J. C. (1982) *Volkekunde en Grense*. Johannesburg: Randse Afrikaanse Universiteit.

KUPER, A. (1973) *Anthropologists and Anthropology*. London: Allen Lane.

MALINOWSKI, B. M. (1922) *Argonauts of the Western Pacific*. London: Routledge and Kegan Paul.

OKOT P'BITEK (1970) *African Religions in Western Scholarship*. Nairobi: East African Literature Bureau.

RADCLIFFE-BROWN, A. R. (1950) *African Systems of Kinship and Marriage*. Oxford: Oxford University Press.

WHISSON, M. G. (1964) *Change and Challenge*. Nairobi: Christian Council of Kenya.

— (1965) *Under the Rug – Drugs in Hong Kong*. Hong Kong: Hong Kong Council of Social Service.

— (1969) Domestic Wages – High Enough? *South African Outlook* July 1969.

— and WEIL, W. M. (1971) *Domestic Servants – A Microcosm of the 'Race Problem'*. Johannesburg: South African Institute of Race Relations.

— and LONSDALE, J. M. (1975) Church and State in Asembo – The Case of Jason Gor. *Africa* 45 (1): 50–66.

— (1980) Port Elizabeth – The Future is Here. *Reality* May 1980. Pietermaritzburg.

— (1981a) Glenmore: A Case Study in Resettlement. In M. Nash and N. Charton (eds) *An Empty Table? Churches and the Ciskei Future*. Johannesburg: South African Council of Churches.

— (1981b) Anthropological Research in Contemporary South Africa. In J. Rex (ed.) *Apartheid and Social Research*. Paris: UNESCO Press.

— (1982a) Glenmore. *South African Outlook* January 1982.

— (1982b) Bathurst. *South African Outlook* August 1982.

— , BEKKER, S. B., FINCHAM, R. J., and MANONA, C. W. (1983) *Tsweletswele: Problems and Prospects for Development in a Peri-urban Closer Settlement in Ciskei.* Development Studies Working Paper 13. Grahamstown: Institute of Social and Economic Research, Rhodes University.

WILSON, M. (1972) *The Interpreters* (The Third Dugmore Memorial Lecture). Grahamstown: The 1820 Settlers' National Monument Foundation.

Robert Layton

9 Anthropology and the Australian Aboriginal Land Rights Act in Northern Australia

Until 1976, Aboriginal traditional title to land was not recognized in Australian law (Rowley 1970: 12ff). In 1976 the Federal Government enacted the Aboriginal Land Rights (Northern Territory) Act which included a definition of land ownership according to Aboriginal tradition. This chapter will illustrate how the application of the Act in particular Aboriginal claims to land has required anthropologists to make practical use of their expertise, with both positive and negative consequences.

The Act was precipitated by the realization that the former policy of assimilation had not worked. Reserves had not become temporary refuges to shelter Aborigines while they prepared to enter the European community. On the contrary, families were leaving the larger settlements created by governments and missions and establishing small 'outstations' on their traditional territories. Until the late 1960s, white economic interest in the Northern Territory was dictated almost entirely by the suitability of land for cattle, but a shift to mineral exploitation had turned attention to different parts of the area.

Two specific events triggered the passing of the Act. One was a strike in 1966 by Gurindji workers on Wave Hill, a cattle station belonging to the international company Vesteys. The strike was for better wages, but the Gurindji set up camp at Waddy Creek on their traditional territory, where they established an independent cattle station without legal security of tenure. The second event was a court action in 1968, brought by Yolngu (Murngin) clans in north-east Arnhem Land against an aluminium company mining their traditional territory. The form of their claim had a direct effect on the subsequent wording of the Land Rights Act.

The case was based on what Keen (1984) described as an orthodox model of totemic society: a timeless interpretation in which patrilineal descent groups each possess an exclusive relationship with a single animal or plant totem and its representation in totemic emblems. Each group holds a territory and its sacred sites through a charter presented by the totemic ancestors, said to confer exclusive foraging rights in the territory. The Gove plaintiffs claimed that their predecessors laid claim to the same land in 1788, and that no surrender or purchase of these rights had since taken place (Blackburn 1971: 58). Since these rights were said to be vested in clans in the form of a 'communal native title', it was an important part of the plaintiffs' case that the same clans had held the same areas of land in 1788. There was, however, considerable evidence that such groups sometimes died out. It was also suggested that the present distribution of sites owned by particular clans could partly be accounted for by displacement of groups through warfare (p. 46). Professors Stanner and Berndt, who gave evidence on behalf of the Aboriginal plaintiffs, could only argue that it was more likely the Rirrarjingu and Gumatj had held the same territories in 1788 than that they had not. Mr Justice Blackburn, hearing the case, found this unconvincing. It was put to Professor Berndt that change in the ownership of particular areas was not inconsistent with a continuing structure and form of social organization, but Berndt replied that there was not much evidence to answer this (p. 54). There was substantial evidence that although access to sacred sites was restricted clans did not exclude others from foraging on their land. In his judgement against the plaintiffs, Blackburn conceded that they possessed a subtle and elaborate legal system which provided a stable order of society (pp. 126–27) but held that this system did not embody proprietary rights. In reaching this decision he recognized three aspects of proprietary right, the right to use and enjoy, the right to exclude others – which the plaintiffs had claimed only with respect to sacred sites, not land in general – and the right to alienate; a right deliberately repudiated by the plaintiffs (p. 132). Thus he held Australian law did not recognize traditional Aboriginal communal title to land.

The orthodox model of totemic society had already been challenged by Hiatt, in 1962, who questioned whether patrilineal descent groups in Aboriginal Australia either formed exclusive foraging units or possessed clearly bounded territories. Stanner replied in a paper published in 1965. He wrote that Radcliffe-Brown's contention, that membership of Aboriginal land-owning groups was exclusively determined by patrilineal descent, was 'about as well-established as any general proposition can be'. There was usually no means for a person to leave his father's clan and be adopted into another. But Stanner accepted the need to distinguish land-owning units, holding *estates*, from the bands their members formed for the purpose of foraging over a wider area, the group's *range* (Stanner 1965: 2).

Following the failure of the Gove case, the Labour Federal government made Woodward, the lawyer who represented the Aboriginal plaintiffs, Aboriginal Land Commissioner, and instructed him to draw up a Bill which would recognize Aboriginal land rights. Woodward was assisted by Nicolas Peterson, whose Ph.D. analysed Aboriginal land use and land tenure in north-east Arnhem Land. Woodward visited Aboriginal communities throughout the Northern Territory, and described his findings in two reports (Woodward 1973, 1974). However, the Act, when formulated, retained an orthodox concept of clan totemism. In his first report Woodward recognized that because clans are of limited size (typically 50–250 people) they can die out, and their spiritual responsibilities be assumed by a closely related clan. He interpreted this, however, through a concept taken from Warner (1958), the authority on north-east Arnhem Land: 'this taking over should be seen as a form of trusteeship rather than a transfer of rights' (Woodward, 1973: para. 46). Only patrilineal descent confers legitimate title.

The Land Rights Act defined Aboriginal land ownership in the following terms:

> 'traditional Aboriginal owners', in relation to land, means a local descent group of Aboriginals who
> (a) have common spiritual affiliations to a site on the land, being affiliations that place the group under a primary spiritual responsibility for that site and for the land; and
> (b) are entitled by Aboriginal tradition to forage as of right over that land.

The Act gave title to existing reserves to their traditional Aboriginal owners, and defined the terms under which mining companies can operate on Aboriginal land.

The Act also made it possible for Aboriginal groups to claim those parts of their traditional territory that lie on vacant crown land; that is to say land over which no-one holds a pastoral, commercial or mining lease, and which is not included in a town boundary or set aside for a public purpose. It also allows claims on leaseholds held by or on behalf of Aboriginal people. Three land councils were set up to administer Aboriginal land and make claims to vacant crown land on behalf of those groups whose traditional land it was. The Act allows opposing interests to claim that the detriment they would suffer from a successful claim outweighs the benefit to the claimants. Mining companies, pastoralists and the Territory government have frequently challenged the claimants' case at claim hearings.

Each claim is heard before an Aboriginal Land Commissioner, who reports his findings to the Federal government. The Commissioner's report provides the basis for granting or withholding a claim.

The Act gives successful claimants freehold title with very restricted rights of alienation. Clearly, it was a milestone in Aboriginal–white relations. The Act was applied in the Northern Territory only because the Federal government was directly responsible for administering the Territory. The Federal government's enlightened attitude differs markedly from that of the Territory government since self-administration, and that of Liberal state governments in Queensland and Western Australia (see Peterson 1981), presumably because these governments are less in the international eye and perceive their own financial interests to be more directly in conflict with Aboriginal rights.

From an Aboriginal point of view the Act presents several difficulties. To obtain legal title, claimants must submit to a procedure defined by whites and administered effectively by white lawyers and anthropologists. The wording of the Act at best crystallizes, and at worst fossilizes unwritten Aboriginal tradition in legal terms. By attempting to match tradition to the Act's terms Aboriginal traditional law is inevitably transformed. The strict criteria for defining traditional ownership were probably essential to the passing of the Bill in parliament: it had to be seen to discriminate between genuine and opportunist claims, and to favour traditionally oriented groups who wanted the land for traditional reasons. This may be why the issue of succession was ignored.

The essential problem with the Act's definition of traditional ownership is that it does not allow for social process. Yet process is intrinsic to the demographic and political dynamics of traditional Aboriginal society (Keen 1984: 24), and has been accentuated by the massacres, epidemics and migrations in search of employment which resulted from white contact in the Territory a hundred years ago, and whose effects are recorded in contemporary territorial allegiances. While the location of linguistically defined tribal units and even their component estates has probably been fairly stable over the last hundred years, it is often remembered that particular clans have died out, or that individuals' fathers married and settled in an area after migrating to find work on cattle stations. Generally speaking, anthropologists have tried to broaden the interpretation of the Act to take these processes into account while objectors have argued for the narrowest possible definition.

The Role of the Anthropologist in Land Claims

In every land claim, the claimants' case has been researched by an anthropologist who, with advice from the claimants' lawyer, has compiled a 'claim book' in which he or she summarizes the case for traditional ownership which it is intended to put in court. The claim book is a published document available to all parties and to the public. At the hearing the anthropologist appears as an expert witness, and is subjected to cross-examination both by counsel for objectors and by counsel assisting the Commissioner. The Aboriginal claimants also appear as witnesses, giving evidence as groups. They too are subjected to cross-examination, so the anthropologist's findings are meticulously scrutinized. The Commissioner is advised by a second anthropologist who provides an independent assessment of the claimants' case. In some hearings the Northern Territory government has also employed an anthropologist.

As a witness, the anthropologist must both report data and analyse them. The latter is more important. Mr Justice Toohey argued in his first report on a land claim that it is only by ordering his material in the light of general anthropological propositions that the anthropologist can avoid the charge of merely relaying hearsay evidence (Toohey 1979a: II). To illustrate the difficulties created, this paper will focus on the issue of interpreting social process, and the translation of process into structure.

Hiatt, in a recent paper, draws attention to the fact that it is exactly this question which has been central to anthropological research in Australia during the last decade (Hiatt 1984). As a general issue in anthropology, the emphasis on process rather than structure has been present since the early 1950s. It is exemplified in the writing of Lévi-Strauss (1945, 1952), Fortes (1949), Evans-Pritchard (1950) and Firth (1954, 1955). In Australia it received considerable impetus from the work of Von Sturmer, Chase and Sutton in Northern Queensland (see Hiatt 1984: 15–19); three writers who also developed careful techniques for mapping the distribution of sacred sites and territorial boundaries. An important contribution was made by Barker (1976) who reviewed the evidence for non-patrilineal modes of accession to membership of the groups responsible for sacred sites. He revealed far more flexibility than had been suspected by Radcliffe-Brown or Stanner.

Positive Aspects

The effect of the Act's stringent criteria for determining Aboriginal land ownership on anthropology in the Northern Territory has been similar to the effect of two world wars on aircraft design. Virtually every available anthropologist working in the Territory has been required to spend months investigating land tenure for a particular claim, mapping estate boundaries, locating sacred sites and documenting their spiritual significance; determining the allocation of spiritual responsibilities and compiling genealogies for all the claimants. This programme was co-ordinated by the Australian Institute of Aboriginal Studies (Ucko 1983: 16). The result has been a rapid, and considerable increase in knowledge about Aboriginal land ownership in the area of the fifteen claims so far heard.

As Stanner suggested (1965), the nature of land tenure changes as one moves from the desert interior of the Northern Territory to the rich tropical woodland near the coast. There is less flexibility in the composition of the land-owning group and greater precision in the definition of suitable marriage partners. There is greater clarity in labelling the land-owning group and greater precision in the definition of its estate.

Through much of the Northern Territory, responsibility for sacred sites and their spiritual traditions is shared between those who have inherited membership of the local descent group from their fathers (the *miniringgi* or *kirda*) and their sisters' sons (the *djunggaiyi* or *kurtingurla*). Thus, from the point of view of any individual, he has responsibilities in two descent groups: his father's (as miniringgi) and his mother's (as djunggaiyi).

A typical pattern is represented by the Alawa data collected for the Cox River land claim (Layton 1980; Bern and Layton 1984). There is no centralized leadership. Rather, the society is divided into a number of overlapping, but corporate descent groups, each of which is spiritually responsible for the sacred sites on a bloc of land which may be termed its estate. However, any Alawa can hunt or gather on any Alawa estate.

In the creation period heroic beings who were at the same time human and animal laid down the laws of social behaviour and left their mark on the landscape. These marks are now the sacred sites. The totemic beings also created songs and rituals which are performed today to commemorate their actions.

In ceremony the miniringgi wear body decoration and perform dances commemorating the heroes who created sacred sites in their father's estate. Miniringgi cannot visit particularly sacred sites in their father's estate because of the spiritual danger to them, but if sacred sites are damaged they must pay a fine to the djunggaiyi. The djunggaiyi prepare the dance ground and decorate the miniringgi. Miniringgi cannot hold a ceremony without the participation of djunggaiyi, and yet ceremonies must be held to preserve the ancestral order. Djunggaiyi must visit sacred sites to clean them of vegetation, restore stone arrangements and check for damage. When the miniringgi are being painted, the sisters' sons of the djunggaiyi, the *dalnyin*, oversee their work to make sure each design is correct. To paint someone else's design would be to claim 'another man's land and his life'.

In general, Aboriginal societies of the Northern Territory have both a continuity (descent) principle, and a contingency principle for group membership. Among the Alawa the contingency principle is that of conception filiation. Any child conceived outside the father's estate can become miniringgi to the estate on which he or she was conceived, if the djunggaiyi consent. Further, estates are allocated to semi-moieties, and someone who is djunggaiyi to an estate of a particular semi-moiety can play the role towards other estates in that semi-moiety in the absence of djunggaiyi with a genealogical connection.

Variation on this pattern may be very briefly summarized as follows (see *Figure 2*). Much of the information derives from claim hearings. *Area 1* is the most arid inhabited zone and here flexibility of group membership is at a maximum. Local descent groups are unnamed and recruited by ambilineal descent: membership is validated by residence and ritual incorporation. Estates do not have clear boundaries. There are no prescriptions for cross-cousin marriage. *Area 2* is the western Aranda system described by Strehlow (1965, 1970). The local descent group is unnamed, and made up of those conceived on the estate and their patrilineal heirs. The role of kurtingurla is not conferred by matrifiliation, but by the decision of group members. Estate boundaries are demarcated by the points at which ancestral dreaming tracks leave the estate ('hand-over points'). There is the prescriptive classificatory

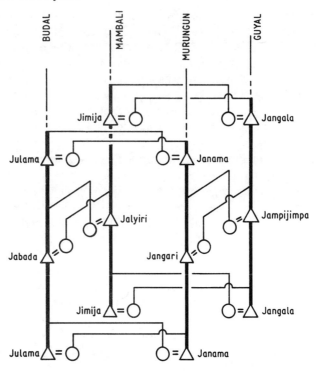

Figure 9.1   Structure of eight subsection/semi-moiety systems from the perspective of patrilines (Mudbura subsection terms, Mara semi-moiety terms)

Within a linguistically defined unit, e.g. Alawa or Warlpiri, there will be several local descent groups affiliated with each semi-moiety or subsection pair. A group holding a Budal estate will have its miniringgi in Budal, its djunggaiyi in Mambali and Murungun, its dalnyin in Guyal. A group holding a Julama-Jabada estate will have its kirda in Julama-Jabada, its kurtingurla in Jimija and Jangari.

second cross-cousin marriage associated with the 'Aranda' system of eight subsections (Radcliffe-Brown 1930). *Area 3* possesses named patrilines, to which the kurtingurla role is played by sisters' sons. The status of kirda can also be gained through conception. Estates have continuous boundaries and 'hand-over points'. *Area 4*, which lies beyond the well-watered ranges occupied by the Aranda, has unnamed descent groups of the same structure as Areas 3 and 5. Sisters' sons are kurtingurla. Conception filiation is recognized. Estate boundaries are marked only by intermittent 'hand-over points'. Estates tend to correspond to sections of Dreaming tracks (Toohey 1980b: 8; 1980c: 11). There is an Aranda eight-subsection system. *Area 5* includes the Alawa. The four subsection pairs which characterize the Aranda system are named: these are the semi-moieties. Estates are bounded by watersheds and,

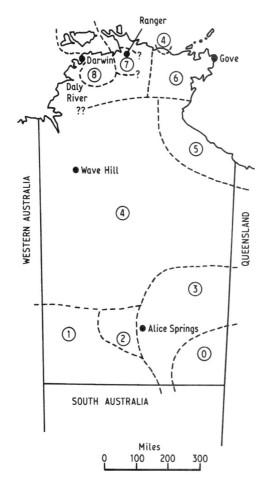

Figure 9.2   Variation in Aboriginal land tenure systems in the Northern Territory

---

(8) *Tiwi, Kungarakany, Limilngun* (Finniss River, Alligator Rivers Stage II claims)
(7) *Kakadju etc.* (Ranger Enquiry, Alligator Rivers Stage II claim)
(6) *Yolngu or Murngin* (Gove case)
(5) *Mara, Alawa etc.:* 'Gulf Country' (Borroloola, Limmen Bight, Cox River claims)
(4) *Warlpiri, Mudbura etc.* (Warlpiri, Willowra, Montejinni, Mt Allan, Daguragu claims) (Gidjingali on Arnhem Land coast are similar. See references in Keen, 1983 and Hiatt, 1962)
(3) *S. and E. Aranda, Alyawarra* (Alyawarra, Utopia claims)
(2) *W., N. and Central Aranda* (no claims)
(1) *Pitjantjatjara etc.:* 'Western Desert' (Uluru claim)
(0) *Simpson Desert* Uninhabited

on rivers, by 'hand-over points'. *Area 6* is that of Warner's Murngin (see Keen 1983). There are named patrilineal clans. All children are conceived at sites on their father's estate. Estates have continuous boundaries. There is prescriptive matrilateral cross-cousin marriage. People still have important ritual links with their mother's and mother's mother's clans (Morphy 1978). *Area 7* has named patrilineal descent groups and continuous estate boundaries. There is no section or subsection system. In *Area 8* the linguistic group is not subdivided into clans. Estates have continuous boundaries. There is a preference for language-group endogamy and no section or subsection system.

Thus, knowledge about regular shifts in the pattern of Aboriginal land tenure across the Northern Territory has been greatly increased by research carried out for land claims. At the same time, the complexity of Aboriginal rights in land has given rise to differences of opinion as to how the Act should best be applied. By reviewing a number of land claims, it is possible to show how the consultant anthropologists have brought their alternative theories of social process to the analysis of the evidence. This has sometimes created problems both for claimants and for anthropology as a scientific discipline.

Interpretation of Principles of Traditional Ownership

Under the Act, only 'traditional owners' can give or refuse permission for mining or any other use or occupation of Aboriginal land. Because their names are entered in a register, identifying traditional owners is also a crucial point in the shift from a non-literate to a bureaucratic system of land tenure (see Maddock n.d. and McLaughlin 1980).

The Ranger Enquiry

The first application of the Northern Territory Land Rights Act was made in the area of the proposed Kakadu National Park. The Ranger Enquiry was established to investigate the potential effects on the environment of proposed uranium mining in the area, portions of which were vacant Crown land. Because the Land Rights Act was about to be passed, the Commissioners decided to include within these terms of reference an investigation of Aboriginal land use and land ownership (Fox, Kelleher, and Kerr 1977: 5–6).

The Enquiry found that there were Aboriginal clans owning estates in the region. Thirteen clans had estates all or partly on vacant Crown land. The clans were individually named, patrilineal, and known collectively as *gunmugugur*. Each was a religious unit, holding several sites of spiritual significance, associated with spirit beings or Dreamtime heroes.

Subsequent research by Ian Keen, for the adjacent Alligator Rivers Stage 2 land claim, revealed that gunmugugur are in fact larger units which cut across linguistic boundaries. Although the Ranger Enquiry correctly identified the landowning groups, these should more accurately have been described as the members of a given gunmugugur speaking a particular language.

The question of where, and how, to delimit the group corresponding to the Act's definition of traditional owners has been a recurrent one.

In the Ranger area several clans had died out during living memory, and their estates were now in the hands of adjacent groups. Peterson, Keen, and Sansom prepared a joint paper submitted to the Enquiry, in which they argued that on the extinction of a clan 'there are rules on the basis of which legitimate succession to the estates is justified' (Peterson, Keen, and Sansom, 1977: 1). Succession 'entails the pressing of rightful claims on principles that are locally recognized' (p. 3): conception or birth on the extinct group's estate, kinship links through the mother or mother's mother, or shared ceremony based on a common ancestral Dreaming track.

In his evidence to the Ranger Enquiry, Peterson emphasized that succession was not a 'cut and dried' procedure, and required discussion and time to complete (transcript, pp. 13, 118), but under cross-examination by counsel for a uranium mining company, he criticized Warner's accounts of 'trusteeship' on the extinction of a clan (pp. 13, 139; 13, 142–46) as speculative. The cross-examining lawyer made the valid point that some of Peterson's cases concerned the incorporation of outsiders into depleted, but not extinct clans, identifying a process which could eliminate the need for subsequent succession. Nonetheless, the Ranger Enquiry accepted that title to an estate could be transferred by means other than patrilineal descent, and recognized four claims by groups within the Ranger area to have succeeded to estates (Fox, Kelleher, and Kerr 1977: 257–70). This was an important decision, because it acknowledged Aboriginal land tenure to be a living system, a concept which dismayed those white people whose ideology held that Aborigines are a dying race. In his evidence to the Ranger Enquiry the majority leader of the Northern Territory Assembly went so far as to assert that recognizing Aboriginal succession 'could have disastrous consequences for law and order in the Northern Territory' (Fox, Kelleher, and Kerr 1977: 260).

Borroloola

The first claim to vacant Crown land heard before an appointed Aboriginal Land Commissioner (Mr Justice Toohey) came from Area 5, the region where semi-moieties operate. This was the Borroloola claim. In his claim book the anthropologist Avery pointed out that, contrary to the system described at Ranger, around Borroloola, there is neither a generic term, nor proper names for landowning groups (Avery and McLaughlin 1977: 26). The Commissioner accepted that the Act defines traditional ownership in terms of descent, and of spiritual relationships; the group holding primary responsibility for a site does not need to be named providing its lineage structure and spiritual responsibilities can be identified (Toohey 1979a: 8).

The position in the Gulf region is complicated by the association of people and estates with semi-moieties. Semi-moieties define real or classificatory relationships of descent and affinity between people in different categories (Avery and McLaughlin 1977: 29, 36). Within any linguistically defined tribe there are several clans belonging to the same semi-moiety. In some senses, however, all members of a semi-moiety do share responsibilities. The obligation to avoid sacred sites affects miniringgi beyond their own clan estate and djunggaiyi of different clans can 'stand in' for one another.

Marie Reay, the anthropologist advising the Aboriginal Land Commissioner in the Borroloola case, argued that among the speakers of a particular language, all members of a semi-moiety could be said to constitute a local descent group according to the terms of the Act (Exhibit 80, p. 10, cited in Toohey 1979a: 20). Avery, however, had pointed out that the patriline associated with each bloc of land possessed a number of unique attributes: a special design to carry on their bodies in ritual, special dances and songs, and a stock of personal names (Avery and McLaughlin 1977: 33–34). It was this smaller group which Toohey accepted as the local descent group, a principle followed in almost all later claims: Toohey, 1979b: 8; Toohey, 1980a: 2–4; Toohey, 1980b: 4; Toohey, 1980c: 13).

The Uluru Claim

The Uluru claim was made over land in Area 1, the area where estates and local descent groups are most indeterminate. It is relatively easy to identify the core, or 'heartland' (Stanner 1965) of estates in this region, because they are named after a conspicuous natural feature near the estate's base camp, but many peripheral sites are shared by adjacent estates. I discovered, moreover, while carrying out research for the claim that a significant proportion of people had not inherited membership of their father's estate. Rather, the following picture emerged:

Estate membership inherited from	father:	69%
	mother:	20%
	parent's sibling:	8%
	grandparent not via parent:	3%
	(total sample: 114 cases):	100%

There was considerable discussion at the Central Land Council before it was decided to proceed with a presentation of the case on the basis of ambilineal descent, but it is clear that had we not done so, almost a third of the claimants would have been excluded from recognition as traditional owners.

During the hearing there proved to be no difficulty in eliciting Aboriginal evidence for non-patrilineal descent, but the picture turned out to be more complex than I had described in my evidence (see Layton 1983). In some later claims the anthropologist's evidence has been withheld until the Aboriginal evidence is complete, so that any complications brought out under the spotlight of court appearance can be analysed.

A further difficulty in the Aboriginal evidence at Uluru arose from my failure to appreciate how crucial, where criteria of descent are relatively indeterminate, would be the issue of identifying primary spiritual responsibilities. The fact that neighbouring groups along a single ancestral track share much of the spiritual responsibility for perpetuating its traditions led me to identify a single criterion for primacy: which men lead the singing of the verses associated with each site. During visits to sites there was thus intense interest among lawyers and the Commissioner to determine who exactly was playing the leading role. Unfortunately I had overlooked not only the fact that uninitiated children cannot join in these songs and might therefore be excluded, on judicial grounds, from membership of the group (transcript, p. 261), but also that the senior man in the estate central to the claim had recently died. Because his adult sons were not confident in leading the singing, his role was taken over by an older man from an adjacent estate. Thus, while the Borroloola claim showed that the group's rights and duties were vital to establishing its identity as a local descent group, it would be misleading to consider the group constituted in action as the local descent group, without reference to the jural procedures motivating behaviour. Eventually we broadened the definition of primary spiritual responsibility by citing other indices (transcript, pp. 990–1) and, happily, the Commissioner accepted that ambilineal descent was indeed the local mode of recruitment to the local descent group. This had a bearing on several later claims.

The Utopia and Willowra Claims

Kenneth Maddock based his Ph.D. on fieldwork at Beswick Creek with cultures having the institution of miniringgi and djunggaiyi. In an unpublished but widely circulated paper written soon after the Land Rights Act was passed he drew attention to the privileged legal position of those identified as traditional owners, and argued that the Act's definition of 'traditional ownership' was so narrow as to risk excluding some of those whom Aboriginal people would regard as members of the landowning group. Among the problems he singled out was that of miniringgi and djunggaiyi (kirda and kurtingurla), arguing that because only djunggaiyi could visit especially sacred sites, and because only they could authorize ceremonies celebrating the spiritual aspects of sites on the estate, they might well be considered (albeit unreasonably) to hold primary spiritual responsibility to the exclusion of miniringgi (Maddock n.d.: 13–14). In a later, published paper, he deplored the fact that neither djunggaiyi in the Borroloola claim, nor kurtingurla in the Warlpiri claim, had been included as traditional owners (Maddock 1979: 19).

In fact the case was simplified in early land claims (Borroloola, Warlpiri and Alyawarra) by putting the contrary position: that only the miniringgi held primary spiritual responsibility. The djunggaiyi were said simply to be their ritual assistants. This was probably the result, in part, of the belief that Aboriginal land-holding groups must be patrilineal, in part due to the Aboriginal English glosses 'owner' and 'manager' sometimes used to characterize miniringgi and djunggaiyi.

The Uluru claim was heard shortly after the Alyawarra claim, the third from the region in which the estate's ritual responsibilities are divided between members of the patriline and their sisters' sons. The Central Land Council was beginning to consider that the importance of their ritual role entitled sisters' sons to legal recognition as traditional owners. The recognition of ambilineal descent by the Commissioner provided support for the idea that the Act could accommodate a descent group containing sisters' sons and it was then put forward in two consecutive claims over pastoral leases which had been purchased on behalf of the resident Aboriginal communities.

In the first, the Utopia claim, the Commissioner was assisted by two anthropologists, Basil Sansom and Diane Bell. Bell's evidence was that the kurtingurla (sisters' sons) played a number of roles: they held knowledge about the estate's sacred traditions; they taught the kirda (members of the patriline), and punished them; cared for and protected the country; supervised strangers entering the estate, and accompanied the kirda to sites; and were custodians of ritual business (Toohey 1980b: 13–14). Kenneth Maddock gave evidence on behalf of the claimants, arguing that their behaviour at sites showed the activities of kirda and kurtingurla to be interlocking: both had some unique roles, and in some spiritual duties they acted together (Toohey 1980b: 19).

Sansom argued the contrary view that only kirda held primary spiritual responsibility, a concept which he saw as a governing one within the Act, and one with the power to exclude (Utopia hearing, Exhibit 65: Toohey 1980b: 19). In Sansom's view the inclusion of kurtingurla required an unwieldy and complex definition of joint and asymmetrical primary spiritual responsibility. His argument had two strands. The first was that the local descent group, as identified by the Commissioner, must be made up of persons who shared a 'single common order' of rights and responsibilities. Not having worked in a region where kirda/miniringgi and kurtingurla/djunggaiyi exist, Sansom referred to his fieldwork around Darwin, where Aboriginal people also talked about 'bosses' and 'helpers'. Only 'bosses' were in danger from the spiritual power inherent in sacred sites, ceremonial objects and performances. Sansom pointed to parallels in Meggitt's classic study of the Warlpiri, where kirda are identified in Aboriginal English as 'bosses' and kurtingurla as 'workers'. Meggitt argued that only kirda identified spiritually with the estate's ancestral heroes. The second strand to Sansom's argument was that the collectivity of kirda and kurtingurla for an estate was not an enduring group. Aboriginal social categories cross-cut one another, allowing groupings to form and dissolve according to context. Kirda and kurtingurla may be 'all the same' for ceremonies, but really they are different. All they share is a common focus for attention. The determination of who play the kurtingurla role to a particular estate depends on the contingencies of marriage in the preceding generation, whereas the identity of the kirda is determined by principled rules:

'The people of Utopia are asking that an emergent grouping that is the product of social process be given primacy over a grouping that is the product of principled rules.'

(Exhibit 65: 15)

It must be said that acceptance of the view that Aboriginal land-owning groups should be based on principles does not necessarily exclude kurt-ingurla. Rules govern the choice of marriage partners and their children's roles. To say this is not so, because one cannot predict the outcome of individual choices, is like saying there are no rules to football because one cannot predict the results of particular matches.

The Commissioner accepted that a local descent group could, in appropri-ate cultures, be composed of both a patriline and their sister's children, all of whom could share spiritual ties to the same land, and that such a unit had been clearly demonstrated by the Aboriginal evidence (Toohey 1980b: 17–18), but he also accepted Sansom's view of primary spiritual responsibility as an exclusive quality. He found that in the Aboriginal evidence there had been no real assertion that kirda and kurtingurla were equally responsible for sites. When asked about their country, Aboriginal witnesses spoke of the estate to which they belonged by patrilineal descent, only mentioning their mother's estate when asked to which country they were kurtingurla. Speaking of the kurtingurla role, Aboriginal witnesses said that they knew the songs and country, and *helped* with the law (Toohey 1980b: 14, 19, my emphasis). For these reasons the Commissioner only accepted kirda as traditional owners.

The outcome of the Willowra case was quite different (Toohey 1980c: 12, 15, 18). David Nash, giving evidence as a linguist, criticized Meggitt's trans-lation of kurtingurla as 'those who may not perform the ritual' (Exhibit 48). Further linguistic evidence was provided by Hale (Exhibit 47). Like Maddock, Hale argued that neither kirda nor kurtingurla can fulfil their spiritual responsibilities without the other's complementary role. He sub-stantiated this with Warlpiri expressions, including two terms meaning 'in unison' or 'jointly responsible', used to describe the relationship between kirda and kurtingurla. Warlpiri, he reported, also speak of both kirda and kurtingurla 'holding' or 'possessing' the land. While the English term 'boss' is sometimes used as a gloss on kirda, where it is opposed to the term 'worker' to refer to kurtingurla, both kirda and kurtingurla are spoken of in Warlpiri as 'boss for the country' (Toohey 1980c: 15).

The Commissioner also found differences from Utopia in the Aboriginal evidence which, he pointed out, derived partly from greater sophistication in the lawyer's questions. If asked, who is *boss* for the country, witnesses would, because of Aboriginal English usage, answer by giving the kirda. When asked for the names of those *responsible* for the country, most answered by giving the names of both kirda and kurtingurla. The Commissioner accepted that both play an essential role in ritual, that the permission of both is needed before strangers enter the country and that in visiting sites, kurtingurla must precede kirda to see if the site has been damaged. Thus, he found, both held a primary spiritual responsibility.

Maddock (1981) discusses the implications of these hearings for anthropologists' involvement in land claims.

Finniss River

The final claim to be considered here is a difficult and controversial one which returns to the question of succession, and raises the issue of whether the Act, when referring to primary spiritual responsibility, was identifying a concept of legitimacy in Aboriginal law, or simply Aboriginal practice.

The Finniss River claim comes from Area 8, but because of the intense disruption of Aboriginal societies by white settlement in the district, it also involved a group which originated from the Daly River, further south.

At the time of white contact, a hundred years ago, the land within the claim area belonged to two language groups, Kungarakany and Warai. By the turn of the century the Kungarakany had been so decimated that all living members of the group now trace descent from one or another of four women, three of whom were married to non-Aboriginal men. Since that low point, however, the group has recovered and the Commissioner recognized 129 Kungarakany as traditional owners of part of the land within the claim. The Warai suffered equally, most of the forty-four successful claimants tracing descent from one woman and her two husbands.

Earlier this century the Warai were forced to leave their traditional territory. They eventually settled at Humpty Doo, in the traditional territory of a neighbouring language group, the Wulna. While the Land Rights Act was still in draft form it was thought that claims based on need as well as traditional ownership would be allowed. At this stage Sansom prepared a report on behalf of the Humpty Doo community. He identified it in terms later developed in his book *The Camp at Wallaby Cross* (1980): it was of mixed tribal origin, and derived its unity partly from the shared work experiences and intermarriages of its members, and partly from the use of a common base camp during the Wet (non-employed) season. Such a unit he termed a Hinterland Aboriginal Community. Only one Wulna survives at Humpty Doo. This man said, in Sansom's words, that he knew 'of no tribal precedent or "law" that would justify the alienation of his traditional rights in a Wulna estate' to the community living on his land, but he had no objection to the *government* giving them rights to that land (Sansom n.d.: 19).

Among the Kungarakany, one surviving family settled at Adelaide River, a traditional Kungarakany–Warai wet season camp in what became the southern end of the claim area. Another family lived, and worked, a tin mine in the northern part of the area included in the land claim. This family was made up of a Kungarakany woman and her brother, the woman's white husband and their five children. On the white man's death in 1918, the government removed his Aboriginal wife and children to Darwin. One son went on to become President of the Federal Committee for the Advancement of Aborigines and Torres Straits Islanders, and another campaigned for Aboriginal rights by establishing an Aboriginal Union in Darwin. In 1960 the oldest surviving son returned from Queensland to Darwin and later secured a mining lease over the old mine site. Since then he, his wife and family have regularly lived there during Dry seasons.

Other tribal groups were also suffering from the impact of white settlement, and Aboriginal people from the Daly were displaced northwards into the region around the claim area.

During the 1920s and 1930s speakers of several Daly River languages were moving seasonally north to the Finniss. By the 1930s, regular camps of Daly River people were established around Batchelor, a European settlement near the centre of the Finniss claim. Two families speaking Maranunggu became associated on a more permanent basis with particular white employers in the Batchelor area. Early in the 1960s a member of one of these white families obtained the lease on a cattle station adjacent to the Wagait Aboriginal Reserve and the west end of the Finniss claim area. Following an argument over conditions of employment, the Aboriginal employees walked off the station to camp on the Wagait Reserve where most remained until the time of the land claim.

In 1969 the group applied for a pastoral lease on part of the Reserve. Following the passing of the Land Rights Act in 1976, one of the younger adults contacted the Commissioner's office to enquire about the grounds for establishing traditional ownership of an area. In the late 1970s there were two inconclusive meetings between Maranunggu, Kungarakany and Warai. After the second meeting the Maranunggu went to Aboriginal Legal Aid in Darwin, 'because' as they said, 'we can't straighten it up in the native way' (transcript, p. 2,066). They obtained a document which purported to renounce ownership of the principal Kungarakany site on the Wagait Reserve. This was taken to Adelaide River, where it was signed by the oldest Kungarakany man. The document did not, however, suggest the man was making this declaration on behalf of anyone else.

Over the period that these Daly people were associated with the area from Batchelor to the Wagait Reserve, names in at least two Daly languages became attached to many local hills and creeks. Dreamings, some having clear connections with Dreamings in the Daly area, were attributed to many sites. The question is, had the Daly people become, in the terms of the Land Rights Act, traditional owners of this country?

When the Finniss River hearings began, the Maranunggu claimed traditional ownership of the western part of the claim area. Although the Kungarakany have several important Dreaming sites on the Wagait Reserve, they had only one on the land claimed by the Maranunggu, whereas the Maranunggu could provide six. The Maranunggu could also claim to forage more regularly over the area.

Nancy Williams and I, who gave evidence on behalf of the Kungarakany and Warai, took the view that traditional ownership was still in the hands of the Kungarakany. Senior members of other Aboriginal groups who gave evidence said (with the exception of one who was living with the Maranunggu) that it was still Kungarakany country and that Maranunggu country lay where Stanner had located it in the 1930s, south of the Daly. We argued that, with the exception of one Maranunggu family who had been adopted by the Warai and lived at Humpty Doo, no recognized traditional mode of succession or incorporation had transferred title to the Maranunggu. It was our opinion that the Land Rights Act was intended to recognize Aboriginal traditional law, and this was apparently accepted by Counsel assisting the Commissioner, who said in his final address that the presence of the Maranunggu near the Finniss 'has not been legitimated' (transcript, p. 3,263).

Peter Sutton, who gave anthropological evidence on behalf of the Maranunggu, took a different view. He presented documentary evidence that a number of Aboriginal groups had in the past forcibly taken over land, although under cross-examination (pp. 2,109–111) he conceded that none of these cases suggested forcible occupation of land was sufficient to confer title. He saw the latter as stemming, over time, from the Aboriginal community forgetting that the occupying group had not always lived there.

Basil Sansom, assisting the Commissioner, accepted Sutton's argument (e.g. pp. 2,747, 2,757), but took it further. He saw politics, not law, as the dominant force in Aboriginal society: 'No clear principles for the final determination of disputed claims to land can be adduced for this would be to put matters of right before matters of politics' (Exhibit 125:10).

Referring to his work in fringe camps, Sansom argued that around Darwin groups were characteristically mixed in composition, mobile and accustomed to using every claim based on kinship, friendship, trade partnership, etc. to establish their presence in an area. In support of this, he submitted the part of his Humpty Doo report which described the formation of Hinterland Communities.

Finally, Daryl Tryon, also assisting the Commissioner, took up Sansom's position and argued that an Aboriginal group is constituted in action: 'that they perform some common act or function, or that they come together for a given purpose' (Exhibit 123: 7).

The Commissioner accepted Tryon's position, not as a basis for identifying local descent groups, but as one for determining whether such groups possessed a common spiritual affiliation or primary spiritual responsibilities (1981a: 62). He found in favour of the Maranggu in the disputed portion of the claim.

Conclusions

Anthropology has played an influential role in the presentation of land claims, but it has been a role with mixed consequences. The fact that the Aboriginal claimants must themselves give evidence means the anthropologist's analysis is tested in a way which, while eminently scientific, is not characteristic of academic research in our field. It obliges one to look very rigorously at data on land tenure, and on one's analysis, to a degree not previously contemplated in Australia. It poses new questions of intrinsic value to anthropology.

Where conflicting interpretations of the data are possible there is a danger that anthropologists will become advocates for particular groups. Nor will those groups merely be Aboriginal ones, for the Northern Territory has already employed a qualified anthropologist and some mining companies would like to do the same. There is, therefore, a danger of anthropologists opposing each other in court and hence potentially damaging the subject's reputation for objective analysis. It is unrealistic not to expect that where the complexity of the situation, or the problems inherent in the translation of culture allow alternative interpretations to be offered, the judicial choice between them may be made to some extent on pragmatic, not academic, grounds.

Notwithstanding these dangers, I believe that, provided 'pure' research is not diminished or compromised, it should in the long run be beneficial to anthropology to use and refine its techniques in such applied fields.

References

AVERY, J. and MCLAUGHLIN, D. (1977) Submission . . . to the Aboriginal Land Commissioner on Behalf of Traditional Aboriginal Owners in the Borroloola Region of the Northern Territory (second edition). Darwin: Northern Land Council.

BARKER, G. (1976) The Ritual Estate and Aboriginal Polity. Mankind 10: 225–39.

BERN, J. and LAYTON, R. (1984) The Local Descent Group and the Division of Labour in the Cox River Land Claim. In L. R. Hiatt (ed.) Aboriginal landowners. Oceania Monograph 27: 67–83.

166   Robert Layton

BLACKBURN, J. (1971) Milirrpum v. Nabalco Pty. Ltd. and the Commonwealth of Australia. *Australian Law Report* (NT Supreme Court) 4–154.
EVANS-PRITCHARD, E. E. (1950) Anthropology and History. *Man*: 118–24.
FIRTH, R. (1954) Social Organization and Social Change. *Journal of the Royal Anthropological Institute* 84: 1–20.
— (1955) Some Principles of Social Organization. *Journal of the Royal Anthropological Institute* 85: 1–18.
FORTES, M. (1949) Time and Social Structure: an Ashanti Case Study. In Fortes, M. (ed.) *Social Structure: Studies Presented to A. R. Radcliffe-Brown*. Oxford: Clarendon Press.
FOX, R. W., KELLEHER, G. G., and KERR, C. B. (1977) *Ranger Uranium Environmental Enquiry: Second Report*. Canberra: Australian Government Printing Service.
HIATT, L. R. (1962) Local Organization among the Australian Aborigines. *Oceania* 32, 267–86.
— (1984) Traditional Land Tenure and Contemporary Land Claims. In L. R. Hiatt (ed.) *Aboriginal landowners*. Sydney: Oceania Monograph 27: 11–23.
— (ed.) (1984) *Aboriginal landowners*. Sydney: Oceania Monograph 27.
HOWIE, R. (1981) Northern Territory. In N. Peterson (ed.), *Aboriginal Land Rights: A Handbook*. Canberra: Australian Institute of Aboriginal Studies.
KEEN, I. (1983) How Some Murngin Men marry Ten Wives. *Man* 17: 620–42.
— (1984) A Question of Interpretation: the Definition of 'Traditional Aboriginal Owners' in the Aboriginal Land Rights (N.T.) Act. In L. R. Hiatt (ed.) *Aboriginal landowners*. Sydney: Oceania Monograph 27: 24–45.
LAYTON, R. (1980) *Cox River (Alawa-Ngandji) Land Claim: Claim Book*. Darwin: Northern Land Council.
— (1983) Pitjantjatjara Processes and the Structure of the Land Rights Act. In N. Peterson and M. Langdon (eds) *Aborigines, Land and Land Rights*. Canberra: Australian Institute of Aboriginal Studies.
LÉVI-STRAUSS, C. (1945) Structural Analysis in Linguistics and Anthropology. Republished in C. Lévi-Strauss (1963) *Structural Anthropology*. New York: Basic Books.
— (1952) Social Structure. Republished in C. Lévi-Strauss *Structural Anthropology*. New York: Basic Books.
MADDOCK, K. (n.d.) Anthropology in the Aboriginal Land Rights Act. Unpublished Paper.
— (1979) Comments on the Aboriginal Land Commissioner's Report in the Warlpiri Land Claim. *Customary Law Group of Australia Newsletter* 3: 16–19.
— (1981) Warlpiri Land Tenure: A Test Case in Legal Anthropology, *Oceania* 52, 85–102.
MCLAUGHLIN, D. (1980) Paper presented at the Aboriginal land rights symposium, Australian Institute of Aboriginal Studies biennial meeting, Canberra, May 1980.
MEGGITT, M. J. (1962) *Desert People*. Chicago: Chicago University Press.
MORPHY, H. (1978) Rights in Paintings and Rights in Women: A Consideration of Some of the Basic Problems posed by the Asymmetry of the 'Murngin system'. *Mankind* 11 (3): 208–19.
PETERSON, N. (ed.) (1981) *Aboriginal Land Rights*: A Handbook. Canberra: Australian Institute of Aboriginal Studies.
—, KEEN, I., and SANSOM, B. (1977) Succession to Land: Primary and Secondary Rights to Aboriginal Estates. Submission to the Ranger Uranium Environmental Enquiry.
— , HAGEN., R., and ROWELL, M. (1978) *A Claim to Areas of Traditional Land by the Warlpiri and Kartangarurru–Kurintji* (third edition). Alice Springs: Central Land Council.

RADCLIFFE-BROWN, A. R. (1930) The Social Organization of Aboriginal Tribes. *Oceania* 1: 34–65; 2: 444–56.

ROWLEY, C. D. (1970) *The Destruction of Aboriginal Society.* Canberra: Australian National University Press.

SANSOM, B. (n.d.) Humpty Doo Land Claim. Unpublished Report.

— (1980) *The Camp at Wallaby Cross.* Canberra: Australian Institute of Aboriginal Studies.

STANNER, W. E. H. (1965) Aboriginal Territorial Organization. *Oceania* 36: 1–26.

STREHLOW, T. G. H. (1965) Culture, Social Structure and Environment in Central Australia. In R. M. Berndt (ed.) *Aboriginal Man in Australia.* Sydney: Angus and Robertson.

— (1970) Geography and the Totemic Landscape in Central Australia. In R. M. Berndt (ed.) *Australian Aboriginal Anthropology.* Perth: University of Western Australia Press.

TOOHEY, J. (1979a) *Borroloola Land Claim: Report by the Aboriginal Land Commissioner.* Canberra: Australian Government Printing Service.

— (1979b) *Land Claim by Warlpiri and Kartangarurru-Kurintji: Report by the Aboriginal Land Commissioner.* Canberra: Australian Government Printing Service.

— (1980a) *Yingawunarri (Old Top Springs) Mudbura Land Claim: Report by the Aboriginal Land Commissioner.* Canberra: Australian Government Printing Service.

— (1980b) *Anmatjirra and Alyawarra Land Claim to Utopia Pastoral Lease: report by the Aboriginal Land Commissioner.* Canberra: Australian Government Printing Service.

— (1980c) *Lander Warlpiri Anmatjirra Land Claim to Willowra Pastoral Lease: Report by the Aboriginal Land Commissioner.* Canberra: Australian Government Printing Service.

— (1981a) *Finniss River Land Claim: Report by the Aboriginal Land Commissioner.* Canberra: Australian Government Printing Service.

— (1981b) *Alligator Rivers Stage II Land Claim: Report by the Aboriginal Land Commissioner.* Canberra: Australian Government Printing Service.

UCKO, P. J. (1983) Australian Academic Archaeology: Aboriginal Transformation of its Aims and Practices. *Australian Archaeology* 16: 11–26.

WARNER, W. L. (1958) *A Black Civilization.* New York: Harper.

WOODWARD, A. E. (1973) *Aboriginal Land Rights Commission: First Report.* Canberra: Parliamentary Paper 138.

— (1974) *Aboriginal Land Rights Commission: Second Report.* Canberra: Parliamentary Paper 69.

Andrew Strathern

10 Research in Papua New Guinea:
cross-currents of conflict

The work of anthropologists in Papua New Guinea has been for some years surrounded by controversy. Opposition to it is strong, particularly among the University-educated élite who hold senior staff positions in government or the public service. Since 1973 I have been closely involved with the issues involved, first as Professor of Anthropology at the University of Papua New Guinea in Port Moresby; second at University College London where I was concerned to ensure that a small group of students should renew the British tradition of fieldwork in Melanesia; and third since 1981 as Director of the Institute of Papua New Guinea Studies, which handles all applications from research workers abroad who wish to conduct projects in this country. I have seen the problem, therefore, over a decade, first as an academic explaining the discipline to classes of students whose senior kinsfolk had been the subjects of earlier research work; second from within the British establishment; and third in the PNG Public Service, where the problems of research are handled on a daily basis. Throughout this ten-year period, and indeed since 1964, I have myself also remained a research worker and teacher committed to the basic values of the discipline of social anthropology, although critical of some aspects of its practice and concerned that its future may be curtailed if certain crucial changes are not affected.

The Institute of PNG Studies maintains an individual file on every known research worker who has visited the country under proper auspices since the mid-1970s. The Institute itself was set up in 1974, just prior to PNG's independence, and its founding Director was Professor Ulli Beier, who had previously spent many years at Ife University in Nigeria. The files are the property of the Ministry of Culture, under which the Institute operates, and information regarding individual cases is not publicly available. In this chapter I shall draw from my working knowledge of these files but it would be improper for me to quote named cases from them, even though these demonstrate exactly the nature of the conflicts in question; they include numbers of letters written by myself to other bodies which have a say in decisions on whether research visas may be granted or refused. The situation here is not very different from the ethical problem of what to do with ethnographic case histories, except that the guidelines are more clear: my 'histories', although in a sense collected by me, do not belong to my field notebooks but to a public service filing system which is subject to bureaucratic rules and procedures. However, as a further check on the files, there is my own 'history', also not extensively recorded in notebooks, but certainly formative of my views and the ways in which I have opposed or concurred with the views of others, whether Papua New Guineans or 'foreigners'.

Accusations

The chief accusations which are made against anthropologists in PNG are:

1. That their work is demeaning to the people, since it is concerned with the category of 'primitive society'. Books written up to the 1950s certainly do give this impression, but anthropology does not need such a categorization.
2. That their work is intimately linked to the colonial order and therefore has no place in the contemporary post-colonial society. This is a misconception based on a half-truth; but it must not be dismissed.
3. That their work is exploitative, designed to secure them degrees and careers rather than assist the people and nation in which their studies are conducted. This is a complex and important issue, central to the whole debate, but the usual formulation of the 'charge' rests on a fallacious zero sum proposition, which must be probed.
4. That their work does not lead to any practical results, because of its academic orientation and because of anthropology's pseudo-scientific claims to objectivity. Again, serious issues are embedded here in a formula which incorrectly argues that there is a radical separation between what is 'academic' and what is 'practical'. One approach is of course to ensure that more obviously practical or 'applied' work is done. But the deeper task is to break down the stubborn and irrational belief of many outsiders that a really detailed knowledge of a people's culture is unnecessary for those who implement programmes for social and economic development.

I will expand on each of these four themes. The first two undoubtedly derive from 'African models' and relate essentially to how the anthropologists of the 1930s and 1940s came to be perceived by the new African élites of the mid-1950s at the time when many African states gained their independence. These were formative years for the middle classes of intellectuals in countries such as Nigeria, Ghana, and Tanzania, and 1960s-trained lecturers and professors have exported their associated experiences and views widely to other universities since then, including to the campus of the University. The standard stereotype of anthropology as the science of colonialism and as the intellectual means whereby colonial domination was achieved is still regularly brought out in public discussions at the UPNG campus and flogged hard by visiting expert sociologists who come to the country from London to offer their wisdom as paid consultants and special guests at seminars. It is hard to avoid the conclusion that this is so much hot air breathed out as a kind of protective device in case the finger might instead be pointed at the speaker: a 'not me, *them*' signal.

More serious argument must recognize that historically anthropology certainly has defined its subject matter as the 'primitive'. Since the 1950s fewer books are written on the 'primitive' and more on 'other cultures', but these cultures do tend to be those outside of, or peripheral in, the spheres of Western industrial capitalism, and the 'primitive' may simply be replaced with the idea of the 'exotic'. Again, this is not all bad, surely. A proper concern with the rights of people to maintain their own ways of living is itself a vital ingredient in any potential fight against the inroads of destructive forms of development, provided that the idea of the 'anthropological zoo' is avoided. Anthropologists have a narrow tight-rope to walk here, as in other spheres, between an unjustified stress on the 'exotic' for its own sake and an equally unworthy capitulation to the values of large scale development. South America (as is shown repeatedly in *Survival International*) is obviously one of the main areas where the problem is felt most sharply. In these cases the anthropologist's *first* duty should always be to the people who have been the focus of study. To return to the accusation itself: is the category of 'primitive' at all necessary to anthropology? I think not, in that anthropology does not have to be *intrinsically* concerned with some hypothetical category of this sort. That does not exclude a legitimate interest in problems of historical evolution of social systems, or a concern, say, with differences between societies with and without literate modes of communication. It is the evaluative (pejorative) dimension of the term 'primitive' which is so unscientific and damaging. It may in fact blind us to the very first principle of a true anthropology: serious respect for other cultures *prior to* any secondary 'judgements' on them.

Here, however, another problem emerges. Even if anthropologists do not call earlier customs 'primitive', present-day Papua New Guineans (often acculturated through mission schooling) may not wish to be reminded of them. It depends: in the Southern Highlands area where I work I now find little difficulty in discussing most aspects of pre-colonial practices although the vast majority of the people are baptized and rather pious Christians. They are even a little concerned now that knowledge of their earlier culture, which was assaulted forcibly from 1960 onwards, may after more than twenty years be in danger of being lost if it is *not* recorded. The anthropologist can only take the situation as it comes, and try to understand, above all, what kind of historical phase the people are undergoing.

These points are relevant to the second (and most well-worn) accusation, regarding anthropology and colonialism. The matter has been well rehearsed in Britain and the USA since the 1970s (see, for example, Asad 1973). What is important to note is that there are at least two levels of debate involved. One is at the level of practice: did/do anthropologists directly assist colonial regimes? Government anthropologists certainly had to do so, as F. E. Williams did in Papua from 1924 to 1943, but these were a small band at best and rapidly became a forgotten relic with the creation of much grander bodies such as the National Planning Office, and the Institute of Applied Social and Economic Research, in independent PNG. More significantly, perhaps, the vast bulk of anthropologists worked as varyingly tolerated temporary outsiders to the dominant colonial cliques in the areas they visited. This was certainly my experience in the 1960s. Mixing with the people was probably regarded as not quite the right thing, even then; and while at headquarters level, the District Officer who kindly gave us the use of his own Land Rover of the reserve pool of labour in the Highlands that might be called on to participate in the Highlands Labour Scheme, no-one at district level ever thought subsequently to press me on this uncomfortable matter. At the local level, the District Officer who kindly gave us the use of his own Land Rover vehicle (plus driver) for a few days, and permitted us to live in a storage shed near to town until we moved further out, made it clear that he wanted us to be as far from the district headquarters as feasible and that he didn't want to hear anything from us while we were in the field. I did not exactly feel, then, that I was at the very hub of the wheel of colonialism at this time. Government Patrol Officers of the day also tended, if anything, to be mildly contemptuous of the young anthropologist's idealistic attempts to understand the people. Through their experience, and their introductory courses at the Australian School of Pacific Administration, given at one time by the Cambridge-trained anthropologist Peter Lawrence, they tended to feel they already knew what there was to know. Perhaps my experience was not typical. In any case, it belonged firmly to pre-independence times. It was just before and just after independence that both Marilyn Strathern and I were called on to play definite practical roles, some ten years after our work had first begun. The kinds of things we were asked about had to do with the administration of justice and plans to set up 'village courts' which would give back to the people some of the judicial and political powers they had lost in the colonial era. We were, therefore, involved in the 'science of de-colonization', if anything. And the knowledge we had gained of how village politics and law operated at times in the past was the key to the role which we were asked to play. Again, the example may not be typical. It does, however, turn upside down the normal form of the accusation regarding anthropology and colonialism. (That there are still many pitfalls can be seen now, in the 1980s, when problems frequently arise with the 'liberal' institutions we devised in the 1970s; but this is a further historical point.)

The second level on which the accusation is sometimes made is a little more firmly based, but like all arguments concerning ideology it is difficult to know how hard it may be pushed. The argument is that the *theory* of anthropology at the time contributed to colonialism by being concerned with social structure and the control of conflict. This concern is especially shown in Radcliffe-Brown's stress on function and harmony in social systems. Change, especially radical change, tends to be left out of the picture. This kind of evaluation of Radcliffe-Brown's work is the stock in trade of introductory courses in social anthropology, and there is little doubt that in some way there was an intellectual link between his theories and the colonial circumstances of his time, but the link is not as simple as is usually maintained at first-year undergraduate level.

There is another problem here. If anthropology really were the intellectual means whereby domination was achieved in the colonial era, why was it not valued much more by colonial administrators? Why were large numbers of anthropologists not regularly incorporated into the structure of the colonial public service? How is it that anthropology managed to outlast and transcend the colonial era? In the case of Papua New Guinea, domination was either achieved long before anthropologists got there to make their studies or else their writings tended to be ignored. Domination was achieved by force, by material inducements, and by religious propaganda, all well in advance of any lessons the Patrol Officers may have learnt from *African Political Systems*.

In fact, the uneasy relationship between Malinowski and Sir Hubert Murray in Papua (on this see West 1968) is mirrored in many other less well-known cases. Glynn Cochrane provides us with an unusual illustration of this point, for he wrote an article from an administrator's viewpoint making this antipathy very clear. Yet Cochrane himself became an anthropologist, and was trained at Oxford (Cochrane 1970).

The deeper issue which underlies the superficial form of the second accusation is contained in the third, that of exploitation. This question is very like the general question of exploitation in social systems at large, indeed it is only a reflected aspect of this wider question. It is a matter of great and legitimate concern to educated Papua New Guineans, who particularly dislike the idea that their people provide the 'raw materials' out of which Ph.Ds are manufactured as commodities, which the refining agents are then able to sell to their advantage. The first point to remember, then, is that this very metaphor derives from the context in which other products are produced in this way, and therefore from the world of development which has been forced on the people. But if we can see this, we can also see beyond it. First, when copper ore is removed from the ground it is removed for ever, and can be sold only once. That is genuine extraction. But because Papua New Guinea needs revenue, such huge schemes as those operated in Bougainville and Ok Tedi are welcomed by the government, while research into the effects of such schemes receives, by comparison, very meagre support. However, when an anthropologist talks to people and learns their stories, they do not lose their knowledge in the same way, nor does he or she gain exclusive rights over it. Nevertheless, to a certain degree the nature of the knowledge does alter at this point: it enters into another sphere of discourse, another culture, and is susceptible to use in ways which the original holder of the knowledge may dislike or object to. What should be done? Ethical rules can be, and have been, drawn up, and these are useful, but there is a certain ineluctability beyond them. The knowledge *is* altered. We have to decide in what ways this is good or bad. In the case of 'salvage anthropology' the matter is fairly simple. The knowledge would otherwise soon be lost. This process of loss is rather far advanced in Papua New Guinea now, and there is a definite and straightforward case for urgent anthropology of this kind. This is also the kind to which national research workers should be encouraged to address themselves. Second, the people have to know the situation and make their comments. These will always be made in the context of perceived reciprocity or the lack of it; another major problem is that genuine, long term reciprocity is something which anthropologists find it hard to keep up. The demands of their career, family, and society see to this. Each practitioner must make a personal struggle in this regard. Conflict between the claims of the field and the claims of career is likely to become acute, and a single formula cannot be laid down. Further, the attitudes of people will vary. In Mount Hagen, my friends recently explained to a visiting team of film-makers, intent on probing the backgrounds of anthropologists, that they thought it was a good thing I had written so many books and articles because these carried their own names outwards, and also brought many visitors back to them. But implicit in the 'success' of this was the fact that I myself have spent time in the field areas practically every year since 1964, and have made myself a longstanding member of the social networks there.

Books and articles are, of course, themselves part of the currency of reciprocity in relation to the educated élites of the countries where research is done. Here again several problems arise. The books may be disliked for giving unflattering or downright critical accounts, or for intruding on privacy. The élite often feel that they should be the ones to write the books, not outsiders. The books may not be written in a language accessible to the mass of the people who were studied. The first two problems have the smack of near-inevitability which I have already mentioned – a situation which can be avoided only by taking careful thought and by avoiding general pontification about what 'a people' are like until one knows them much better than can be achieved in a one-year stint. The third point, however, is one about which a great deal can be, and very little has been, done. Booklets designed for educational use; translations of life stories; songs, or poems with texts; vernacular texts: all the conventional panoply of traditional scholarship can be brought to bear here, but how many anthropologists receive encouragement to do this? Such works do not advance 'theory'. They are treated as professionally secondary. They may be dismissed as 'antiquarianism'. This attitude needs to be combated very vigorously. It is an example of a deeply ingrained professional ethnocentrism from which anthropologists have a duty to shake themselves free, and it inhibits a genuine humanism within our discipline (cf. A. J. Strathern 1982: 28–9).

The problem of reciprocity, then, resolves itself into two points: (1) reciprocity must be long term, and (2) reciprocity must operate at many *different levels* over time. That we do not, or cannot, or will not, attain these ideals is not just regrettable: it poses a considerable danger to the future accessibility of areas for fieldwork. It should therefore be of concern to institutions as well as to individuals.

Another dimension of reciprocity is that of reciprocal accessibility and interest of field areas. To many Papua New Guineans it appears as though their island has some unique attraction for the many foreign scientists who apply to do research there. Does the Western world hold the same attraction for Papua New Guineans as a research area? It is more likely that they, too, wish to work in Papua New Guinea itself, and they are concerned that research topics will be exhausted if foreign workers are permitted endlessly to carve up the ethnographic terrain among themselves.[1] Reciprocity is therefore liable to be replaced by rivalry. The attraction which the outside world does appear to have is in terms of programmes of further study for higher degrees. Perhaps this can lead to a kind of generalized, if not specific, reciprocity.

Finally, here, I must refer to the problem of zero sum thinking. A Ph.D is seen as an absolute gain to the person who obtains it and in that sense somehow an advantage wrested from the people studied. Yet this is not how the matter *has* to be looked at, since a Ph.D rests on a thesis and a thesis can be written so as to be interesting to those who are its subjects. The prevalence of negative zero sum thinking nevertheless must be a pointer to matters which have gone wrong or are wrongly understood. If reciprocity is being maintained on a broad front, such thinking will be reduced. Hageners, as I have noted, think it is an excellent thing that they have books dealing with their life because it makes them well known, but they also want to have a share in the material wealth of those who produce the books. In this, they are simply following their own established cultural ideals. My older friends in this area also point out that through my writings people from elsewhere seem to have gained a good understanding of them, but what about *their* understanding of the outside world? They want to see England, Cambridge, London, and be told about it. In the case of the leader Ongka, who has now appeared in four different films and has his own autobiography published (translated by myself at his behest), this has in fact become a pressing ambition. Unfortunately, at the time the autobiography was published he had an even more pressing desire to purchase a new vehicle, and it was this that I assisted him with at the time, using up money which might otherwise have been set aside for at least a visit to the 'white men's places'.

Quite a different range of objections comes from those who think that anthropology is 'of no practical use'. This fallacy has been disproved many times over, so its roots must be sought. In its most common form it consists of a belief that what engineers, economists, and geographers say is 'practical', but what anthropologists say is esoteric and useless. Here fault lies on both sides. Much of anthropological writing *is* esoteric. This does not mean to say that it is in fact useless, but its potential usefulness to those outside anthropology itself needs to be made clear. On the other hand, most of what economists write is equally esoteric and sometimes wrong as well, and a good deal of 'pure' rather than 'applied' research is done in, say, geography. Why, then, the special hostility towards anthropology? Perhaps this is because anthropology does tend to make rather special claims for itself, as both a generalizing kind of science (whose generalizations are actually rather few) and a unique method for getting at the inside details of ethnographic study (although attention to empirical detail is by no means a special possession of any one of the social sciences). Anthropology, in short, can be irritating: to administrators it may seem 'impractical'; to other scientists it may seem not scientific enough. But there are plenty of examples where its practicality, if not its scientific status, can be demonstrated. In 1981–82, for instance, one province in PNG (Milne Bay) publicly banned anthropologists from abroad from visiting to do further research there, using a mixture of arguments from all four of the categories discussed. The centre of the problem lies in the Trobriand Islands which are within the Milne Bay province. Malinowski became world famous, but the Trobrianders stayed as they were before. (In fact, they too are world famous.) Other research workers followed and became professors as well. They talked and wrote about exchanges of shells and mortuary rituals and art and cosmic ideas and virgin birth. What had it all to do with health, education, political development, and agricultural production? (Probably a great deal, but refer back to my argument on making such connections clear.) The Provincial government laid down its new guidelines that research must be relevant to these administrative aims. Most anthropologists then had no difficulty in making the case that their work *was* relevant, but it was a pity that they had to do so only after the ban and had not succeeded in communicating this earlier. In the event, the Provincial government even hired an established anthropologist to conduct a survey of villagers' views on a proposed large scale agricultural project, and the anthropologist wrote a detailed consultant's report for them (see Young 1981). In another case from the same Province, an anthropologist was able to show convincingly that she could give advice on agriculture because of her unique study of a system of taro growing (see Kahn 1980). In yet another case, a team of workers from the Forschungsstelle für Humanethologie in Seewiesen, West Germany, including a medical anthropologist and two linguists, arrived, and they were able to offer health services, and the eventual production of a dictionary as 'useful' products. The province thus gradually re-opened to research workers, but in each case a definite kind of return had to be offered. In 1983 the Premier reiterated his earlier stand and personally banned further foreign anthropologists from working in Milne Bay. (Provinces do not have the legal power to do this, but in practice their decisions have to be respected.) This example brings me to another major area for discussion. In the past two years it has become clear that in many cases where a crisis regarding research workers has blown up at province level, this has coincided with political problems and often outright conflict between the province and the PNG National government. This coincidence is not, I think, accidental, as the following cases will indicate:

Province and Politics

1. In the case of Milne Bay Province, the 'research workers crisis' coincided with a challenge to the leadership of the Premier by a rival from the Trobriand Islands themselves. In so far as research workers had been allowed in, this was held against the Premier. The Trobriand Council of Chiefs was not consulted officially by the Provincial government authorities regarding the issue, and they objected to such decisions being taken from the provincial as opposed to the islands level. The Premier's rival was none other than Lepani Watson, the Trobriander whose criticisms of Malinowski's account of chiefship were published many years ago in *Man* through a letter from Murray Groves.[2]
2. In another province the Premier is strong, sophisticated, and radical in his approach to social problems. He is also a political science graduate from the UPNG. He has predictably been suspicious of self-seeking research workers, but he did not institute any ban on research until an unsuspecting American anthropologist arrived (with full permission from the province's own administrative secretariat) and became associated with a main rival to the Premier through wishing to work within the rival's electorate. The Premier had not been briefed on this, and when he met the research worker, he ordered her out of the province on the grounds that 'he was not convinced of her study's usefulness' (even though it had to do with the problem of rural–urban migration which certainly is relevant to the question of how to administer the province's growing capital port town). The anthropologist left and permission for her to work in another, neighbouring, province was obtained through myself at the Institute. Many months later, the province set up its own research committee and a co-operative relationship was re-established. As background to the above, 1981–82 was the period immediately preceding PNG's national elections, at which the PANGU party of Mr Michael Somare was returned to power after being ousted in 1977 by a coalition led by Sir Julius Chan and his People's Progress Party. In both cases conflicts within the province reflected also pre-election struggles within the provinces and between their Premiers and national government parliamentarians. In Milne

Bay the Premier was actually ousted by a vote of 'no confidence' in 1982, and replaced by Mr John Tubira. The latter was in turn replaced by Mr Lepani Watson himself. In the second case the Premier is from the pro-Melanesian Alliance, a party with socialist leanings. PANGU is very strong in his province, but he continues to oppose its policies, and to ward off attempts to unseat him by the pro-PANGU bloc in his own Provincial Assembly or Tutumang.[3]

3. In another province the opposition to research workers resulted partly from a split within itself. To the north, a huge copper and gold mine is being developed at a site known as Ok Tedi, specifically at Mount Fubilan (see Jackson 1982). The mine requires a vast capital outlay and promises eventually an equally enormous return. The lives of village peoples all around it have been disrupted, and at the same time all are keen to have a share in the wealth which will flow from it.[4] This is a classic area, therefore, where basic ethnography, salvage anthropology, and social impact studies are obviously needed. Several research workers, from various disciplines, but chiefly anthropology, applied to go there. About this time officials in the provincial headquarters at Daru, far to the south of Ok Tedi, refused to process any more applications for research on the grounds that their own workload was too heavy, that they did not place priority on anthropological investigations, and that results of work were never sent back to the province (this last was untrue; the Milne Bay Premier had made the same claim – indeed, it is a standard and recurring claim, which results from poor filing systems and frequent changes of personnel at provincial offices). However, these grounds were by no means the only reasons involved for this policy switch. The political background was that there was a struggle between the Premier, representing the south, and the Deputy Premier, representing the north. All the 1982 applications were to do work in the north, but at the same time the northern people were trying to split away from the south and form a new province centred on the mine site, much as some years earlier the whole island of Bougainville had attempted to secede from the nation state of Papua New Guinea, and for the same reason: that of securing maximum returns from having the mine in their area. Officials in the south were disgruntled with the north and their refusal to process research applications reflected their feeling that the south was being left out. IPNGS has been able to alleviate this situation by sending its Ethnology Research Officer to do a six-week survey of the Wipi, a previously unstudied people in the southern area, on request from the Provincial Planner. The National Government earlier took over direct responsibility for the administration of the mine area and research applications are therefore channelled through its administrative authority, with copies for information to the officials in Daru. These compromises have eased the situation, and applications are again going through, but obviously there remain awkward possibilities for the future.

4. A further example from a province which has experienced much

development and has a sophisticated and able premier will help to highlight another problem: that of national versus expatriate research workers. This issue was also of concern to the Milne Bay province, and it is legitimately grounded. It will also appear in my fifth and final case. In the present case, an experienced American anthropologist, who has previously worked in Polynesia, wished to do a study on one of the atolls which form a part of this province. The Premier's first response was that the people were upset with a film which had been made about them and didn't want anybody more to come and look at them; his second was that the USA has not been responsive to the aid needs of the Pacific outside its own sphere of domination, so why should its scholars make their names out of studies done in his province? And his third was that according to his assessment the study could be done well enough by young educated people of the island itself. He asked the applicant to explain what special contribution he could make, and the latter replied that he felt his previous research experience would enable him to make such a contribution. The Premier has not to date replied, and it seems very unlikely that research permission will be given. (1985: permission *was* ultimately given and the research done.)

This province has not been hostile to research in general. Indeed, it is highly aware of culture matters, and has in fact financially sponsored the IPNGS to make both music recordings and a very successful film in its territory.[5] The point is that once a certain degree of awareness is reached, a desire by local scholars themselves to make the relevant studies automatically emerges. Anthropologists must learn how to co-operate with that aim, because it is positive: the people are saying, 'We want to be our own anthropologists now.'[6]

One word of caution here. Experience indicates that national researchers are not automatically exempt from problems when they work in their own areas. IPNGS has sponsored a Siuai student, Alex Dawia, to work in the same area where Douglas Oliver worked a generation ago. Alex Dawia found that he was greeted with suspicion; that people thought he was trying to steal clan secrets, and make money out of them. Some thought Oliver had done this; others that only Dawia was doing it. A provincial politician accused him of trying to campaign against him in the elections. Dawia explains that he felt like 'a stranger in my own land' during this affair; but his strength was, of course, that he could not be turned away because he had a basic right to be there (see Dawia 1982).

5. Some research workers from abroad stay for lengthy periods of time and also achieve in some measure a local identity and a 'right to be there' in the eyes of the local people with whom they actually live and pursue their investigations. Such an achievement is contingent on overall reciprocity, as I have explained earlier, and its price is certainly eternal vigilance, to say the least. But this contingent right does not necessarily coincide with policy views, or personality clashes at national and provincial levels. In the final case

history, this is precisely the problem which has arisen for a committed and very able American worker who spent thirty-six months on the actual field-work phase of her Ph.D project. Her problems are (1) that she is disliked by a senior official, who is also a committed and very able practitioner in the provincial government; he feels that her approach is too 'mentalistic'; (2) that she has accused another long term American scholar of plagiarism, and this scholar may be more acceptable in the province than herself; (3) the provincial officials do not seem to be responsive to the fact that her friends in the local area very much want her to come back. This is a serious point. Provincial governments are supposed to consult local people. The fourth case shows a Premier who did so; but in this present case it has not apparently been done. Underlying it is a longstanding opinion of the leading official, expressed many years ago in a paper for the IPNGS, that foreigners should not do too much research, since this will reduce the topics available for Papua New Guineans later (another zero-sum idea, this time partially true). The case is still under negotiation through the IPNGS and other interested research institutions. IPNGS can only act in a low-key manner in this as in other examples; first, because all issues are complicated, and second because it is necessary to defuse rather than set light to the antagonism which can exist between provincial and National government bodies like the IPNGS itself, and the Ministry of Culture which it serves. (1985: after suspension of the Provincial Government, a National Government Administrator gave permission for the research to take place.)

Types of Research

What sorts of research should be done to ensure that our work is genuinely useful to the peoples and nations in which the work is carried out, as well as to our academic discipline? This is itself a large topic, and here I am concerned only to sketch some points in answer to the question:

1. First, there is obviously a need for anthropologists to show that their work *is* relevant to policy concerns of administrators. They may not have given much thought to showing this, perhaps taking it for granted, or feeling that someone else can adapt their work to such ends. Their technical language and the ethnographic detail into which they enter may seem both impenetrable and perhaps impolite to an administrator who is from the area itself. One of the best ways to force anthropologists to do something about all this is precisely for them to be denied further field access until they do so! Perhaps the Milne Bay cases show, then, the way to a positive outcome (cf. Weiner 1982). Anthropologists must be prepared to write in more than one style for more than one kind of readership, and the institutions which sponsor them must recognize this as legitimate and necessary. This applies regardless of the exact

focus of their research and the degree to which it itself is policy orientated or otherwise.

2. There is always room for good policy-directed research, but no room at all should be made for bad research masquerading under a 'policy' or 'problem' banner. Research cannot be made good simply by focusing on a matter seen as 'relevant'. The best type of policy research is that which is backed up solidly by experience in the use of research skills in general and by good basic research data. Anthropologists are in a position to offer research of this kind. They can do effective short-term studies *only if* the long term work has been previously done. The debate on policy research is rather like that about subsistence versus cash-cropping in agriculture. Cash-cropping is praised as modern and is expected to replace subsistence cropping, at least within the terms of modernization theory. But underdevelopment theory shows the catch in this: people can be impoverished rather than enriched over time by such a process. In effect, cash-cropping is subsidized and supported by subsistence agriculture. In the same way, policy studies require to be subsidized by basic studies. An example of how this can be successfully done is provided by the work of Ric Scaglion of Pittsburgh University (Scaglion 1981). He first did a general study of social structure and dispute settlement in the East Sepik Province (Abelam people); this was underpinned by earlier studies in the area done by Kaberry and Forge. Second, he worked for the Law Reform Commission of Papua New Guinea on dispute settlement and the workings of village courts, set up by the government to bridge the gap between indigenous and introduced legal institutions. Third, he is now focusing back on his field area to evaluate the progress over time of village courts there, and the East Sepik provincial government has welcomed this as an example of applied research. My point here is simple, and one I have made before. First do the anthropology, and then apply it. Without the initial study, anything 'applied' is unlikely to stick!

3. The boundary between what is seen as pure or applied, and what does or does not contribute to 'practical' concerns, shifts historically. Thus, almost all of the pure or conventional anthropology done since Europeans came to Papua New Guinea can now be seen as contributing to one definite policy aim as expounded in PNG's Cultural Development Act, first passed in 1974: that of cultural preservation. One of the National Cultural Council's staff, Tony Crawford, was able to re-stimulate a whole art form among the Gogodala people of Western province, destroyed earlier through missionary evangelism, by showing them a set of old photographs taken before the massive burning and abandonment of their artefacts had taken place. The people who took those photographs were certainly doing their own 'pure' research at the time (including themselves making artefact collections for foreign museums which contributed to the Gogodalas' cultural loss at the time, but preserved at least something from the later evangelistic onslaught from the Asia Pacific Christian Mission). In Crawford's hands, however, the photographs became

an 'applied' tool for cultural revival (Crawford 1981).

This does not mean that Papua New Guineans should simply accept all that has been written as a part of their heritage. They may be equally concerned to throw it out or deny it or re-evaluate it, as John Waiko has done in his thesis on the Binandere people of Oro Province (his own area). The point is rather that it is *there*, something to be re-evaluated, a set of clues against which oral traditions can be explored or re-explored to reveal new versions of history or ethnography. The process of criticism and re-evaluation is, after all, normal in anthropology, and it can become very acrimonious, too. It must include the critical comments of nationals, themselves engaged in research work.

Here again, the IPNGS is able to play a role. We sponsor research by young nationals to obtain oral traditions which may run counter to received anthropological accounts of areas previously studied (although we do not specifically suggest this or go looking for it). We publish their writings in two journals, *Oral History* and *Bikamus*. And we are attempting to train our own national staff to an international level of competence so that they can fully participate in all debates which take place. The Institute of Applied Social and Economic Research does exactly the same kind of thing, and on a larger scale than us. An example is its project on alcohol drinking, run by Professor Mac Marshall with two national Research Officers, Francis Sumanop and Antonia Piau-Lynch. This resulted in a volume, *Through a Glass Darkly*, edited by the IASER team, and containing a host of ethnographic studies by anthropologists, coupled with survey results obtained by the team themselves and a set of policy recommendations. This is another example of a good combination of basic and applied research (see Marshall 1982).

As the training of national scholars develops, they are certainly going to add considerably to our stock of insight into Papua New Guinea's cultures. The general point here is that this process is to be welcomed because it means our subject is transmitted and lives again in new hands, most appropriately the hands of those whom we ourselves have studied (see Morauta 1979).

Summary and Recommendations

The first and most lengthy part of this paper consisted of an examination of four leading accusations made against anthropology. These were that it is demeaning to the peoples studied, that it is linked to colonialism, that it is exploitative, and that it has no practical relevance for the peoples of the countries where its fieldwork is done. Without attempting to deny the grains of historical truth in these accusations, I have been concerned to sift them and also to point out how the accusations are themselves partial, outdated, and ideologically motivated. Anthropology does not have to be the monstrous creature depicted in these charges, nor has it always in fact been so. But the accusations are a necessary backdrop to self-reform: this is your image; now change it.

The next part of the paper is an intermezzo. It shows that these accusations are not made in a vacuum. They are, to the contrary, made in definite political contexts, where anthropologists appear often as easy scapegoats for politicians' manoeuvrings or fulminations. Research Institutes *within* Third World countries, such as the one of which I am Director, must learn to live with this and to operate as well as possible despite it. Not all results are negative, as the case histories show.

Finally, I made some points about policy-related research. What is related to policy depends on what policy is, and this changes over time. Basic research may feed into later policy research, and policy research is useless unless it is informed by insights from basic research and by the principles of the discipline as a whole. The recommendations which I draw from all this are as follows:

1. Long term and multiplex reciprocity is the only means to ensure anthropology's good linkage with field areas.
2. To achieve this, institutions need to provide a number of posts from which such reciprocity can be obtained. In my own case, I have experienced the difficulties of achieving this end painfully and at first hand, to the extent of resigning from a professorship in London University in order to remain in touch with the people in Mount Hagen.
3. Anthropologists must write directly for the people and countries they have worked in as well as for academic readers in their home countries. They also in general need to communicate their findings more widely. Film and television can work wonders here.
4. Anthropologists should be prepared to, and seek to, serve in active roles outside university posts, and in the countries where they do their formal research.
5. Every encouragement must be given to the emergence of national scholars/ indigenous anthropologists. 'Encouragement' may include refraining from making a particular study if a national anthropologist wants to do it, but in general 'zero sum' thinking has to be combated.

By way of final summary, the spirit in which these lines have been written is that anthropologists must not beat their breasts, erase their names, or crawl away when faced with accusations of imperialism or exploitation. They must face these and answer them. If they do not, this is tantamount to admitting that their discipline has no right to continue. Anthropology is not a dirty word, but the name of a genuine humanistic discipline, and we must maintain and develop it as such, even if others attempt to destroy and swallow it.

Notes

1. See K. K. Talyaga 1974. The argument of this strongly-worded paper rests heavily on the colonial context in which fieldwork was carried out before 1975. There is also a strong feeling conveyed in it that research workers have insulted the Enga by speaking superficially of them: 'If you want to be precise, then better stay longer in the Enga area, say for six years rather than just six months.'

2. In this case the situation was exacerbated by a complicated incident in which a research worker appeared actually to have violated procedural rules at national government level in proceeding to her field area without permission from either the national or the provincial levels. However, she had in fact obtained a valid 'business' visa, but not one for 'research'. The dividing line between 'business' and 'research' is a fine one, but it is occasionally invoked. At local level she would be identified as visiting for research, regardless of the type of visa used for her entry into the country. But at local level, also, she was able to show her acceptability to the people by attending a meeting held by the chief and receiving his approval.

    The issues in Milne Bay Province run deep. It is the officials of this province who show the most repeated dislike of anthropologists, and it cannot be coincidence that this is also the area where Malinowski worked. This is a bitter legacy indeed for the fieldwork tradition which Malinowski so successfully created in British social anthropology. In April 1983 the Premier wrote to a young applicant from the University of Texas at Austin (where Annette Weiner previously worked), declining to give his permission for her to work on Dobu, and stating that 'our records show that the simple, poor, humble people of this country and indeed this Province have contributed more than enough in educating big-time academics from the States and from the continent . . . Since the days of Malinowski, Fortune and the lot the brains of our simple people have been picked by the western academics.'

    There is a lot of truth in these observations. Only two problems remain with them. First, there is no indication here that the Premier has consulted the actual Dobu people at all. Perhaps as a Trobriand chief he feels that such is unnecessary. Second, the letter repeatedly refers to the province's people as 'simple' and 'humble'. There is more than a slight ring of paternalism about this choice of words. Perhaps if the people were asked, their story would be different. Since then, the Premier has decided to ban all further applications by foreign anthropologists to work in his province.

3. Nevertheless, the co-operative relationship mentioned above has been established during a time when PANGU is actually in power at national government level. Personal meetings with the Premier and his senior officers have contributed to this. His province is one of two (from a total of twenty) which actually gave the IPNGS travel funds to assist this collection of traditional music. The other is the province mentioned below, in the fourth case, this section.

4. This has been some busy re-fashioning of traditional myths in the area, done in order to link as many groups as possible with the mountain which contains the gold and copper deposits (Eytan Bercovitch, personal communication. Mr Bercovitch is doing an intensive study of narrative in this region).

5. There is the feature film *Tukana*, made by Chris Owen. It shows the history of a young man who leaves his village to work in the Bougainville copper mine, his marriage choices between a town and a village girl, the village wife's death by sorcery, and his 'reform' from hard drinking.

6. A further question arises, however: how likely is it that the studies *will* be made? IPNGS has encouraged provinces actually to put resources and personnel where their policy statements indicate these should placed.

References

ASAD T. (ed.) (1973) *Anthropology and the Colonial Encounter*. London: Ithaca Press.

COCHRANE, D. G. (1970) *Anthropologists in the Field: An Administrative View*. *Journal of the Polynesian Society* 79 (3): 349–53.

CRAWFORD, A. L. (1981) *Aida: Life and Ceremony of the Gogodala*. Port Moresby: National Cultural Council, in association with Robert Brown Associates, New South Wales.

DAWIA, A. (1982) Report on Stone Monuments or Sacred Stones (Siwai, North Solomons Province). *Oral History* 10 (3): 86–97.

JACKSON, R. (1982) *Ok Tedi: Pot of Gold*. Port Moresby: Word Publishing Company.

KAHN, M. (1980) Always in Hunger: Food as a Metaphor for Social Identity in Wamira, Papua New Guinea. Ph.D. Thesis, Bryn Mawr, USA.

MARSHALL, M. (ed.) (1982) *Through a Glass Darkly: Beer and Modernization in Papua New Guinea*. Port Moresby: Institute of Applied Social and Economic Research Monograph 18.

MORAUTA, L. (1979) Indigenous Anthropology in Papua New Guinea. *Current Anthropology* 20.

SCAGLION, R. (1981) Samukundi Abelam Conflict Management: Implications for Legal Planning in Papua New Guinea. *Oceania* 52: 28–38.

STRATHERN, A. J. (1982) Fieldwork and Theory in Social Anthropology (Inaugural Lecture, University College, London). Published by the College.

TALYAGA, K. K. (1974) Should we allow Research Workers and Tourists into the Enga Area? Port Moresby: *Institute of PNG Studies Discussion Paper 1*.

WEINER, A. (1982) Ten Years in the Life of an Island. *Bikmaus* 3 (4): 64–75.

WEST, F. (1968) *Sir Hubert Murray of Papua, Australian Proconsul*. Melbourne: Oxford University Press.

YOUNG, M. (1981) Oil Palm for Milne Bay: A Social Feasibility Study. Port Moresby: Institute of Applied Economic and Social Research.

Alan Rew

11 The Organizational Connection:
multi-disciplinary practice and anthropological theory

The Bearing of Practical Advice on Theory

This is a paper written, in the first case, for would-be consultant anthropologists by someone now using social anthropological concepts and methods within the context of a multi-disciplinary consultancy. From time to time, a number of colleagues and students send me their personal details, telling me how much they want to use their anthropology in practical, applied work. One aim of the chapter is to tell them what adjustments they will need to make in order to contribute to practical problem solving in the context of development projects and programmes.

The second aim of the chapter is to argue for an additional, specifically anthropological, perspective on development policy to augment those existing analyses which use a general social science or 'development studies' perspective. An expanded perspective of this kind can be achieved using the full range of social anthropology and need not imply merely the restricted use of a narrow sub-discipline – 'development anthropology', 'applied anthropology', and so on – specially created for the purpose. Nor does the achievement of this larger perspective pose, in my experience, any unusually demanding ethical conflicts for the researcher. But it does demand that the discipline compromise some of its cherished traditions concerning the nature of fieldwork and look a little more intensively (with time honoured methods) at the complete range of actors and ideologies involved in development work and policy making; and that the discipline and its researchers tackle power relations head-on rather than fleeing them in distaste.

For the would-be consultant, the chapter offers a set of axioms designed to focus attention on the process by which anthropological knowledge is actually applied to practical problems. They are rules of thumb which I have evolved on a piecemeal basis to make the form of analysis and report writing I use intelligible to non-anthropologists. So often what may well be an acceptable piece of anthropological work when viewed in academic terms lacks both point and clarity when measured by the very different but usually equally demanding standards of, say, an engineering study.

A certain lack of awareness of, or interest in, the formats used by other technical specialisms no doubt creates impressions such as that reported by Chambers, a specialist in rural development, who has worked with a number of anthropologists. Discussing the use of key informants in the appraisal of rural development programmes, he writes that: 'Some of the most useful are social anthropologists who are in the field. *They often do not know what they know . . .*' (1980: 13, my emphasis).

These questions of technique and presentation for individual advisers and consultants are also firmly related to the creation of a social anthropological approach to public policy on development questions and involve both methodological and theoretical implications.

First, there is both need and opportunity to introduce the anthropologist's concern with intimacy of enquiry into organizations and situations where public policy is formulated and where key factors influencing policy outcomes can be researched. The basic premises of this kind of enquiry, usually known as participant observation, are mutual trust and the definition of the subject matter of the enquiry through an interaction between the theoretically informed scholar and the 'respondents' expressing their ideas and beliefs in their own terms. To undertake this kind of research in policy circles and governmental institutions requires empathy between the scholar and the policy-maker.

It also requires a fieldwork location from which to examine policy formation and implementation at close range. One good vantage point for this kind of observation is the development project or programme, which may be first presented as wholly technical or financial but is also a segment of administrative and policy making action with consequences for both statements and movements concerning institutional power and resources. While there are certainly other approaches to public policy appraisal, the methodological needs of a social anthropological perspective on policy require close camera work, and therefore a focus on definable pieces of policy action and intention. Close observation of projects and programmes as units of policy choice and administrative planning will allow the simultaneous analysis of policy outcomes and policy resources. This offers the best option for an effective social anthropological contribution at both theoretical and practical levels.

Second, there is a theoretical implication. The aim of being effective as an individual adviser, and the aim of developing social anthropological theory concerning public policy both revolve around the central importance of the connection between political and administrative mechanisms on the one hand and communities and individuals on the other. The key to the kind of social anthropology I have in mind, that is, revolves around the idea of 'the organizational connection'. In my advisory work I have found this concept to be full of both practical and theoretical significance. It focuses our attention on the relationship, in the planning and policy process, between the institutions of the 'decision makers' and those of the 'decision takers' (Lipton 1976): to the relationship, that is, between those who make policy and those who receive its outcomes. In order to document, analyse, and illuminate this relationship it is necessary to be able to move backwards and forwards across the connection. To function as both participant and observer in these situations is difficult but presumably within the skills and interests of at least some anthropologists. Effectiveness in the dual role will depend on the practitioner's ability to gain and use an understanding of the sociology of development work. In the next sections, some rules of applied sociological method are listed as guidelines for potential recruits to this kind of activity.

The Opportunity to Give Advice

Increasingly, social anthropologists are making significant contributions to applied subjects such as health, irrigation scheme development, land settlement, pastoralism and livestock development and agricultural decision making. Many of these contributions are in the form of feasibility study reports, master plan documents and so on, for which there are often considerable publishing constraints. Notable reviews, in a more conventional academic sense, of these areas of enquiry include those on agriculture by Bartlett (1980), on nomadic pastoralism by R. and N. Dyson-Hudson (1980), on administration and public policy by Hinshaw (1980), new land settlement by Scudder (1981) and on more general issues by Hoben (1982).

Two factors usually encourage the inclusion of social scientists in development work. One would be that there is uncertainty about the project or programme's potential beneficiaries, or of the impact on the distribution of income and wealth in the area. The second would be the failure of earlier development schemes directed to a particular population or economic sector.

Nonetheless, even in cases such as these where immediately congenial or recognizable issues will be found in the terms of reference there may well be no specific mention of social science, let alone social anthropology, nor necessarily any labelling of a component as distinctively 'social'. This means that other related disciplines can as easily claim to be able to tackle the problem indicated as the anthropologist. Certainly, there can be no assumption that anthropological concepts will mean anything at all to those evaluating what is to be undertaken in a study, and if the concepts are not recognizable they will probably be treated with doubt or hostility. Once the anthropologist has a reasonable understanding of the expectations of the other disciplines and the others have a reciprocal familiarity with the anthropologist's work they can usually agree to differ as to which factors to examine and on questions of interpretation.

The major difficulty of adjustment for anthropologists, once they have won initial acceptance but are, so to speak, only neophyte consultants, will centre around their urgent need to develop sensitive sociological and institutional analyses of the project or programme frameworks while their basic anthropological training usually channels them into concentrating on the relationships internal to the local populations or groups caught up in the scheme. What is necessary, however, is that the two sociologies should be developed simultaneously and, in the final analysis, integrated conceptually. Put in somewhat different terms, the first and primary task in anthropological research on development policy is the ethnography of the total project rather than the ethnography of an ethnic group or set of local populations. This is a most crucial point but no doubt difficult to sense in its full implications unless one has actually undertaken work of this kind.

For would-be consultants lacking any experience of project work, a major difficulty, at least in the British context, will be whether or not it is desirable or possible for them to use the label 'social anthropology', with the disciplinary boundaries implied, to describe the combination of data collection, analysis, and advice which constitutes consultancy work. The fact is that social anthropologists wishing to contribute to the analysis of development policy do not write on a *tabula rasa*. Social and behavioural factors are already implicitly considered in most development policy questions. They are examined under many headings: for example, in studies of market arrangements; in studies of labour productivity and training requirements; in the determination of user requirements prior to architectural design; in the preparation of schedules for supply of agricultural inputs; and so on.

Experienced economists, engineers, and planners usually have a wealth of travel and project expertise to draw on if they are required to appraise these implicitly social issues. Often they will do so because no-one, except social scientists, sees any particular advantage in having another specialist to work on these matters. Moreover, other social science advisers have also reported being on a team where one of the technical specialists has been in the country for some years, speaks the local language, appears to have good fieldworking skills, and knows the technical subject matter inside out. If such a person is already contributing to the project it is usually hard to argue, whatever the deficiencies of his sociological imagination, that an untried social anthropologist has a unique contribution to make simply because of his or her discipline. It is particularly hard to argue in this way if it is claimed that a substantial period of fieldwork is needed in order to realize the anthropological contribution. In other words, while the discipline has had the academic authority, at least in the main universities, to make the necessary disciplinary and methodological distinctions it requires to operate in a teaching context, it will have to argue its case very closely indeed and with specific attention to the way projects are formulated and evaluated if it is to claim a special role in policy-related research.

It is usually a hindrance to effective anthropological research on policy rather than a help for would-be practitioners to label their studies too emphatically as social anthropology and to strive for a unique identity within an appraisal team when the terms of reference they are being asked to comment on speak of, for example, 'land settlement planning', 'agricultural decision making', 'livestock husbandry', or 'evaluation and monitoring'. Too much emphasis on the claims of 'social anthropology' before project-hardened engineers, agriculturalists and economists may detract from the need to convince them that what are in fact anthropological perspectives and methods are required in order to assess specific ambiguities and uncertainties in project design and appraisal. If there were a sufficient number of successful attempts to include what were in effect, but not necessarily in name, social anthropological contributions to development project work, it would be easier to convince decision makers that it is social anthropological training which is important rather than 'being sociable', 'wanting to live in the village', or the other mottos and clichés which could be used to describe anthropological fieldwork.

The Synergy Rule: You Are Not Alone

One major challenge and opportunity for the development of theory and methods arising from development policy work comes from the greatly increased need to engage in multi-disciplinary teamwork. Development schemes and projects lead almost inevitably to multi-disciplinary enquiry: indeed, no practical problem has yet occurred to me which could be solved by a single discipline. Multi-disciplinary research is not, of course, restricted to development. Nonetheless, the scale and scope of collaboration with contrasted disciplines in policy-related work does mean that there are repeated requirements for both new methodologies and for the analysis of fresh areas of enquiry. However well prepared the consultant is by a previous pattern of work there will always be problems to tackle for which there are few methods available and for which explanations are not well developed in the disciplines or sub-disciplines involved.

Again, there are implications for both the individual researcher and for the discipline as a whole. The individual anthropologist need not feel he is alone in the need to be creative when facing these challenges. Synergy does help in defining unprecedented study tasks and the means of addressing them. At a collective level, moreover, new properties and methodologies often arise from the interaction of different disciplines, and larger systems of study with new possibilities of integration occurring can be created. To use the distinctions coined by Streeten (1976), *multi-disciplinary* development work, in which disciplines co-operate to find an integrated solution to a practical problem but without affecting the methods used in the contributing disciplines, gives way to either the *cross-disciplinary* loan of methods and concepts or to new *supra-disciplinary* enquiry. The reasons for cross-disciplinary work centre on the use of the assumptions, concepts, and methods of one discipline in another. Supra-disciplinary work develops because, for a particular time or region, the justification for maintaining separate disciplines does not hold, and there is a case for merger.

For the would-be consultant and adviser I can best illustrate the process of multi-disciplinary teamwork, the 'synergy rules' axiom, and the growth of larger systems of study by reference to my own experience of commissioned research on soil and water conservation in the Murang'a and Machakos Districts of Kenya.

The problem was defined for me as principally one of establishing the administrative and management considerations to be taken into account in developing a soil and water conservation programme for the catchments of the Masinga Dam. With very few exceptions – notably the work of Mbithi (1977) – soil and water conservation and erosion issues in Kenya have received scant mention indeed in Kenyan social anthropology or rural sociology. When erosion control measures are referred to in the rural development literature it is within the context of resistance to colonial rule and enforcements. Kikuyu political prisoners were used to construct bench terraces (Sorrenson 1967) and mention is made of Kikamba obstructing tractors and work gangs carrying out erosion control in Machakos District (de Wilde 1967).

In the absence of other information, the first proposition to be investigated was the extent to which the administration's interest in soil erosion control was a realistic concern, an unexamined continuation of colonial themes, or a kind of inappropriate transfer of technology arising from purely administrative enthusiasms circulating among the international development agencies. In fact, it was possible to find, from location to location, a real interest in erosion questions among rural residents. Farmers in the densely populated coffee growing zones, for example, were usually very mindful indeed of the sometimes devastating effect of gullying from concentrated flows of water along farm boundaries, since quite significant strips of their small farms could be washed away in this process. Periodic amounts of money from government sources to support rural conservation work have also supported a certain amount of welcome employment of the rural public works kind.

As fieldwork continued it became clear that the many variables which could influence the perception of both erosion hazards and the importance of conservation for rural livelihoods could not be arrived at with purely anthropological or sociological tools, or simply by an untutored questioning of farmers and household members. Interaction with other team members and rural residents and the use of insights from social science *and* agronomy and soil science showed that a complex assessment procedure and sampling strategy was needed to specify the many relationships between social and environmental factors. These included, for example, differences and similar-ities in farms according to: their position in relation to the ridge and valley bottoms; soil types; agro-climatic zones; farm practices concerning livestock movement; the pattern of rural movement and transport by road and foot-path; and, most importantly, the relationship of gender to both small-holder commercial and foodcrop agriculture.

The co-operation between the disciplines went far beyond a purely parallel listing of social and physical constraints and variables, or even collaboration to arrive at an agreed sampling frame for questioning rural households. Far-reaching and new questions about rural residents' understanding of the causes of erosion, its impact on agricultural systems, and available options in terms of future population levels and changing levels of social and economic activity, were now encompassed within the boundary of the study.

In outline, the problem which emerged centred on the extent to which existing on-farm conservation works – which consisted of digging deep trenches along the contours to break up accumulating water flows – should be supported or discouraged in favour of other approaches. Alternative con-servation works would involve collecting and shedding the water from farms as quickly as possible through the construction of, say, stone and grass waterways and, in the long run, more elaborate rural civil engineering in what was becoming an increasingly urbanized countryside. The existing 'cut-off drain' methods will prove difficult to sustain in the long run yet the adoption of new waterway systems will require an upheaval in only recently acquired conservation habits, and considerable negotiation between adjacent farms.

To make recommendations concerning the merits and disadvantages of either approach required, first, an assessment of how members of farm households understood the causes of soil loss. Was erosion simply a con-sequence of high rainfall, and thus an act of God, or did they see that their own, their neighbours' and government's actions, both on and off the farm, influenced land use and flows of water? The work also raised the question of whether or not, and how, responsibility was allocated between the genders for conservation work in farm management systems prior to land consolidation and before that period. Answers to this question would affect the emphasis to be placed on a separate agricultural and conservation extension effort for women farmers.

Multi-disciplinary work can often enlarge the scope and methods of social anthropological enquiry. In the next section, however, I examine how the reporting procedures of planning and policy-related work often pose limits on the ability of social anthropologists to write in an untrammelled way.

An 'Iceberg Axiom'

Anthropologists who have been involved in development projects or con-sultancies often complain that their findings are not taken seriously or are edited out of recognition. I suggest that this is, in part, because they have not appreciated the 'iceberg axiom' which can be found underlying the reporting structure of multi-disciplinary planning and policy work.

This axiom states that about seven-eighths of the studies undertaken for a particular appraisal should be kept submerged in annexes in order to keep the remaining portion, or 'main report' part of the studies visible. The contrast intended is with the extended scholarly discussion in a book or lengthy paper, where there is no particular merit in submerging large amounts of successful, highly individual work in volumes of subsidiary importance; nor are appendices usually a significant part of the total bulk of the manuscript. This cultural divide in reporting style is, in part, because of a more intimate relationship in social anthropology between 'data' and 'analysis' than in many of the technical disciplines involved in multi-disciplinary planning work. In this kind of enquiry, moreover, there is an emphasis on authoritative but specific and limited conclusions. In the case of a feasibility study, for example, the need for definite conclusions is tailored to benchmarks concerning project timing and cut-off points for the estimation and review of proposed expenditure and technical assistance.

What the axiom means in practice for anthropological advisers is that their writings will only rarely be individual, personal creations reviewed by anonymous reviewers on publication. The planning or policy report is a more anonymous product built up layer by layer through the interaction of team members with different disciplinary perspectives. Once individual drafts are written they will be amended or qualified as the results from other specialists are assembled. This process requires both teamwork patterns and perspectives developed from collective working and, where the project requires a dominant discipline, good synthesizing and editing skills on the part of its representatives.

The end product is a composite one requiring specialists to subdue or subordinate the normal reporting and analytical style of their primary discipline. This degree of compromise for the discipline is necessary to achieve the extension or *vulgarisation* (as it would be expressed in French) of social anthropological insights to other policy-related specialities. The 'iceberg axiom' underlines the fact that the 'compromise' is a logical requirement and challenge and not a wounding loss of disciplinary status.

Both process and axiom can be illustrated by a study, carried out in the UK, to assess the potential for energy conservation through community heating systems based on combined heat and power technology. The poor reputation of many previous attempts at community heating schemes was felt to require an investigation of the potential social and consumer impacts. The report on these issues ran to some 239 pages. The major empirical study commissioned was our in-depth field investigation of 500 households on a distinctive scheme in Nottingham. Even though the write-up of this study provided the key field data, it appeared as an annexe of some 200 pages to the report of 39 pages titled *Social Acceptability of CHP/DH*. Findings from the detailed empirical study, together with conclusions from relevant engineering and financial analyses, were then further reduced to eight pages. These were in turn synthesized to allow an answer to the question of feasibility on social and consumer grounds, and this took up only half of the first page.

In fact, the *Social Acceptability of CHP/DH* was only one of nine supplementary reports which included studies of topics such as thermal storage vessels, polyurethane foam insulation, environmental disturbance and so on. The nine supplementary reports taken together required, of course, a further summary.

Finally, results from the social acceptability report were used in the overall study's main report which ran to 138 pages. The highlights of the work on social and consumer factors were reported in one of its chapters, entitled 'Consumer, Planning and Environmental Issues', and received attention in seven of the 34 paragraphs. The conclusions on social acceptability were then taken through to the 90-*sentence* summary of the summary report, where they received one sentence of conclusion and one recommending further social research.

These two sentences which appeared in the summary of the summary report which summarized the summaries of the nine supplementary reports etc. were perfectly satisfactory for the task and for our conclusions. The social and consumer work on the technology was subsequently noted by the Select Committee on Energy, and at least one of the recommendations stimulated extensive debate in the public arena. If would-be consultant anthropologists are anxious about surrendering control over what is written in multi-disciplinary projects, they must be forewarned that the tip of the iceberg is frequently beyond their control (although their turn to sit on the top may come if the social and institutional aspects of a project are very prominent). This makes it very important for the social research specialists to draft their conclusions with such care that other team members can take over and reduce their contributions, often severely, to the few pages of key conclusions which is all the policy maker will have time to read.

Rew's 'Cracking' Corollary

Development projects are a little like the 'cracking towers' used in the petroleum industry. The oils with their heavy carbons are heated and passed over a catalyst, and in the process the heavy chains of carbon are 'cracked' and the lighter products taken off at the higher levels of the tower, with the heavy sludge dropping to the bottom. The heating process of the development project together with the presence of one's colleagues as catalysts creates the conditions for the varied outputs that are needed at differing levels of the activity. The metaphor emphasizes, moreover, that the output expected from a social adviser is not some seamless web of creativity, the framework for which is dictated by the traditions of the parent discipline, but often very simple answers which can look insubstantial when written up, but require considerable research effort to produce them.

'Organigrams' come immediately to mind as a 'light' project output for the social researcher. These are the organization charts which set out the manning and staff function requirements of a project or programme. To establish them authoritatively, considerable investigation of the sociology and anthropology of public administration is required. For example, relationships between farmers and extension agents, between extension agents and their superiors, and those of district to national organizations are matters which can be and have been illuminated by social anthropological investigation. The major reason for such research within a project is not, however, to show Crozier, Selznick or Weber alive and well in policy-relevant research. Organization charts are needed for more than purely descriptive purposes in project appraisals and the reason for them varies according to the stage in the project cycle. At the feasibility stage, a main aim will be to establish that trained manpower in the necessary categories is in fact likely to be available, and its cost; another aim will be to indicate if there are possible legislative requirements. At subsequent stages of the project cycle the aims will shift to more detailed considerations of workability and, for example, what standards to apply to housing and other infrastructure provision for project staff and participants.

The Bearing of Theory on Practical Advice

The notes and rules of thumb now reviewed emphasize that while some disciplines will treat development planning work as a set of wholly technical exchanges and examinations, the social anthropologist will want to place such research within a sociological context and examine the social relations of the team, its enterprise, its clients, and how groups within society will be affected by the studies and the decisions taken in their light. This is an area in which there have been very few empirical studies. Their absence means there are correspondingly few anchors, other than general theory or prejudice, with which to stabilize the search for explanations of, say, the performance of development projects or the reasons for policy formulation in particular or general cases. The concept of the organizational connection is such an anchor and can lead to a recognizably social anthropological understanding of development work and policy.

Understanding the organizational connection is analogous to the process of translation. In order to translate effectively one must speak at least two languages fluently. The researcher-cum-translator of development policy must equally be able to cross and recross the cultural divide between community institutions on the one hand and the administrative and technical institutions of development on the other. The difficulty for social anthropology in this respect is that so much of the existing and required descriptive and analytical material is, or would be, carried out by anthropologists and their students who lack much experience of either public policy or administrative/planning work. Moreover, many appear ideologically or aesthetically opposed to it anyway, and thus suffer from a trained incapacity to empathize with the administrative, policy and technical roles which decision makers assume (Wallace 1972: 195). It can be argued that these questions of judgement and choice are for each would-be anthropological adviser alone; an extension, that is, of the rule of the scholar's sovereignty of interest. Nonetheless, it is well to recognize that the area of debate is, at least in the British context, a sensitive one, leading to ambiguity and apparent discrepancies between the public attitudes and individual practices of some members of the discipline.

There are recognized theoretical attractions in understanding the social worlds of the development agencies. There is, however, a somewhat more grudging acceptance that, in order to understand an agency, you have to be prepared to develop an empathy with its officials and its organizational life. Perhaps that is why a colleague, who had both read *The Nuer* as a student and attended some anthropological gatherings asked me, with a full sense of irony, why it was that Evans-Pritchard was prepared to buy cattle in order to participate more fully in Nuer social life, while contemporary anthropologists baulked at buying pin-striped suits for their policy-related researches. I doubt that he meant this question to be taken *too* seriously but merely to indicate that there would be benefit in being a little more aware of the semiology of the presentation of self in policy-related research methods.

Many researchers will feel they are indeed not well suited to research of this kind and so will rightly pass on to follow their own interests. For others it is an apparently fascinating but most uncomfortable area to inhabit, which leads to much questioning about 'ethics', reflecting an anxiety that the moral problems of an adviser may prove more intractable than those of an apparently unapplied researcher.

This paper starts from a different understanding and a different set of anxieties. The major dichotomies which should be drawn are not so much between ethical tension and its lack as between, on the one hand, a kind of Morris or Kropotkin anarchism and escape from power relations (Schaffer 1975: 5), and an acceptance, on the other, that 'anthropologists, whether they like it or not, are working in a context of power and have little chance of improving man's lot except through influencing directly or through the force of ideas the uses to which power is put' (Belshaw 1976: 257).

Admittedly, as Belshaw goes on to add, power corrupts, and there is a risk that social science will be drawn into the corruption. Yet, at the other extreme there is the possibility of the complicity and moral cowardice of living as an ineffective, silent witness to failures to satisfy human needs and rights, or of opting out by choosing less demanding areas in which to work.

This debate is not by any means wholly new. Some, indeed, will see in it the same, familiar set of stances towards applied work as in earlier periods of the discipline. This view is mistaken, since it ignores a major change which has occurred since those earlier discussions on the relationship between the economic, political-administrative and socio-cultural systems of most national societies. In particular, there has been a major expansion in the administratively processed aspects of social life through the penetration of an assortment of rural, urban, population and family planning, agricultural, transportation and cultural development programmes and projects. Schaffer (e.g. 175), together with Lamb (1975), and Rew (e.g. 1977), has discussed this greater institutional presence in development and social performance in terms of 'access' and 'the organizational connection'. The research it generated examined how administrative and planning mechanisms structure the distribution of the social product to different social groups and categories and the effect of this structuring on the politics of access. Habermas (1976) provides an integrated, theoretical discussion of the growth and implications of the administrative planning of contemporary social life. A key point in his discussion is that 'cultural affairs that were taken for granted, and that were previously boundary conditions for the political system, fall into the administrative planning area' but, while incorporated, are nonetheless 'peculiarly resistant to administrative control' (1976: 71). Educational and curriculum questions, regional and city planning and the private ownership of land, health matters and areas of family, marriage and sexual relations all become subject to governments' intentions to create 'the direct administrative processing of cultural tradition'.

Only by intimate enquiry will it be possible to fill in the lacunae between institutional powers and resources, formal organizational structures, decision making at each level, and the policy outcomes which make up development policy. These lacunae are very often covered with general propositions such as 'officials are instruments of the ruling class', 'the rich always win', 'reform is impossible', or 'Third World bureaucracies are corrupt'. Any of these could be true, maybe universally. They do not, however, explain. Those who would wish to start their enquiries with these particular hypotheses would do well to examine the mechanisms by which, if they are general truths, they are realized, and what this implies for their subsequent practice.

References

BARTLETT, P. F. (1980) Adaptive Strategies in Peasant Agricultural Production. *Annual Review of Anthropology* 9: 545–73.

BELSHAW, C. S. (1976) *The Sorcerer's Apprentice: An anthropology of public policy.* New York: Pergamon.

CHAMBERS, R. (1980) Short cut Methods in Information Gathering for Rural Development Projects. Mimeo, Institute of Development Studies, Sussex University.

DE WILDE, J. C. (1967) *Experiences with Agricultural Developments in Tropical Africa*. Baltimore: Johns Hopkins Press.

DUMONT, L. (1979) The Anthropological Community and Ideology. *Social Science Information* 18 (6) 785–817.

DYSON-HUDSON, R. and N. (1980) Nomadic Pastoralism. *Annual Review of Anthropology* 9: 15–61.

HABERMAS, J. (1976) *Legitimation Crisis*. London: Heinemann.

HAMNETT, I. (1970) A Social Scientist among Technicians. *Institute of Development Studies Bulletin* 3 (1): 24–9.

HINSHAW, R. E. (1980) Anthropology, Administration and Public Policy. *Annual Review of Anthropology* 9: 497–522.

HOBEN, A. (1982) Anthropologists and Development. *Annual Review of Anthropology* 11: 349–75.

LAMB, G. B. (1975) Access, Marxism and the State. In B. B. Schaffer (ed.) The Problems of Access to Public Services. *Development and Change* VI (2).

LIPTON, M. (1976) *Why Poor People Stay Poor: Urban Bias in World Development*. London: Temple Smith.

MBITHI, P. M. (1977) Responding to African Family Service Needs. *In Family Welfare in Africa*. International Association School Social Work.

REW, A. W. (1975) Without Regard for Persons: Queueing for Access to Housing and Employment in Port Moresby. In B. B. Schaffer (ed.) *The Problems of Access to Public Services*.

— (1977) Urban Water: Access, Delivery and Institutional Scarcity. *IDS Discussion Paper* 113. Institute of Development Studies, University of Sussex.

SCHAFFER, B. B. (ed.) (1975) The Problems of Access to Public Services. *Development and Change* VI (2).

SCUDDER, T. (1981) The Development Potential of New Lands Settlement in the Tropics and Sub-Tropics: a Global State of the Art Evaluation with Specific Emphasis on Policy Implications. New York: Binghampton.

SORRENSON, M. P. K. (1967) *Land Reform in the Kikuyu country*. Nairobi: Oxford University Press.

STREETEN, P. (1976) Why Interdisciplinary Studies? In D. C. Pitt (ed.) *Development from Below*. Chicago: The Beresford Book Service.

WALLACE, A. F. C. (1972) A Day in the Office. In S. T. Kimball and J. B. Watson (eds) *Crossing Cultural Boundaries: The Anthropological Experience*. London: Chandler.

M. R. Redclift*

---

12 Policy Research and Anthropological Compromise:

should the piper call the tune?

Alan Rew's paper is an important contribution to the discussion of anthropology and development. He opens a number of new doors and urges anthropologists to enter new terrain. But he also closes a number of doors, by failing to tackle some fundamental ethical issues which cannot be ignored.

Rew's paper makes a number of valid points. He argues that anthropologists show little ability to utilize their own findings and turn them into policy-relevant conclusions. This is attributed partly to anthropological habits of thought, and partly to an unwillingness to sell the skills that the anthropologist does possess. The habits of thought die hard, and anthropologists, according to Rew, still tend to write about development without including development interventions in their analysis. The practice of development, and its associated agencies, is seen as a constraint on good analysis rather than a means towards it. Anthropologists are held to possess a 'trained and sustained ability to put (themselves) in other people's shoes', but this has not enabled them to see themselves as other professionals see them.

In addition Rew makes some useful observations about development consultancy. He indicates that few policy agencies *seek* anthropological advice, and those that do are uninterested in whether it comes from anthropologists as such. Other technical consultants often possess sociological skills which are put to use in projects. When anthropological advice is sought it is usually to do one (or both) of two things: to provide data on a project's impact and a profile on its beneficiaries, or to correct past mistakes by ensuring that projects reach beneficiaries.

Like the anthropologists that he is criticizing, many of Rew's most percipient comments are made *en passant*. He shows, for example, how some

---

*This chapter is an expanded version of remarks presented to the ASA Decennial Conference as part of a panel discussion of Rew's paper, Chapter 11. Other panellists on that occasion were Professors L. Baric, J. Boissevain, and T. S. Epstein.

anthropological 'facts' are only interesting to anthropologists, while others, not immediately interesting to anthropologists (like salary schedules and organizational matrices) are especially interesting to fellow policy professionals. He also provides good advice on report writing, observing that only two sentences of a 239-page report on social factors are likely to reach the organization that commissioned the report. He insists, rather less convincingly perhaps, that it *is* possible to draft conclusions with such care that they can be condensed without losing their point.

In reproducing the 'authoritative conclusions' that policy agencies seek, anthropologists inevitably compromise their skills and interests in the cause of the greater good. This compromise is a challenge which anthropologists ignore at their cost. If engineers are prepared to be seen by non-engineering colleagues as a parody of their true professional selves, why not anthropologists? If Evans-Pritchard was prepared to buy cattle to enter Nuer society, why are not anthropologists willing to don pin-stripes and enter the corridors of power?

Rew's conclusions are based on considerable experience of consultancy but they beg as many questions as they answer. First, it is necessary to disentangle his own motivation for being interested in both anthropology and consultancy, from the professional guidance he is offering others. His own motivation to combine academic seriousness with practical resourcefulness is entirely convincing, but his advocacy of this position on wider grounds is not. If anthropologists are as ill-equipped as he suggests for practical development work, why does he continue to believe 'that social anthroplogy can survive and thrive in the perambulations' of the consultancy world?

In making his case Rew leaves out of his account a number of important considerations. Clearly, the motivation to be an anthropologist is quite different from that of an engineer or accountant. Power and mastery of technical skills come into it, of course, but one of the main things that continues to draw young people to anthropology (notwithstanding the constrictions imposed by the University Grants Committee) is the desire for personal displacement or alternation, to leave one's own society and its values behind, both physically *and* mentally. People who study social anthropology usually do so to avoid having to wear pin-stripes, in the belief that other societies' conventions are more interesting than their own. They are uninterested in visiting Babel with or without their anthropological skills, and may be excused for asking whether it is their principles that Rew is seeking to alter, or their personalities.

Second, he seems to confuse the issue of how anthropology can be of greater use to development consultancy with the related, but separate, issue of whether anthropology should approximate to development consultancy in its methods and goals. If anthropologists are to play a larger part in practical development work, they must surely address the first issue with some urgency. The second issue deserves to be treated with a good deal more caution. The current political context, and disregard for honest but critical research in many of the developed and developing countries, make it imperative that anthropology defend itself against assaults from the commercial world of the development consultant.

There is an inevitable tension between the need to communicate the message to those outside the discipline and the need to ensure that the message is not lost in the medium itself. Development consultancy – which, incidentally, Rew treats as synonymous with applied anthropology – can probably make use of some anthropological skills and at the same time force anthropologists to recognize the realities of the 'real world'. The world of politics and profit is transforming the societies which anthropologists study, including their own. But the anthropological enterprise is not only about relevance, it is also about rigorous intellectual standards and the painful balance that is to be achieved between this objectivity and the observer's subjective interpretation. In most developing countries (and, for that matter, many developed ones) ideological justifications are increasingly sought for development policies, with scant regard for intellectual consistency or humanitarian considerations. Anthropology should seek to provide coherence and ethical resolve, however uncomfortable the results. In countries where there is no critical research tradition, or where critical research is not tolerated, the expatriate anthropologist advising on practical development work has an obligation to consider his responsibilities to the society in which he is working, as well as to the contractor who is paying for his services. This makes it difficult for him to decide where his loyalties lie, and may take priority over both his obligations to the consultancy and the professional community of anthropologists.

The issue of the role of critical research is one facet of a wider matter: one of the most fundamental issues in anthropology, that of ethics. Rew makes scarcely any reference to the ethics of applied anthropology in his paper. At no point does he discuss whether the consultancy assignment was necessary, or ultimately beneficial, whether it was based on social values inimical to the anthropologists and others involved. Whether he is discussing soil and water conservation in Kenya, or community heating in Nottingham, irrigation in Zimbabwe, or central heating in Clapham, the matter is never raised. Is it better that anthropologists get involved in development on the wrong side, for the wrong people, for the wrong reasons, than that they stay motionless at the touchline? Rew clearly thinks it is. In his view, the recognition that settlement planning will not work as assumed is of more consequence than whether it should be attempted at all. Thus, the most that the anthropologist can expect to get out of shortcomings in project design is the promise that they 'will be modified a little' in response to his criticism. The people who decide the essential elements in this design are the paymasters: governments, international agencies and private entrepreneurs. The anthropologist may also be well equipped to ask searching questions of these bodies, but apparently he should not trouble himself to do so: it is outside his remit. He had better be clear from the beginning that ethical objections cannot be entertained, because nobody else in the consultancy team is going to stay awake at night worrying themselves about them.

It is also interesting how little Rew has to say about the anthropologist in another role familiar to many of us, that of insurgent in the system, siding with the inarticulate against the system's managers, with the powerless against the powerful. Evaluating the needs and strategies of groups of people for whom the development process affords few benefits, can be an important contribution to mapping out the alternative development which many anthropologists and non-anthropologists alike believe in. Many situations come to mind in which anthropologists have been of use to people in developing countries, but in which they also refused to meet the 'commercial criteria' discussed in Rew's paper. The responsibility of the anthropologist, like other academic researchers, is to his host society, which often needs to be confronted with worthwhile social research under difficult conditions. Obligations to this society include a need to train local people to cope with the pressures imposed on their society by development agencies, some of which may be staffed by anthropologists. A longer view of development needs to be taken, in which the decision to abide by commercial criteria is weighed carefully, together with other ethical and professional choices.

The need to be more conscious of the use to which anthropological work is put should not be equated with the commercial 'usefulness' of anthropology. The first goal may require anthropology to venture further into prediction and forecasting, an area which has hitherto been neglected. It may also require that anthropologists make it their business to contact other professionals, persuading and lobbying if necessary, always being prepared to argue their corner. It will undoubtedly mean that anthropologists learn more about the tools of other trades and examine whether these can be utilized within anthropology. Anthropology needs to be more ecumenical and less self-regarding than formerly, and to avoid endless agonizing about whether or not it has anything to offer those outside its boundaries. At the same time it needs to be more careful about which of these 'relevant others' are worthy of attention and, consistent with its own intellectual inheritance, more concerned with what is being exchanged within the gift relationship.

'Taking sides' in development need not mean choosing between commercial interests and *engagé* political activism, although this is the choice which often worries anthropologists most. There are more subtle ways of changing the world than those currently being canvassed by either development professionals or revolutionary leaders. One of these is to bring local people's indigenous knowledge to a wider audience, providing a research component in practical interventions that is sorely needed. Several avenues for work of this kind are already clear. For example, farming systems research has attracted widespread interest in development circles, but anthropologists have seldom made it their job to help articulate the farmers' preferences to the policy professionals.

In addition, following in the spirit of Rew's paper but changing its emphasis, anthropologists can identify from the outside ways in which development processes affect societies and seek to turn the lessons of these changes to the benefit of local people. For example, the vertical integration of small agricultural producers within agribusiness complexes has begun to attract the attention of a variety of social scientists, but practical interventions on behalf of the poor seldom make use of these experiences. Should it be left to transnational companies like Nestlé and General Foods to learn the lessons of the market place? As new technologies threaten to displace existing technological applications, opportunities exist for anthropologists to investigate their potential for the social groups with which they have often traditionally worked. An industrial alcohol programme based on cassava production rather than sugar cane, would benefit millions in rural Brazil. Should not anthropologists be the advocates and 'educators' that such a programme requires? More generally, the opportunities presented by biotechnology research are often greatest when they are in the hands of venture capital, as at present, rather than the huge pharmaceutical and food industry complexes which are buying their way into research in an attempt to forestall the crisis in the petrochemical sector. Should not anthropologists interested in development be monitoring these trends and examining their implications, especially for small farmers in resource-poor tropical environments? The critical issue is how far anthropology, in seeking to intervene, can do so to the benefit of the peoples it has traditionally studied, and without sacrificing its critical, objective edge.

Looking back at the 1973 ASA Conference, I am struck by the contrast with the 1983 meeting. In 1973 the prevailing attitude seemed to be, 'we will only join the development fraternity on our terms'. Today, the employment crisis among anthropologists, and the self-searching which has accompanied cuts in research spending in the universities, have triggered a different response. The call seems to be to join the development brigade at almost any cost. Are the blockages which exist within anthropology today the result of an inability to make compromises with reality, or a symptom of something deeper? Must the anthropologist compromise only to *be* compromised?

Name Index

Subject Index